TROUBLESHOOTING YOUR NOVEL

Essential Techniques for Identifying and Solving Manuscript Problems

STEVEN JAMES

Foreword by Steve Berry

WRITER'S DIGEST
BOOKS

WritersDigest.com
Cincinnati, Ohio

For more resources for writers, visit www.writersdigest.com.

20 19 18 17 16   5 4 3 2 1

Distributed in Canada by Fraser Direct
100 Armstrong Avenue
Georgetown, Ontario, Canada L7G 5S4
Tel: (905) 877-4411

Distributed in the U.K. and Europe by F+W Media International
Brunel House, Newton Abbot, Devon, TQ12 4PU, England
Tel: (+44) 1626-323200, Fax: (+44) 1626-323319
E-mail: postmaster@davidandcharles.co.uk

ISBN-13: 978-1-59963-980-2

Edited by Rachel Randall
Designed by Alexis Estoye
Production coordinated by Debbie Thomas

DEDICATION

This book is dedicated to my friend and Novel Writing Intensive co-instructor, Robert Dugoni, a great author, a great teacher, and a man of integrity and faith.

ACKNOWLEDGMENTS

Thanks to Jessica, Rachel, Phil, Justin, Pam, Trinity, Andrew, and Liesl for all of your helpful insights, suggestions, and ideas.

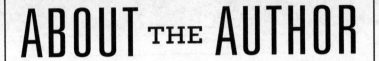

ABOUT THE AUTHOR

Steven James is the best-selling, critically acclaimed author of thirteen novels. He has a master's degree in storytelling and is a contributing editor to *Writer's Digest*.

Best known for his psychological thrillers, he has received more than a dozen honors and awards for his novels, including three Christy Awards for best suspense. His book *The Queen* was a finalist for an International Thriller Award.

His groundbreaking book on the craft of fiction, *Story Trumps Structure: How to Write Unforgettable Fiction by Breaking the Rules*, won a 2015 Storytelling World Award, recognizing it as one of the year's best resources for storytellers. He is the host of the podcast "The Story Blender," where he interviews great storytellers from the world of cinema, oral performance, and writing about the craft of great storytelling.

Throughout the United States, Steven hosts regular Novel Writing Intensives that provide in-depth instruction for serious novelists. For information on these seminars, visit www.novelwritingintensive.com.

For information on his fiction, visit www.stevenjames.net. To book him to speak, e-mail info@stevenjames.net.

TABLE OF CONTENTS

PART I
Story Progression

PART II
Characterization

PART III
Narrative Techniques

PART IV
Reader Engagement

PART V
Style and Finesse

FOREWORD

Steve Berry

When my friend Steven James asked me to write a foreword to this book, I was flattered. Steven is one of the best writing teachers I know. In 2014, when we started Master CraftFest, which involves a day of extensive training with a small group of students at ThrillerFest each year, Steven was our first choice to be an instructor.

Our instincts proved correct. His classes have been widely popular.

Steven sent me the manuscript, and I thought, *Okay, I'll skim through it to get the gist of things and then write a few kind words.* I started on page 1 and read a little. Then a little more. Then a little more after that. A few hours later, I finished the entire book. Every word.

And was amazed.

For years I've said that someone should write a practical, hands-on, how-to guide on polishing a manuscript. So many writers bang out that first draft and then have no idea what to do next. The art of self-editing is a lost one. Writers today are in a hurry. The world of independent publishing has ushered in a generation of impatience and, to some degree, carelessness.

In my day the gatekeepers were New York editors. They decided what was published. Those days are gone. The gatekeepers today are you, me, and every other reader in the world. We determine what's popular, what endures, and what comes next. And if you thought New York editors were tough, the entire world makes them look downright kind.

All of which means that now, more than ever, writers have to master the art of self-editing. And it is an art. In the following pages Steven whittles down that task to a clear, concise, and succinct form. He's created a book that needed to be written, and thank goodness he was the one who wrote it. Steven holds a master's degree in storytelling, which in and of itself is impressive. He's taught writing all over the world. He's published fifteen novels, along with another terrific book on writing, *Story Trumps Structure*. This man just doesn't talk the talk; he walks the walk.

From the day I wrote my first word to the day I sold my first word was a span of twelve years. During that time I completed eight manuscripts, five of which were submitted to New York publishing houses. They were rejected a total of eighty-five times. It was on the eighty-sixth attempt that things happened for me. Unfortunately, in the 1990s, no book like this existed. You learned manuscript polishing through trial and error, writing every day, and taking heed of the many rejections that came your way. That path was both instructive and painful. Steven has now taken some of the pain out of the process.

I encourage every writer out there—whether published, about-to-be published, or just with the desire to be published—to read this book. Then apply its principles to your own writing.

I assure you, the finished product will be a thousand percent better.

I'll definitely be doing that.

And we'll all have Steven James to thank.

STEVE BERRY is the *New York Times* and #1 internationally bestselling author of sixteen thrillers. His books have been translated into forty languages, with more than twenty million printed copies in fifty-one countries. He also teaches writing as part of his History Matters foundation, which raises money for historic preservation. To date, nearly three thousand students have taken his course.

INTRODUCTION

When I first became a writer, I had an editor who taught me more than just the principles of fiction; he taught me how to analyze my manuscript and fix it myself. Most of that troubleshooting depended on asking the right questions.

So, here's the philosophy I learned from him and that guided me as I worked on this book: "Don't just tell me what I should do; teach me what I should ask."

In these pages, you'll find hundreds of questions to press against the clay of your story to help you shape it into the kind of novel that will ring true to readers, impact them, entertain them, and leave them anxious for your next book.

Just as with any troubleshooting process, we'll identify the problems, pinpoint the issues that need attention, and then address them head-on with specific, targeted solutions. Each chapter will also include ideas for fine-tuning your manuscript.

Incidentally, every chapter topic has had, or could have, an entire book written about it, so (thankfully for both of us) rather than trying to be comprehensive I've focused on being as succinct and insanely practical as possible.

So, enough.

Let's get to work and make this manuscript of yours the best it can be.

PART I
STORY
PROGRESSION

1

ORIENTATION

You're walking home late one night when two men leap out of the shadows, pull a hood over your head, and shove you into a van.

You can't see anything, and as the vehicle takes off, though you sense movement and hear hushed voices, you don't know how many people are in there with you, what they look like, or what they want. When you demand that they tell you what's going on, their only reply is silence.

At last, the van stops, you hear the door open, and a man grabs your elbow and leads you outside.

"Alright," he says. "It's time."

Someone yanks off the hood.

Now—what happens?

If you're anything like me, you'd immediately scan the area and take in as much as you can, as quickly as you can, to identify where you are and what danger you might be in. Who's there? What do they look like? Did they bring you to your house for a surprise party? Did they take you to a deserted warehouse to torture you? Are you in a parking lot? On an isolated country road? What do you smell? Hear?

When readers flip to (or scroll to) the first page of your book, the hood comes off. Based on word of mouth and the book's title, they might have a vague idea of what your story is about, but they need you to orient them here, at the start, when you tug off the hood.

Readers need to know (1) who they're supposed to cheer for or against, (2) what threats are present, (3) why the story's outcome matters, and (4) if they can trust you with their time. They need to be able to picture the scene, care about the outcome, and meet characters that they find intriguing and will want to spend time with.

They'll be lost until you show them where they are. The longer you keep the hood over their eyes, the more frustrated they'll become.

....

Readers don't want gimmicks, they want orientation.

....

FIXING ORIENTATION ISSUES

Set aside what you already know about the story and what's coming down the pike—like that great twist on page 300 or the big reveal in the final act. Instead, enter the mindset of your readers. Look at the story with first-time eyes.

Imagine that someone has led you into the opening scene and pulled off the hood. What do you see? Who's present? What are they doing? Why are they here?

There are a myriad of things to keep in mind regarding your story's beginning, and we'll look at them in the coming chapters, but for now, simply ask if your opening orients readers or disorients them.

Print out your first fifteen pages. Go to a location where you normally don't write—a coffee shop across town, a state park, a tree house, your attic. I want you to do this exercise old school, with a pen in hand. Trust me. You'll notice things on the printed page that refused to reveal themselves on the computer screen.

Now, imagine that someone has just tugged off the hood. Open your eyes. Step into that scene and look around.

Mark up the page with notes and reactions.

Then go back to your computer and evaluate those edits. See which ones fit with the emerging context of the story. Recast the opening to orient readers so they can be more emotionally engaged, more curious, and, of course, intrigued enough to keep reading.

DO I NEED TO START THE STORY WITH THE MAIN CHARACTER?

By introducing a character early on, you make a promise about his meaningful contribution to the story. Unless you include a prologue, readers will assume that the protagonist is the first person introduced in the story. If he's not, clarify who the main character is as soon as possible.

QUICK FIX: Avoid opening your book from the point of view of someone who ends up being insignificant to the story's outcome. Reshuffle the opening chapters as necessary to provide promises that are congruous with the story you're actually telling.

FINE-TUNING MY MANUSCRIPT

- If I start with *dialogue*, how soon will readers be able to see how many people are present, what they look like, and where they are? How can I make this scene more visually striking to better orient readers?
- If I start with *description*, from whose point of view is the scene rendered? Based on this, will readers make assumptions that will turn out to be untrue? How can I solve that?
- How quickly will readers be able to know who's telling this story? Should I alter that to avoid confusion? Does this point of view really serve the story?
- Does my first chapter (or my prologue) include a twist? If not, how can I reshape the scene so it's not so predictable or clichéd?
- Based on where the story ends (and the path it takes to get there), is this opening essential, emotionally charged, and true to the tone and mood of the rest of the book—or is this simply where I've been assuming the book should start?
- If I were to set my presuppositions aside, would I still choose this beginning? If not, what does the context call for me to do?

2

CAUSALITY

A game of billiards begins with the cue ball striking the racked balls, which then scatter across the pool table. After that the players take turns trying to clear the table by pocketing another ball (either stripes or solids), all while keeping the cue ball out of the pockets.

We all understand that the game must start somehow. Normally that happens when one player hits that cue ball to break the triangle of racked balls. And from then on, every time a ball hits another, that contact results in an effect.

It's the same with a story.

One opening event causes things to splinter apart for the main character in your novel. After that, there's a chain of events that are all linked and caused by the ones that precede them.

A story moves from choice to consequences, from stimulus to response, from cause to effect. This happens on the macro-level, as the results of each scene set the stage for the next, and on the micro-level, as every action and every line of dialogue affects what comes next.

Cause: One ball strikes another.

Effect: That ball rolls across the table.

An event's effect on a character should be immediately evident to readers. Even if the character is trying to ignore or repress a response, he'll be impacted somehow. He must be. If he isn't, readers will lose trust in the story's believability.

Every action should be justified by the intersection of setting, context, pursuit, and characterization. They all need to make sense. They all need to fit.

> **If you have to explain why something just happened, you're telling the story backward.**

FIXING CAUSALITY ISSUES

Causality is closely related to believability and flow. If an event has no cause, readers will find the scene unbelievable. If there isn't a strong enough stimulus to cause a certain event, it'll seem contrived. Neither unbelievable nor contrived events serve your readers or the story.

When you write a scene that doesn't follow from cause to effect, you create a gap that requires readers to ask, "But why didn't he …?" and requires you to explain what just happened.

And most of the time, that's the opposite of what you want.

If a story moves from effect to cause, rather than from cause to effect, the flow will be disrupted. For example:

> Reggie crossed through the kitchen and opened the cupboard. He was starving and wanted some canned ravioli.

Note how action occurs (Reggie crossed through the kitchen and opened the cupboard), and then an explanation is given for why it happened (he was starving and wanted some ravioli). This is backward. Rather than driving the story forward, the movement of the narrative stops as the author backtracks to explain. The sequence would be better cast like this:

> Reggie was starving and wanted some canned ravioli. He crossed through the kitchen and opened the cupboard.

Here, action moves from cause to effect. There's no need to explain afterward why Reggie opened the cupboard. The narrative flows naturally.

Too often, novelists show an event and then explain why it happened. This disrupts the pace and disorients readers. Unless you have an overwhelming contextual reason to reverse the order, show the action and then the result—in that order.

Here's another example of how not to do it:

> Suzanne stepped into the shower. She needed to relax. As the water washed over her, she thought of the time she nearly drowned when she was nine. She let the water rinse across her skin. Finally, shuddering, she hastily toweled herself dry after turning off the faucet, and tried not to think about that traumatic day at the lake.

As it stands, most of the events in this paragraph happen out of order and sometimes inexplicably. (For instance, Suzanne remains in the shower instead of leaving it right away when the painful memory returns.)

Here's the edited version:

> Suzanne needed to relax, so she stepped into the shower. She let the water rinse over her, but it made her think of the time she nearly drowned when she was nine. Shuddering, she turned off the faucet and hastily toweled herself dry, trying not to think about that traumatic day at the lake.

Written in this way, no follow-up explanations are needed for why she does what she does. The actions make sense and move the story forward, and readers don't have to ask why things are happening.

Study your story. Can readers see how one ball affects the movement of the others? If not, try reversing the order of events so they string together causally. Move the narrative forward, action to reaction, rather than action to explanation.

DOES EVERYTHING IN A STORY HAVE TO BE CONNECTED?

Unless your novel centers on the absurdity of life, every subsequent event (after the initiating one) should follow naturally and logically, otherwise the story won't be cohesive.

QUICK FIX: Analyze every scene, as well as every paragraph, to weed out cause-and-effect problems. Pinpoint the connections between events. Does each action have an appropriate consequence? Does the emotional resonance of a scene fit in congruently from the actions within that scene?

FINE-TUNING MY MANUSCRIPT

- Do realizations or insights occur after the event that caused them (as would naturally happen), or do I have things in the wrong order?
- Does this scene move from cause to effect? If not, why not? Can I tweak the story to show the natural flow of events rather than stop after they've happened to explain why they did?
- Does context dictate that I reverse the order to effect to cause? Rendering the story this way will force readers to ask, "Why?" Do I want them to do so at this moment in the book? Would lack of clarity about the character's intention help readers engage with the story at this point? If it won't, how can I recast it?
- What will I do to ensure that each ball rolls naturally away from the one that just hit it, both in action sequences and in dialogue?

3

SETTING

Think about the details this time stamp communicates in regard to genre and setting:

> Year: 2224
> Planet: Aikolon 7

Most readers will naturally be thinking of science fiction. Or this one:

> 0302 hours
> Ten miles east of Las Vegas

Here, the setting is both specific and intriguingly nebulous. Since the time is written military-style, readers will probably imagine that the story has some type of military connection, perhaps a training exercise in the desert surrounding Vegas.

Setting is not simply the backdrop of the story. It's the context within which the pursuit unfolds. This journey encompasses both space and time. When you conceptualize your story, don't just think about its location. Remember that it travels through the unfolding fabric of time. Whether or not you use a time stamp, it's vital to orient your readers to the setting early in your story.

Time. Location. Character. Desire. All four can be encapsulated in just a handful of well-chosen sentences:

> Noon.
> Our fourteenth day on the raft.
> Only three of us are left, and Janice isn't waking up.

The setting affects the characters' mood, outlook, and decisions.

Your character might love going out for coffee in the afternoon but may not be a morning person. So, the central question, the one that reveals characterization, is not how she feels toward coffee shops but how she feels about being in *this* one, here, today, *at 5:02* A.M.

Think about intention and the effect the event has on her: Why is she here? Why now? Based on what she just experienced (immediately preceding the story's inception), what is she hoping to accomplish in this scene? What's going through her mind? How does this time of day or this location make her feel, change her attitude, or influence her actions?

....

Character is the *who*. Pursuit is the *what*.
Intention is the *why*. Plot is the *how*.
Setting is both the *where* and the *when*.

....

FIXING SETTING ISSUES

Study your first scene. Ask yourself if you can picture that specific place at that specific time with those specific characters. If you haven't included a time stamp, would it perhaps be helpful to do so? If you have, do you really need it?

What clues or information have you included that will orient readers to the setting? What crucial information have you failed to provide? What essential promises have you made?

If your readers will likely be familiar with this location, you don't need to describe it in detail. Instead, show by contrast how it is unique and distinct:

> Unlike most hospitals, the hallway walls in this one were painted pitch black from floor to ceiling.

> The gated community might have been one of a thousand just like anywhere else in the South, except this one didn't allow whites.

> Room 1142 smelled more like a morgue than a hotel room that had been serviced four hours ago.

As you evaluate your setting, think about how well you leverage it in terms of impressions, misconceptions, and orientation of both your characters and your readers. Does the juxtaposition of these characters in this setting allow for intrigue, bring up fascinating questions, and drive story development?

Movement is dynamic—a character has a destination and encounters a different environment or set of circumstances. Because of that, movement creates the natural opportunity for introducing more storylines. So, don't just describe the world in which your character exists. Let him move through it on his way toward (or away from) something that matters to him.

When you transition to a new setting, keep your readers locked in. Add clues in the text or insert time stamps to help them continue to track the movement of the story through time and space.

HOW MUCH DO I NEED TO DESCRIBE THE SETTING?

Common locations don't require much description: "There was nothing unusual about the modest, beige, two-story house." Do readers need to read about the color of the shutters? The style of rain gutters? No—unless those become vital to the story later on.

However, when you introduce an unusual setting, you'll want to make it come alive to your readers. They need to visualize the world of your story. In particular, they expect fantasy, science fiction, historical, and mythic novels to contain detailed descriptions of setting.

QUICK FIX: Use your descriptions to evoke a mood or feeling rather than just create mental images. Don't get carried away with sensory descriptions. Appealing to one or two senses is enough. Include what's essential, drop what's superfluous. Give your characters a reason to be here in this scene at this time and, if appropriate, an ardent desire to be somewhere else.

TROUBLESHOOTING YOUR NOVEL

FINE-TUNING MY MANUSCRIPT

- Is it clear where and when this story is taking place? What incorrect assumptions might readers make regarding this setting or genre? How can I address or quell them early on?
- How can I better show the impact that this setting has on the characters? How will it affect their goals and the way they try to accomplish them?
- Is the setting integral to this story? If not, how can I make the time and location more vital to the character's and the story's development?
- What potential assets does this setting provide that will facilitate the protagonist's pursuit? Can I organically weave them in to better integrate the setting with each scene?
- What attributes of this setting will hinder the protagonist in the pursuit of his goal? How can I better utilize the uniqueness of this setting to create more obstacles to his success?
- Have I used vivid details to create an impression rather than just describe a location? How can I use more evocative language (while remaining in this voice and point of view) to generate readers' empathy and emotion rather than just visual images in their minds?

4

HOOK

You're psyched.

The novel you just picked up to read has started off with a bang. It has an incredible hook, an intriguing first sentence, a gripping opening image, a fascinating premise. You devour that first chapter and flip to the second one—which turns out to be a snore-worthy yawn fest that details the main character's entire life story.

Or maybe the novel *starts* with the yawn fest, and you never make it to chapter two at all.

In the first case, the escalation failed. In the second case the hook did.

Readers should always want to read the next page—and never want to skip any of them.

An intriguing hook is important, but it must do more than simply grab attention. It also needs to be honest to the story, to the voice, and to the direction you're taking things.

The length of the hook is determined somewhat by your book's length. The longer the story, the more latitude readers will give you in setting things up at the start.

A hook that doesn't provide the impetus for escalation will sabotage the progression of your story.

....

Often, the more clever you try to make your hook, the less effective it will be. A strong hook is authentic, not just memorable.

....

FIXING ISSUES WITH THE HOOK

For each of the following types of hooks, think about your story's current opening—and how you might be able to strengthen it.

Use Intrigue

Jump right in with a brief, gripping, evocative sentence:

> They say the scars will fade.

> It all began with a phone call.

> No one knew how long the man had been dead.

> Murder never goes as planned.

Introduce the Protagonist

Show him in a specific setting, facing a specific problem:

> Detective Harrington was angling across the abandoned warehouse, 9mm Glock in hand, when he heard the woman scream.

> It took a little work to pry open the trapdoor, but Angie managed. She tilted her flashlight beam down to illuminate the wooden steps that disappeared into the square, obsidian hole.

> The air is cold—I'd say right around freezing. I shiver and realize that if I don't bleed to death from the gunshot wound in my side, hypothermia will get the best of me soon enough.

Start with Dialogue

Dialogue can be an effective hook because it clues in readers that more than one character is present and offers the immediate opportunity for conflict. Just be sure to give enough visual cues early on so that readers can picture the scene. (Note: These are five separate examples, not one conversation.)

> "We shouldn't be doing this."

"Will I ever see you again?"

"I figured I'd find you here."

"I told you never to call me at this number."

"The only way for this to work is if each of us uses the knife. Here, give it to me. I'll go first."

Imbed Promises

Indicate that the character is already facing problems that will eventually escalate:

> Your mind does strange things when it's dying.

> The whole way to school, Mom was totally quiet, and I knew something was up with her and that guy she's been seeing. The one who looks at me funny.

Set the Genre

Often, this is best done through the narrator's point of view:

> The last human body died eighty-two years ago, leaving the five of us here alone. Their scientists had called us humanity's greatest hope, but even we couldn't stop them from killing each other off.
> To us, eighty-two years isn't a long time.

Lock in the Voice

Introduce a character who has a unique way of looking at the world, a distinctive attitude, or a captivating voice (comedic, sarcastic, etc.):

> I hadn't blown anything up in two weeks, and I was getting a little antsy.

Is your hook doing its job? If not, look for a way to employ one of those six techniques (or a combination of them) to snag your readers' interest right off the bat.

HOW CAN I COME UP WITH A GOOD HOOK?

Don't fall in love with the hook you currently have. A novel is fluid until it's published, so try some hooks on for size, but don't pressure yourself to come up with one before moving forward. Only when you've finished your book will you know where it should ideally start, so quite possibly the opening line is the last thing you'll write as you complete your first draft.

QUICK FIX: Since story openings make significant promises that relate to the main character's pursuit, use them to your advantage. Solidify (1) the promises your hook makes regarding the protagonist's struggles; (2) the clarity and resonance of sensory impressions; (3) the presence of strong, visceral emotions; and (4) the uniqueness of the voice.

FINE-TUNING MY MANUSCRIPT

- Is my hook an appropriate length? Does it make accurate promises for this story's direction and take into consideration what readers will already know about the novel from its title, cover, back-cover copy, blurbs, and reviews?
- If I start the story by introducing someone other than the protagonist, do I have a compelling reason for doing so? How will readers react when they find out that this character isn't the main one?
- Will this opening make readers want to keep reading? Is it too clichéd or overwrought? How can I make it more gripping and memorable?
- Does my book lock in the mood, clarify the narrator's point of view, and introduce the voice soon enough?
- Is my opening sentence concise and evocative, or have I tried to do too much, turning it into its own paragraph? How can I pare it down to a more effective length?

5

OPENING

The Latin phrase *in medias res* means "in the middle of things." For thousands of years, authors have been taught to start stories this way: to begin while meaningful action is occurring and while something significant is at stake.

This is helpful—as long as your opening provides the opportunity for natural escalation.

In your opening chapter you'll want to introduce an intriguing character with a worthwhile pursuit; give readers a feel for the mood of the story, its texture, and its world; and then provide a surprising twist or plot pivot to move things forward in an unexpected way.

When the curtain opens, the actors should already be onstage.

Ideally, they'll be in the middle of the opening scene.

The opening scene is the most vital promise in your book. The climax is when you'll pay it off.

FIXING ISSUES WITH THE OPENING

If you start with *action*, orient readers so they can see who's present and realize why it's important for those characters to succeed or fail. Make it clear whose corner readers should be in—who to cheer for, who to cheer against.

If you start with *description*, it should come from a significant character's point of view and should reflect the tone, introduce the voice, and evoke an emotion.

If you start with *dialogue* or *internal reflection*, add visual cues to ground readers in a specific place. Your readers need more than just disembodied voices; they need concrete images if they're going to picture things in their mind's eye.

Until they know whose point of view they're in, they won't understand whose eyes to see things through, so lock in the narrator's or protagonist's viewpoint as early as possible.

Avoid starting your story too slowly and then letting it descend into the quagmire of irrelevant character history in the second chapter. And steer clear of the three most common openings for novels:

1. **A VEHICLE COMES TO A STOP.** Someone drives up to an office building, a cabin, a military barracks, etc. The vehicle might be a sports coupe, a creepy van, a World War I biplane, a cruise liner, or an intergalactic starship. Doesn't matter. It's all the same. Readers have seen it a million times. Recast your scene.

2. **A PERSON WAKES UP.** Her alarm goes off or her phone rings, awakening her before she's ready. She slumps out of bed (where she's probably alone or with someone who means nothing to her). She gets dressed (for work, for school, to go for a jog), then makes breakfast, feeds the dog, checks her e-mail, whatever. (No, I'm not kidding. As overused and trite as this opening is, some authors still use it.)

3. **A POINT-OF-VIEW CHARACTER GETS KILLED OFF.** Readers learn about his background, start to care about him, and then—*here comes the amazing plot twist!*—he's killed at the end of the scene! How original. That's never been done before. Fix it.

Why start with an overdone idea if you don't have to? Give readers something different. Something better. Think in terms of the M.E.A.T. that you're offering: Mystery, Emotion, Action, and Truth. Let your opening introduce a mystery, appeal to emotion, include action, or touch on a poignant truth of human nature. If your story doesn't start with some M.E.A.T., why not?

Consider beginning with a challenge that:

1. reveals what your protagonist is capable of.
2. gives her a place to progress from during the story.
3. shows that she's intriguing enough to warrant your reader's time and attention.

Too many authors default to using the opening they wrote months or even years ago—even though the broader context of the story has since made it clear that the scene (1) doesn't match the tone of the rest of the book, (2) doesn't make the proper promises in regard to the direction of the plot, (3) is too long or too short for that story, or (4) shines the spotlight on something that isn't ultimately significant.

If any of those things are true about your story's opening, recast it by adding more M.E.A.T.

HOW DO I KNOW WHERE TO START MY STORY?

"Where does my story begin?" is a far different question than "Where do I begin my story?" Exploring the first question will help you understand your character's backstory, pursuit, and unmet desire. Examining the second question will help you zero in on the opening sentence, scene, or sequence of your novel.

QUICK FIX: Once you know your character's pursuit, you'll be able to narrow down the options for the opening scene. Follow the journey of the protagonist's struggle, his choices, and their consequences. Tilt the trajectory of the story's opening scene to the best angle to hit the climactic target you're aiming at.

FINE-TUNING MY MANUSCRIPT

- Does the first scene accurately promise what the book will be about? If not, how can I shade the promises to be more honest to the true direction of the story?
- Is the opening memorable? Does it lock in readers' expectations about who the main character will be? Does it include a twist that

provides opportunity for escalation? (If not, see chapter thirteen for practical ways to develop effective twists.)

- Does my opening draw upon mystery, emotion, action, or truth? If not, what will I do about it?

- Have I given readers enough detail to help them picture the protagonist and the setting, while also trusting them by curtailing my descriptions of nonessentials?

- Does this story need a prologue to introduce a subplot or to give essential backstory about the protagonist? Knowing that some readers have hang-ups about prologues and just skip over them, how will I address that in the structure or format of my novel?

6

DISRUPTION

The sea is calm—but a squall is gathering on the horizon.

The sea is angry, and the boat is about to sink.

Either opening could work for your story because they both involve the inevitability of things getting worse.

• • •

A story's inception occurs when normal life is disrupted—typically when a calling is offered or a crisis occurs.

The *calling* might be an invitation to sail across the sea.

The *crisis* might be the arrival of the storm.

Of course, the calling might also be *professional* (the detective is assigned the case), *personal* (the character seeks spiritual awakening), or *epic* (a prophet announces that the protagonist will become king of the land).

So, clarify in your own mind what disrupts your main character's current situation—his emotional, physical, psychological, or relational life. Why does the boat leave the shore, or what will he do now that it's about to sink?

By the way, when stories begin with the calm sea, readers know the calm is not going to last.

For instance, your protagonist gets a raise, or the home loan goes through, or she wins the election, or the prodigal son comes home. All of these, by themselves, are good things—but if they occur at the start of a story, they serve as the precursor of an impending crisis that will initiate the protagonist's pursuit. In a sense they are gifts. If you start your story with your main character receiving a gift rather than experiencing a crisis, readers will realize that the problems are about to come.

> For the moment, he's riding the wave.
> But it's about to crash.
> Let it.

....

To get things started in your story, something will turn your protagonist's life upside down in a way that cannot be ignored or immediately solved.

....

FIXING DISRUPTION ISSUES

Once your protagonist's life is disrupted, there's no turning back—but that doesn't mean he won't try. In fact, if he *doesn't* try, you have no story. (And if he's able to succeed right off the bat, you have no story either.)

Stories often begin in one of eight ways for the protagonist:

1. Something is not quite right.
2. Something is so right that it can't last.
3. Something undesirable is overwhelming him.
4. Something desirable is just out of reach.
5. Something that matters is right in front of him, but he doesn't notice it.
6. Something needs fixing.
7. Something terrible happens and he tries to recover.
8. Something incredible happens, but the blessing ends up being a curse in disguise.

Examine your story. Which of the eight types of disruption did you use?

However you may choose to get things started, make sure your opening includes a disruption or the implicit promise that one is about to occur.

Readers get bored by reading about success, but they find failure intriguing. So, rip apart the fabric of your protagonist's life before they get tired of reading about how great things are. Think in terms of his status quo prior to the disruption. Also, consider how his situation will be transformed because of his pursuit to find balance or resolution.

A story has struggles in three realms: internal, external, and interpersonal. (More on this in chapter thirty-four.) For now, verify that you've included the initiation of the central, overriding struggle in at least one of those realms on the pages of your book.

In essence, things will either start out well and go wrong, or they will start out wrong and get worse.

Bring on the storm.

DO I NEED TO KNOW MY BOOK'S ENDING BEFORE I KNOW THE BEGINNING?

Novels will start in a way that introduces the significant promises that follow, and you probably won't know what all of those are until you've seen how the story plays out. Because of that, your story's beginning might not clearly emerge in your mind until the ending does. Many novelists hone the opening after the editing process rather than before it.

QUICK FIX: As you analyze your story, ask if you've made clear what the character (1) loses and tries to regain, (2) desires and pursues, or (3) suffers through and must overcome.

FINE-TUNING MY MANUSCRIPT

- The status quo is no longer the status quo. Something has altered the character's life in an unavoidable and impactful way. What is it? What crisis or calling has he experienced?
- What will he do to try to return to normal? How does he fail? What will he do next? Where will that lead him?
- If the story begins by showing his normal life, does the disruption (either a crisis or a calling) occur early enough to satisfy readers?
- What does this character's life look like prior to the disruption? How will that affect his pursuit as he tries to solve things?

- Does the disruption occur in the first ten to fifteen pages? If not, how have I made certain that readers will remain engaged? What do I need to clarify, change, or add to draw them deeper into the compelling emotion of the protagonist's struggle?
- Is the main character's crisis or calling clear? If not, how can I show how bad things are because of the crisis or how good they could be if only it were resolved?
- Is there a place on the page where the main character's life is disrupted either with a struggle or with a calling to achieve more or become more than he ever thought possible?

7

PURSUIT

When my daughters were young, I told them a continuing bedtime story. Most nights, I would close by saying, "I'll tell you more tomorrow," but once in a while I would say, "And they all lived happily ever after."

Immediately, my girls would cry out, "No they didn't! Something *bad* happened!"

Even when they were four and five years old, my daughters instinctively knew that if nothing else went wrong, their story (which eventually extended several thousand nights) would be finished—and that was the last thing they wanted.

• • •

Stories aren't about people living happily ever after—they're about the pursuit of happiness. Once it's found (or lost forever), the story is over.

The path your character chooses in order to pursue happiness or success (however she might define it) might include the pursuit of justice, love, truth, adventure, security, peace, revenge, or more.

It might involve rethinking priorities, starting over, or moving on.

It might be a quest to do something noble or great; an invitation into a new relationship; an attempt to conceal (or solve) a crime, save a kidnapped victim, or stop the genetically altered mutant gorilla invasion; or any number of things.

Whatever the goal is, things will not go as planned.

As he pursues that thing (story theorists sometimes call it the Object of Desire), obstacles will arise and the resolution will never occur *at the time* or *in the way* that the character expected when he began his pursuit.

A story isn't just a list of sequential events. Every event is caused and results in an intention-infused choice.

Story is more than conflict—it is desire in a specific direction. Story is pursuit.

Plot is the by-product of the pursuit, not its precursor.

FIXING PURSUIT ISSUES

Pursuit is action with intention.

Without it, you don't have a story.

Rather than trying to figure out your story's plot, focus on rendering your character's pursuit—what does he want? What steps does he take to get it? What hinders him? How does he respond?

If the story is fueled by believability, causality, and escalation, the plot will emerge naturally, without you ever having to look for it.

Readers will be engaged as long as the action is believable, the character's intention is clear, and tension continues to escalate.

- If readers witness action but don't know its intention, they'll be lost and ask, "Why is *this* happening?"
- If they know the character's intention but don't see her taking logical steps to accomplish it, they'll be confused and ask, "Why isn't *that* happening?"
- If things get easier rather than harder for the protagonist, they'll be bored and complain, "Nothing's going wrong!"

The concept of pursuit encompasses all the central aspects of a story.

A character is present. There's unmet desire, or she wouldn't be pursuing that thing in the first place. The pursuit happens through time and space, so there's a setting. Something is hindering the character from getting what she wants (otherwise she would get it right away and a pursuit would be unnecessary), so there's an obstacle. And in the end, she'll either get the Object of Desire or fail to do so, and there'll be closure.

Character, unmet desire, setting, obstacles, resolution—it's all there, all captured in the concept of pursuit.

As we write, we engage readers by (1) engendering their trust, (2) keeping things believable within the unique universe of this story, and (3) making sure things continue to make sense as the tension and difficulties escalate.

Clarity of intention keeps readers grounded in a story.

Regarding pursuit, as your protagonist tries to achieve something, she also might be trying to elude something or someone. In other words, as she pursues, she might also be pursued.

Readers need to know what the character wants and how he's going after it—and they need to care about (and even worry about) whether or not he'll eventually reach his goal.

So, identify what's out of your protagonist's reach and why it matters that he obtains it. Spend more time focusing on the ways he pursues it (which are concrete) than the reasons why (which might be amorphous and even inconsequential in the grand scheme of the plot).

HOW DO I CLARIFY THE PURSUIT TO READERS?

Often, you can just let one character tell another character what he wants: "I'm going to swing by the bank and pick up that check before they close," or "I'm here to meet Mandie. Is she in?"

QUICK FIX: Fuse action with intention in every scene. Use dialogue, narration, or the character's thoughts to clarify the intention to readers. In. Every. Scene. Then verify that the characters are pursuing their objective in believable ways.

FINE-TUNING MY MANUSCRIPT

- How can I reveal my protagonist's characterization, her passion, or her priorities through actions and choices while something is at stake rather than simply telling readers that she is a certain type of person?

- Do I effectively specify the pursuit to readers, either by stating it outright or by unequivocally showing it?
- Have I led the protagonist into a place where his life will never be the same again? Am I showing his purposive, meaningful attempts to get back to normal?
- Have I made the importance of her pursuit evident by delineating the catastrophic consequences of failure? Why is it important that she overcome this? What's she trying to prove? To hide? To reveal?
- If he obtains his desire, is it what he *really* wants, or does he subconsciously desire something else?
- Will readers care about this pursuit? If not, what wounds or secrets can I give the protagonist to help readers more closely identify with him?

8

TENSION

When I was twelve, I went fishing with my dad on a remote lake in northern Wisconsin. A three-foot-long muskie struck my lure and started taking out fishing line.

I tried to reel that fish in, but it was dead-set on swimming in the opposite direction.

Two opposing forces. Each driven by desire, each resulting in action. And only one of us was going to get what we wanted.

That fishing line became more and more taut.

Until it seemed like.

It just might.

Snap.

• • •

That's the kind of tension you want to generate in your fiction.

It comes when readers care about characters, understand the stakes, and invest emotionally in the outcome.

Simply piling problems onto your character isn't enough.

On its own, conflict doesn't create tension. For instance, if there's conflict in a marriage but neither spouse cares enough to seek change, there's no tension, just resignation. That's different from pursuit. It's static rather than dynamic. It's not story worthy.

So, although conflicts might occur within your story, they're not enough to drive it forward. Only struggles will. Only pursuit.

Tension is born when conflict meets desire.

It might come from an unfulfilled dream, a passionate yearning, a daring quest, a deep wound, unrequited love, comedic misfortune, or a longing for freedom or self-expression, but tension *always and only* results from the pursuit of an unmet desire.

....

Tension is the lifeblood of a story.
Let it pump through every scene.

....

FIXING TENSION ISSUES

Tension is the only narrative force that drives a story forward. Not description. Not exposition. Not dialogue. A character doesn't drive a story forward (unless that character is in tension). Plot doesn't drive a story forward (unless that plot includes a pursuit).

Usually, tension comes from a character trying to do one of five things: obtain, avoid, overcome, achieve, or withstand something that matters. Perhaps he wants to *obtain* the gold, *avoid* getting eaten by the shark, *overcome* societal constraints to marry the person of his dreams, *achieve* success, or *withstand* the interrogation without giving up the secret base's location.

If someone or something is pulled in only one direction and doesn't meet with any resistance, you don't have a story. Tension is heightened when two characters want what only one of them can have.

Don't confuse action with tension, or movement with story. They're not the same thing, and they may even stand in opposition to each other.

Picture a chase scene: A police cruiser is pursuing a suspect in a stolen sedan.

They zip through the city, whipping around corners, barely missing pedestrians.

Then they pass through the suburbs.

Then the countryside.

The chase goes on for five pages.

Then ten.

Fifteen.

Fifty.

Is there action? Yes.

Movement? Yes.

Tension?

Well ... maybe at first, but then, not so much. Repetition cuts the heart out of escalation.

If the peril is real, and if the close calls get closer and the stakes get higher, then, yes, the tension would increase. But action alone, movement alone, will not create tension and could very well bore readers instead of thrill them.

Anxiety doesn't come from activity; it comes from breathless anticipation and escalation.

If your story is short on tension, you may need to take one (or more) of these ten steps:

1. Cut down on the action.
2. Include more promises of peril.
3. Milk the moments between the promise of impending danger and the payoff when it arrives.
4. Remove repetition.
5. Tilt scenes away from frenetic activity and toward justified transformation.
6. Insert escalation.
7. Have someone turn the tables on the protagonist right when it looks like things are going his way.
8. Clarify desire.
9. Sharpen that desire.
10. Obligate someone in two directions—make him choose between two beliefs, two sacrifices, two desires, or two convictions. Make him decide not just *what to do* but *what to give up.*

What's on the other end of the fishing line? How can you make it tug your character out of the boat? What would that mean for the story?

(Incidentally, I did catch that muskie. But it wasn't long enough to legally keep, so I had to release it. And because we didn't have a camera that day and I wanted to prove I'd caught it, this created its own form of tension and unmet desire.)

HOW DO I CREATE MORE TENSION?

Accentuate empathy, peril, desire, and stakes. Readers won't emotionally engage if they don't care about a character, or if they don't sense an impending and significant threat to him. Remember, worry has two strands: (1) concern for the character and (2) anxiety about his situation.

QUICK FIX: Help readers empathize more with the character's struggle. Make the danger more imminent, set up bigger obstacles, raise the stakes, or add unforeseen tragedy.

FINE-TUNING MY MANUSCRIPT

- Are the obstacles or hindrances to the protagonist's success believable? Does it make sense that she's responding to them in the way she is?
- Do I manage to turn *conflicts* into *struggles* by showing the protagonist's unmet desire? How will his choices affect the story's progression and deepen the struggles?
- Have I made sure that my story is tension driven rather than character driven or plot driven? If it's not tension driven, how can I deepen reader engagement through clarity about the struggles and the stakes?
- How does my character react as the tension builds? How does it affect him? What does it draw out of him? Frustration? Anger? Desperation? Resolve? Self-sacrifice? Is that really what readers want? If not, how can I recast the story to meet or surpass their expectations?

9

SCENES

Before I started using my phone for directions, I borrowed a friend's GPS unit. Whenever I went off-route the voice would tell me, "Recalculating … recalculating … recalculating …" and then offer me a different route (which usually involved making a U-turn as soon as possible).

That's a good picture of how stories progress.

A character comes to a roadblock, a washed-out bridge, a traffic jam, or a moose standing in the middle of the road, and she's forced to recalculate her course in order to continue her pursuit.

Except in this case, a U-turn won't work.

She can never go back along the same road that led her here. There is no turning around. There is only moving forward, further into the escalating tension.

Your character has a specific intention when a scene begins, but something happens to turn things in a direction she didn't anticipate. From there, she needs to regroup. This sequence of *scene* (action) to *interlude* (reflection) is how stories are built.

When you think of a scene, don't think of location or events or chapters. Think of unmet goals that result in recalculation.

Scenes fulfill promises.
Interludes sharpen or interpret them.

FIXING SCENE ISSUES

If a scene isn't working, it's probably because (1) nothing was altered, (2) you rendered what should have been summarized or summarized what should have been rendered, or (3) the character's desire wasn't clear to readers.

For each scene, ask yourself the following questions.

Is Something Altered?

Once when I was watching a movie, I realized how rare it is for meals depicted in films or on television shows to be finished onscreen.

I think it's so infrequent because screenwriters know that mutually exclusive desires between different characters need to clash, and when they clash, something will change. Typically, that means at least one person getting up and leaving the table.

What's the "meal" in your scene? What's the clash? Who ends up "leaving the table" as a result? If no one does, can you recast things so they do? If there is no clash, what point does the scene serve?

Is the Scene Properly Rendered?

If nothing significant is altered, you can just summarize the scene. If two characters are simply having a discussion that conveys background info to readers, rewrite the scene so that it's centrally about a character overcoming an obstacle rather than simply passing information along to readers. (For more specifics on when to show and when to tell, see chapter sixty-one.)

Is the Intention Clear?

Have the character state his intention *before* the scene begins, remind readers what he wants *during* the scene, and then, *after* the scene concludes, evaluate the implications of not getting what he wants. This will keep the scene on track, ground readers, and move the story logically forward.

• • •

You'll be tempted to write your way into scenes and interrupt your way out of them.

For instance, at the very moment a decision needs to be made, a character gets a phone call, a timer buzzes, the doorbell rings, another person bursts into the room, a bomb goes off, a shark flies through the window, etc. Or, right as the two star-crossed lovers are about to kiss, they're interrupted and will have to pick things up later.

Since interruptions don't depend on the choice of the protagonist or grow naturally from the context (but rather rely on chance and coincidence), they undermine believability.

Instead, start scenes *in medias res* or with a clear call to action, and avoid using interruptions to end them.

Allow yourself one coincidentally interrupted scene per book. Readers will tolerate that. Otherwise, foreshadow the interruption to make it more inevitable.

A FEW MINUTES BEFORE …	FORESHADOW THE INTERRUPTION:
the phone rings …	"I can't come in the water. I'm expecting a phone call any minute now."
the paramedics arrive …	The ambulance sirens rang in the distance. "They're on their way," Maggie said urgently. "Hang in there, Mom. Help is coming."
the boss walks into the break-room …	"I saw Mr. Bickman's car out in the parking lot. I know he's around here somewhere."

Often, a character enters a scene with a goal and leaves with a wound. This doesn't need to be a physical wound, but ask yourself what this character is taking away from the scene and what he has been forced to leave behind.

As you shape your scene, ask, "How will this result in pain?" When you know that answer, you'll know what the scene is primarily about.

Your story will naturally follow a rhythm of tension and reflection as your protagonist faces increasingly more difficult challenges in the pursuit of his goal, fails to surmount those challenges, processes the failure, and makes a choice that propels the story forward.

A scene is a story played out in miniature, but rather than providing resolution, it sets up the impetus for detouring the ongoing pursuit and escalating the tension. It ends when something significant is altered—that is, when the character has failed to reach his goal and now has to deal with the consequences.

QUICK FIX: Render the failure, show the results, clarify the closure, and then immediately move into the interlude.

FINE-TUNING MY MANUSCRIPT

- Is an attitude, perspective, situation, or relationship altered in this scene? If not, how can I (1) revise things to show the tilt or (2) summarize the events rather than render them?
- Does the scene move the story in a new direction by showing how the struggle has deepened? If not, why is it in my book?
- Have I resorted to clichés to begin or end scenes? Where can I foreshadow interruptions so they're not coincidences, or end scenes with decisions or revelations?
- How has the character been changed by the scene? What has he lost or had to give up to move to that new place in the story?
- If this scene contains a major resolution, have I promised enough peril or inserted enough new struggles to keep readers engaged? If not, where can I add promises of peril earlier in my manuscript?

10

INTERLUDES

The protagonist's boyfriend has left her; the aliens have laid waste to Chicago and are taking aim at New York City; the police have failed to catch the terrorists, who have slipped away into the crowd.

The action sequence has finished.

Now what? Do you just move on immediately to the next scene?

No. Before doing so, let the characters take a breath, evaluate what just happened, assess the situation, and determine how they will deal with what has occurred.

During interludes, characters will think through the implication of the scene's setbacks or the emotional impact those setbacks have caused. They'll regroup and then decide on an action that will initiate a new intention-infused scene.

A scene/interlude couplet moves through four stages: goal, setback, reorientation, and decision. In other words, the character will seek something, fail to get it, process what happened, and proceed in a new direction.

Seek. Fail. Process. Proceed.

If your story sequence is missing any of those four steps, take a closer look at how the scenes are connected. You may need to recast things to include more interludes of reorientation.

These interludes are essential. Without them you have only *movement*. With them you have *progression*.

....

Interludes are moments of recalibration that (1) orient readers to the new situation and (2) propel characters toward their next challenge.

....

FIXING INTERLUDE ISSUES

Stories progress as characters make intentional decisions, face struggles that detour the pursuit, and then take a moment to recalibrate before moving forward again.

Typically, interludes involve a brief conversation or a few moments of internal reflection. Just avoid always having characters process things during a phone call, during a meal, over drinks or coffee, or in a car.

Stories often falter when the interludes (1) don't appear at all and the plot contains relentless, tedious, and eventually meaningless action; (2) go on too long, weighing down the story in rumination; (3) don't end with a clear decision; or (4) aren't the appropriate length, tone, or mood for the story.

Any of these issues can bore or confuse readers.

To avoid that, insert obstacles and add mutually exclusive goals to your scenes. Give your characters a deadline or an urgent choice to make, a consequence for indecision, and an action to reveal the escalation evidenced through their reflection and response.

Genre will dictate how much of an interlude is necessary, but even action novels contain them. For example, let's say the scene ends with an explosion going off and the building collapsing. Here's what the interlude might look like:

> "So, fill me in. Was anyone hurt? I want to know where they got those explosives! Andy, get your team in there and look for possible victims. Laramie, start checking your sources to find out where that C-4 came from. Let's move!"

Study the end of your scenes or action sequences. Have you allowed the characters an opportunity to think through what just happened, review the events, and process the emotions? If not, fix that before moving on with more action.

Evaluate whether you're allowing the characters enough time to process the event that just occurred. The emotional impact will reveal the value of what was lost in the scene.

For instance, someone in your story is murdered. Do the other characters move on immediately, or do they mourn? If so, for how long? Often, cozy mysteries and action stories have little or no grieving. As a result, they run the risk of devaluing human life. After all, if death is cheap, life is cheap. If death matters, so does life.

The bruise of death on a soul takes time to heal.

Or at least it should.

How much do the characters grieve? That will tell you what the writer is stating about the value of life.

So, identify the tragedies or setbacks that your character experiences. Make sure that in each case he takes a genre-appropriate amount of time to process what just happened, and then makes a decision to move forward in a relevant direction in pursuit of his goal.

WHAT'S THE BIGGEST POTENTIAL WEAKNESS OF AN INTERLUDE?

Most interlude problems come in terms of proportion. Remember, the bigger the promise that led to the scene, the more loss the scene should contain. The deeper the grief, the longer the interlude.

QUICK FIX: Build the scenes during your first draft. Then, on later revisions, work on the interludes. After you have a feel for the pace and direction of the story, you can determine how long the interludes need to be. The broader context of where they appear in the story and what they need to accomplish will determine their length. Show your character fail. Show the results. Then have him evaluate and process things so that readers understand his intention as he moves into the next scene.

FINE-TUNING MY MANUSCRIPT

- Is there an interlude or moment of reorientation between each scene?
- Does the protagonist (1) assess the situation, (2) make a choice, (3) take an action, and then (4) deal with the ever-escalating consequences? If not, can I rethink the storyline to better show the journey of the character through the scene/interlude sequences? Are the in-

terludes the right length to allow the characters to process the scene's emotional impact or psychological implications, but not so long that they detract from or slow down the story?

- Is the mood of the interludes genre appropriate? If not, what words (typically verbs and adjectives) can I change or omit to fix that? (See chapter forty-five for more on this.)
- Is death, loss, or grief dealt with honestly during the interludes, or do I swing to another scene or back to normal life too fast? What will I do about that?
- During each interlude, is at least one promise made or kept? If not, how can I better integrate this interlude into the story's underlying framework of promises?

11

SETBACKS

A magnificent rose bush is in full bloom right in front of you on the edge of the jungle.

Man, you love roses.

Even though you can't identify this specific type of rose, you've never seen any as beautiful as this before. You lean over to pick one—but a cobra slashes out of the bush and bites your hand.

Okay, that's bad.

Or maybe there's no cobra and you pick the rose, but when you smell it, you realize you're deadly allergic to this type of pollen.

That's bad too.

In the first case you didn't get what you wanted and your situation became worse. In the second case, you obtained what you wanted, only to find out that it wasn't really what you wanted after all.

● ● ●

In real life, you'd do all you could to remove the roadblocks between your friends and their happiness. But in a novel you'll treat your characters the opposite of how you would treat your friends. You're going to make things as painful and difficult as you can for the characters you care about the most. This is done through setbacks that might be:

1. **EMOTIONAL:** The character can't find the peace, the answers, or the hope he so desperately needs.
2. **PHYSICAL:** The villain escapes, the bridge blows up, or the hero gets stabbed in the leg.

3. **RELATIONAL:** Misunderstandings, external pressure, or broken promises plague the relationship.

You'll shape situations that make success seem further and further out of reach. Or you'll offer bright promises that are seductively *within* reach—but when the character grabs for them, he finds them maddeningly elusive or covered with scar-forming thorns. These setbacks detour the story toward a climax and an eventual solution that neither your protagonist nor your readers saw coming.

....

With every escalating scene, you'll be making things as frustrating as believably possible.

....

FIXING SETBACK ISSUES

Dead-ends stop a story in its tracks. Setbacks reroute it.

Reaching a complete dead-end would simply mean failure. On the other hand, reaching a final destination would mean success. If you die from the snakebite or pollen, or if you simply wander off into the sunset smelling your wonderful rose, the story is over. It has nowhere else to go.

Readers know this, so when it looks like a character has come to a complete dead-end or has arrived at his destination too early in the story, they'll assume that things aren't what they seem, that more is going on than meets the eye, or that the scene's deeper significance will later be revealed.

And they are right. Those things will happen, or you're not doing your job as a storyteller.

That leaves us with a limited number of ways to move a story forward:

1. **APPARENT DEAD-ENDS THAT TURN OUT TO BE DETOURS.**
These are setbacks that seem like dead-ends but lead the story along a path that neither readers nor characters can predict. The driving narrative force is *surprise*. This is the cobra in the bush. Whiplash—the story takes off in a whole different direction.

2. **APPARENT DESTINATIONS THAT TURN OUT TO BE PAINFUL DETOURS.** These seem like good things at first (you were able to pluck and smell that rose!) but lead toward greater complications and pain (the pollen might kill you!). The driving force here is *escalation of tension*.

3. **CLEARLY DELINEATED DETOURS.** The story events make it clear to readers and characters alike that this new, unforeseen direction is the only available option. The secret here is *a promise of peril*. This might be a friend by your side pointing out the cobra before you're bitten and edging carefully with you past the bush and deeper into the tangled jungle. But now readers know the jungle is harboring cobras ...

Setbacks hold a magnifying glass up to your character's priorities, which readers get to examine closely. Even if the character is unaware of what his choices and actions reveal, readers will get an impression of them.

Examine your scenes. You might need to go back and insert clues, add red herrings, foreshadow storylines, redirect suspicion, or introduce twists that naturally lead to this new route. If so, do it.

Add the cobra.

Or add the pollen.

Or lead readers deeper into the jungle.

HOW DO SETBACKS MOVE A STORY FORWARD?

If things get easier for your character, readers will assume that you're setting him up for a big fall. If that fall never comes, they'll feel betrayed that they invested time and emotion in a storyline that "didn't go anywhere." But, of course, it did go somewhere—it just did so *without any setbacks*.

QUICK FIX: Rather than move the story forward through a series of small victories that all incrementally lead to the resolution, look for ways to create a series of small defeats that incrementally lead toward more hopelessness. In essence, allow your protagonist to fail his way forward toward the climax of the story.

TROUBLESHOOTING YOUR NOVEL

- At the end of this scene, do the characters find a detour—or simply a dead-end or destination? How does that affect the flow of the story and the choices I need to make when I revise it?
- Do the obstacles and setbacks reroute the story's progression, or bring it all to a crashing halt? How can I use overlapping promises and dip into the three realms of struggles (internal, external, and interpersonal) to solve this?
- What does my protagonist want to achieve or accomplish? Is that something my readers will either identify with or cheer for? If not, can I reshape the character's desire so readers can relate to it on a more personal or emotional level?
- Have I let my character relax too much, or am I pressing her—through escalating tension and setbacks on every page—toward change? What is constraining her from reaching her goal?
- Am I trying to move the story forward through scenes of dialogue, exposition, or description that hinge on *explanations* (a weaker storytelling choice) or on *misunderstandings* (much better for creating tension)? What obstacle can I put in the character's way to avoid explanation-burdened scenes?

12

INEVITABILITY

If readers are reacting in any of these ways, you're in trouble:

> "I don't get it."

> "This doesn't even make sense."

> "Those characters would never do that!"

> "What in the hell does that have to do with anything?"

> "So, whatever happened with the notebook? I thought that was supposed to be important in helping them find the treasure."

Readers *want* stories to make sense, they *need* stories to make sense, they *get irritated when they don't make sense*—but what does that really mean? What are the ingredients to a story "making sense"?

Events that make sense are:

1. believable, given the character's personality and pursuit.
2. logical, growing naturally from the scene's tension and the character's choices.
3. contextual, fitting organically with everything else that is going on.

Nothing will drive readers out of a story faster than the Three Killers of Reader Engagement: Unbelievable Events, Illogical Choices, and Coincidences (otherwise known as the Convenient Solutions That Come out of Nowhere).

A story unfolds as a character is pressed into corners and forced into difficult situations, and then responds in a natural way as he tries to deal with those setbacks.

Scenes will end with the *unexpected outcomes* of *believable decisions.*

Your story is constructed from a sequence of believable events that develop into inevitable storylines. In fact, the more an event seems like the only logical or legitimate option, the tighter the story will be.

....

Every choice, every action, should make sense to the character when he takes it—and it should also make sense to your readers.

....

FIXING INEVITABILITY ISSUES

Inevitability is the natural extension of believability.

In regard to believability, readers will think, *Okay, sure, I can accept that.*

In regard to inevitability, they'll think, *I can't imagine any other way this could play out.*

That's the place you want to take your readers.

As soon as the inevitable doesn't happen, disbelief creeps in. Usually, this occurs when you're trying to follow your predetermined plot outline rather than the characters' contextually emerging pursuit.

If your story isn't currently working, ask if the events within the scene, or the scenes within the novel, are believable, logical, and contextual. If they're not, fix them, change them, or cut them.

The story needs to keep making sense.

Always let your characters act authentically based on who they are and what they want in that setting, even if that means taking the story places you hadn't planned.

Be aware that if a storyline is inevitable but holds no surprises, it'll be predictable—which isn't what you want either. In the next chapter we'll look at ways to weave in surprises to create twists, but the first step to creating that twist involves constructing a world of inevitability that plays to readers' expectations (after all, if readers don't expect one thing, they won't be surprised when something else happens). Surprises rely on carefully honed expectations.

An inexplicable event is one that happens for no apparent reason. Remove all of them from your book.

Yes.

All of them.

But what if the story's progression dictates that something inexplicable needs to happen? Then justify the event by appealing to a higher virtue.

IT WOULD MAKE SENSE TO …	BUT YOU'LL APPEAL TO A HIGHER VIRTUE IF YOU …	TO CREATE A BELIEVABLE RESPONSE:
call for S.W.A.T.	let urgency trump precaution.	"There's no time to wait for backup. He'll kill her unless we move in *now*. Let's go!"
release the suspect.	let compassion trump procedure.	"If we release him, he's going to kill again before nightfall. Find something to hold him on. I don't care what. I'm not going to have innocent blood on my hands."
declare a mistrial after the disruption in the courtroom.	let justice trump red tape.	"I will not allow antics like these to derail the judicial process," the judge said. "Not in my courtroom. This trial is moving forward."

Identify every inexplicable event, brainstorm ways to appeal to a higher virtue, and then clearly communicate to readers why this subsequent action makes the most sense after all.

Beware of letting anything encroach on your story's inevitability. If it looks like it has, verify that events are moving from cause to effect, that characters are responding believably, and that the context is appropriately altering the scene's outcome.

TROUBLESHOOTING YOUR NOVEL

You can eliminate predictability by looking at the story through the readers' eyes, anticipating what readers will expect (based on the genre and the promises you've made earlier in the story), and then turning things on their head.

QUICK FIX: The believable, logical, and contextual chain of events that began at the story's inception and leads to its conclusion must remain intact throughout every scene. Cut events and decisions that happen for no apparent reason, that don't happen for a believable reason, or that don't move the story forward.

FINE-TUNING MY MANUSCRIPT

- Is the scene predictable? Or, on the other hand, is it too ridiculous? How can I recast things to make sure that the logic holds up at this point in the story, as well as later, when the twist occurs?
- Does the sustained cause-and-effect movement of the events create a sense of inevitability? If not, how can I address those problems through foreshadowing or justify the actions by appealing to higher virtues?
- Does the story stand on its own without any twists (ideal), or does it depend on the eventual twists to feel complete (not so good)? How can I make the story depend more on what *has* happened than on what *will*?
- Have I built up the inevitability of the story so the clues and revelations that occur both before and after the twist make complete sense?
- Does the character take action at the moment when readers assume that he should, or is there a delay between stimulus and response? How can I show him responding immediately to the stimulus in a way that makes sense?
- What is the most reasonable response for this character to take, given the circumstances?

13

TWISTS

When a basketball player pivots, he keeps one foot in place while spinning to the side to change direction.

That's what a plot twist does.

The story's new direction doesn't come out of nowhere. It's rooted in the overall context of the story, but it takes everyone by surprise.

Also, the momentum that appeared to be moving the story in one direction actually propels it into a new, even more meaningful one.

Look for ways to make every scene pivot away from expectation toward satisfaction.

> **A twist gives readers what they didn't know they want.**

FIXING TWIST ISSUES

A contingent event grows out of what just occurred—it depends on it and is caused by it.

A twist is simply a series of contingent events that lead readers to a place they didn't expect—but are glad they ended up in.

When we create twists, we first play to readers' expectations and then turn things in an unexpected, yet inevitable, direction.

The more that events happen by chance, the less contingent they are. So, to make your twist work, you'll include contingent choices and their consequences even as you remove chance occurrences.

When you pivot a story, you also reveal. The storyline doesn't just go in a new direction, but in a direction that reveals more about where it's been.

Pivot. Reveal. Propel.

Readers shouldn't have to think, *Oh, now I get it.* They should've "gotten it" all along.

Focus more on the twist's plausibility than on its cleverness. A minor but believable twist is more satisfying to readers than a huge one that comes out of nowhere.

1. **CHOOSE STORY ELEMENTS THAT CAN HAVE MULTIPLE MEANINGS OR SUPPORT MULTIPLE STORYLINES.** Plant seeds that could grow into two types of plants. Think in terms of *what this could mean later.* However, when those events first occur, readers shouldn't notice that they might have another, deeper meaning.

    Are there phrases, pauses, characters, clues, scenes, or actions in your story that could point in more than one direction? If not, weave some in. If so, capitalize on them. This doesn't mean that you should make these elements ambiguous when they first appear. They should always be clear, but they should look different when seen through the lens of retrospection.

2. **DISCARD THE OBVIOUS SOLUTIONS.** Brainstorm ways readers will guess that the scene will end, and then discard those ideas. All of them. Then brainstorm again, and discard those ideas too. (You might think I'm kidding, but I'm not. Once you've exhausted this second list, you'll be closer to finding your twist.)

3. **UNEARTH THE "INEVIDICTABLE" WAY.** Every scene has at least one possible ending that is inevitable but also predictable, as well as several possible endings that are unexpected but aren't inevitable. Strive to end every scene in an "inevidictable" way, or in a way that is both inevitable *and* unexpected.

    Ask, "Is this scene's ending justified? Is it logical? Is it unpredictable?" When you can answer yes to all three questions, you've found the inevidictable way to end the scene.

    Move readers from, "Man, I have no idea where this is going!" to "Oh, sweet! I should've thought of that!"

4. **DEEPEN THE MEANING OR TENSION.** Twists add meaning to the events that precede them by showing that things were not as they appeared. They also add tension. A twist that doesn't do this (such as someone waking up from a dream) will let readers down.
5. **KEEP THE STORY BELIEVABLE.** Everything before the pivot needs to make sense.

When you withhold information from readers in the hopes of surprising them later on, you'll probably end up confusing them now. Instead, let the twist grow from details you've already revealed but that readers didn't realize the significance of.

Since many authors find the challenge of coming up with a twist intimidating, it might be helpful to simply look for ways to pivot your story forward. Use the narrative momentum you have, but change course by including events that readers didn't anticipate but that are justified by the context and the flow of the story.

WHAT'S THE DIFFERENCE BETWEEN A SURPRISE AND A TWIST?

A surprise comes out of nowhere and shocks readers. A twist grows from what came before and pleases readers. A twist reveals deeper meaning or tightens the tension. A surprise doesn't necessarily do either.

QUICK FIX: If the story doesn't make sense without the twist, the twist isn't going to solve the problem. Instead, go back through the manuscript and layer in believable and logical clues with dual meaning. A twist is an integral part of a well-told story; its purpose isn't to prop up or salvage a poorly told one. The bigger the twist, the more vital it is that the story makes sense without it.

- If I include a twist early in the story, does it set things up for escalation later on? If not, how can I rework the sequence so that the twist doesn't let readers down but propels the story forward?
- How inevitable are these events? Does the story turn in an unexpected direction that'll seem even more reasonable than the direction it seemed to be heading?
- Can I improve my twist's inevitability by shading character responses to make those people seem guiltier or more innocent?
- What events have I included that could, retrospectively, contain more than one meaning? Without them, twists are impossible. Where do I need to add events that support two divergent storylines?
- What would astute readers anticipate or predict? Have I surpassed their expectations?

14

SUBPLOTS

Imagine you're a pole-vaulter.

Carrying that pole, you sprint down the track, plant the pole's tip against the ground, and let the momentum propel you up and over the bar, twenty-one feet in the air.

Nicely done.

You just broke the world record.

So, what muscle groups were necessary for this incredible feat?

Legs. Abs. Chest. Arms. Back.

Actually, I'd wager that with all the running and twisting and vaulting, it would require pretty much every muscle group in your body.

And if they weren't all working in sync, you wouldn't be able to vault very high at all. Certainly you wouldn't break any world records.

In fact, you probably wouldn't even get off the ground.

In a similar way, all of the storylines, all of the plot threads, contribute to your story's impact and success.

Think of subplots as those little-known muscle groups that help you vault.

Subplot problems occur when authors (1) add more storylines than necessary to "fill out" a novel, (2) don't resolve the struggle of each storyline, (3) allow minor storylines to overshadow the main one, and (4) don't allow the storylines to contribute to each other—which results in parallel plots rather than one integrated, multidimensional story.

Subplots that aren't vital to the main story will only distract and confuse readers.

Work toward a cohesive whole in which the different sinews that attach the details to the plot are inseparable from each other. If you were to remove them, the story's main promises would never get fulfilled. If a storyline can be cut, then cut it. You'll vault higher without the extra weight.

....

Subplots are layers of promises, not simply subordinate plotlines.

....

FIXING SUBPLOT ISSUES

Rather than focus on developing a main plot and several subplots, (1) introduce diverse, interesting characters that contribute to the story's progress, (2) make overlapping promises that will keep readers engaged, and then (3) fulfill those promises in ways readers will appreciate.

Every relationship your protagonist has provides you with an opportunity for a subplot. This doesn't mean you'll pursue all of those potential story threads, but it does mean that you can capitalize on the most important relationships to deepen your story.

Making it appear that there are parallel plots can be a way of drawing readers in as they wonder, *What do these storylines possibly have to do with each other?* Then, in a way that takes readers by surprise but also grows naturally from the narrative, bring those story threads together in the climax.

Shoot for more than just a coincidental or tangential connection between storylines. The more central the connection later in the story—and the more inconspicuous it is at first—the more satisfying it'll be when it's revealed.

Readers are carried through stories on the current of promises.

Every storyline will have its own pursuit, its own trajectory toward resolution.

The most significant promises will be fulfilled at the climax, or in your story's final moments. Readers understand that the depth and breadth of a storyline (that is, the number of words you use to develop it), is proportionate to its significance to the story.

So, condense the storylines that aren't as important, and accentuate the ones that are.

Read your book from the beginning and track each promise, each pursuit, each payoff. As you revise your story, make sure that each storyline's promises line up with and are congruent with their overall significance to the narrative.

Consider carefully how many people you bring onstage in your story, what purpose they serve, and how their storylines intertwine with the main muscle groups.

HOW MANY SUBPLOTS SHOULD I INCLUDE?

Don't worry about the number of subplots. Instead, focus on the essence and depth of the main characters' intertwining struggles. Think in terms of promises and payoff—what promises have been made? What will readers be looking forward to? What don't they care about at this moment in the story?

QUICK FIX: Make sure that all the storylines are interrelated, interdependent, and nonrepetitive. If they're too similar (for example, the three main characters all learn the same lesson about forgiveness), readers won't be satisfied. Rather than add or subtract subplots to meet a certain word count, examine where to add depth to the story and where to eliminate sections for the readers' benefit and in the service of the story's narrative promises.

FINE-TUNING MY MANUSCRIPT

- Is every point-of-view character essential to this story? Does every one of them have her own struggle, unmet desire, pursuit, and resolution?
- Are all of the storylines crucial? Do they each conclude in a satisfying way? Could I get by without one of them? Is so, why don't I?

- Have I included any storylines simply to set up another book? Will readers cheer or grumble about this?
- Is each storyline indispensable, intriguing, and inseparably connected to the main character's central struggle(s)? If not, what pivotal scene or scenes can I add to fix this?
- By the story's end, is it clear whether each character has succeeded or failed at attaining his goal? How can I work backward through the book to foreshadow the emotional or psychological place each character will reach at the end of the story?
- Is the introduction of my characters spaced appropriately, or do too many come onstage at once? Are the storylines and characters that matter most introduced early enough in the story to dial readers' expectations in the right direction?

15

ESCALATION

Picture a snowball rolling down a mountain.

Picking up speed.

Gaining momentum.

Eventually becoming an avalanche.

As it travels along, it grows in magnitude, just like the tension of your story will.

The narrative momentum of the promises you make early in the book will continue to build, creating endings that hurtle into unforgettable climaxes. Tension will tighten, complications will arise. Unavoidable detours will crop up.

The snowball is going to smack into something at the bottom of that mountain. It's not just going to quietly roll to a stop.

Stop thinking of a story in terms of something that has "a beginning, a middle, and an end." Of course it does. That's obvious. Everything has a beginning, a middle, and an end. Instead, think of the story as a progression of increasingly difficult setbacks that escalate the tension until it reaches a satisfying conclusion, regardless of the number of acts that might require.

In a story, every moment is a point of no return.

FIXING ESCALATION ISSUES

Escalation isn't about the *number* of things that go wrong; it's about the *depth and force* of that specific avalanche on that specific mountain.

So, identify your mountain, get things rolling, and escalate the avalanche.

1. **PROMISE EARLY THAT AN AVALANCHE MIGHT OCCUR.** Use implied and explicit promises that this story will move in the direction of a potential avalanche. The avalanche shouldn't come out of nowhere. As early as possible in your story, show how precariously the snow is perched on that mountain.

2. **START SMALL, GET BIG.** It seems obvious, but if you start with the avalanche, how will you escalate from there? Don't insert too much tension in your hook or your opening, or you won't have anywhere to go and the story's tension will de-escalate. Stories aren't about sustained conflict, they're about escalating struggles. Let your characters' struggles grow.

3. **SHOW READERS THE VILLAGE AT THE BASE OF THE MOUNTAIN.** Make the danger more imminent and the devastation increasingly unavoidable. You'll create even more tension if you allow readers to see the avalanche, but for the time being, keep the villagers oblivious to the danger.

4. **STAY ON ONE MOUNTAIN.** Don't just add random setbacks. Deepen your protagonist's primary struggle—the one that was introduced at the beginning of the story and revolves around his central pursuit.

5. **INCLUDE SOME SKIERS TRYING TO OUTRUN THE AVALANCHE.** When you put more characters in peril, or bring the danger closer to the people you've already introduced in the story, you'll escalate the tension. Show the skiers early in the story, heading up the mountain, to avoid the book seeming contrived when they're put in danger later on.

6. **LET THE VILLAGERS TRY TO SOLVE THINGS, BUT FAIL.** Maybe they attempt to reroute the snow, but it doesn't work. Maybe they try to flee, but the bridge collapses. Everything they try will either fail or make things worse.

7. **STEEPEN THE SLOPE.** Guess what? Things are worse than the villagers thought. When that one section of the mountain gave way, the avalanche picked up even more speed. Repetition undermines

escalation, so make sure that events progress exponentially rather than steadily. Eliminate repetition. Let things keep getting worse.

8. **THROW IN A BLIZZARD.** Why not? Foreshadow that the storm is rolling in, and then reveal the rising helplessness and hopelessness of those poor, stranded villagers.

Often, writers fail to provide variety and escalation of emotion. For example, a character is always yelling or always pounding the table or whining or gasping or sighing or crying. Instead, have the character express *escalating* emotion to show how things are continuing to get worse.

Take your protagonist, for example. In a notebook, list three ways he could show anger, impatience, or jealousy *in escalation*.

HOW MUCH ESCALATION DO I NEED?

As much as believably possible.

QUICK FIX: If a scene is stalling out, go back earlier in the book and promise pain or danger, and then remind readers of how close that danger is right now. Insert an obstacle that the characters must avoid, but by doing so they end up closer to the brink. Verify that each scene contains an appropriate sense of urgency based on the context, the pursuit, and the current time frame.

As you get closer to the climax, include shorter paragraphs and sentences, and avoid unfamiliar words that might trip up readers.

FINE-TUNING MY MANUSCRIPT

- Have I successfully brought the danger closer and closer, sharpened the promises of peril, and clarified the consequences and stakes?
- As the story builds toward its climax, have I focused more on tightening the tension than on rising action? Have I mistaken movement or action for escalation? How can I include less action but imbue it with more meaning, using fewer events but giving them more narrative significance?

- As the tension escalates, have I made things personal for the protagonist?
- Is the escalation undercut by too much repetition? Where do I have similar events (chase scenes, murders, sex scenes, etc.) that don't escalate? How can I eliminate some or ratchet up the tension, danger, or stakes of others as they build toward the climax?
- Is the unmet desire of the characters clear in each scene? How can I add more complications to drive the story forward?
- Do the struggles intensify as the main character tries to solve her problem and fails, scene by scene, until she either achieves her goal (or fails to achieve it) in a way that is unexpected and inevitable?

16

DESPAIR

Is there a way out for your character?

It better not look like it.

If it does, readers will just assume that the character will do That One Obvious Thing That Solves All His Problems—and if they realize the solution before he does, they'll think he's stupid for not noticing it.

Also, if the solution was available all along (the "Gosh, Dorothy, you could have gone home at any time with those wonderful shoes! Instead, I just kept that knowledge from you and let you and your friends almost get killed over and over again! Wasn't that so kind of me?" approach), it'll annoy readers. If the problem could have been solved earlier, why wasn't it?

Additionally, if readers can think of a way the situation could believably get worse for the protagonist, they'll be disappointed if it doesn't.

So, here's your job: Make the situation for the protagonist worse than readers anticipate, yet as hopeless as they can fathom—and then solve it in a way they would never expect but are thrilled to see.

Sound like a challenge?

It *absolutely* is a challenge.

That's one reason why great novels are so hard to find.

(And write.)

....

Just when it looks like things can't get any worse, they will. The more impossible the situation seems, the more satisfying it'll be to readers when it's believably solved.

....

FIXING DESPAIR ISSUES

As the tension reaches its highest point, your protagonist will reach his lowest.

The darkest moment in your story will come right before the greatest discovery or epiphany, or that final climactic encounter between good and evil. Often, your character will reach a point of despair—or at least a situation in which it appears that she has no way out.

It'll seem as if nothing more could go wrong.

But then it does.

And when it does, it'll be something believable, it'll make sense, and it'll leave readers wondering how in the world the protagonist is going to get out of this terrible mess.

- If the story is a mystery, all the obvious solutions will be discarded. The solution will seem impossible, the riddle unsolvable.
- If it's a romance, it'll appear that the misunderstanding cannot be resolved, that the relationship can't be saved, or that the two lovers won't end up together.
- If it's a thriller, the hero might find herself in a life-or-death struggle with the clock ticking down and the lives of thousands of innocent people hanging in the balance.

Readers want a hopeless moment.

When your protagonist reaches the end of her rope, cut it. Let her fall. See what happens then. That's when the story's truest conclusion will emerge.

Along the way, consider her fears, her disadvantages, and her isolation.

1. MAKE HER CONFRONT HER GREATEST FEAR. Snakes. Heights. Needles. Drowning. Whatever it is, if it's contextually appropriate, bring it on.

Often, the issue isn't so much about what she's afraid of experiencing but what she's afraid of losing—perhaps the life of a loved one.

When you begin writing your story, you might not know what this is, or who matters most to her, but as you discover what she *loves* most you'll also learn what she *fears* most—losing that person (or thing) she cares so much about.

Usually, the thing that your character believes to be her greatest fear at the start of the story won't turn out to be her greatest, *greatest* fear.

For example, if being buried alive is the worst thing she can think of, what if she were buried alive with a cell phone that shows footage of her daughter being buried alive an hour earlier?

Take it all the way.

2. PUT HER AT A DISADVANTAGE. At the hopeless moment, your character will likely be in a situation where she has the least amount of control, or the lowest amount of situational status, for the whole book. (For more on status, see chapter thirty-three.)

3. HAVE EVERYONE ELSE BETRAY HER OR ABANDON HER. Put her in a place where others have left her physically, emotionally, or psychologically. Press her to the limit, and see how she responds.

- What will this dark moment impel her to do? (Think of something she would never have been prepared to do at the start of the story.)
- What will the darkness cause her to become? (A hero? A villain? A hero who must become a villain to vanquish evil?)
- When she's hopeless, where will she turn? Will that person let her down? (You better believe it.) What will she do then? (I don't know, but things have started to get interesting ...)

Stack the deck against her, and force her to face the evil alone. Why can't she just wait for the cops, call 9-1-1, or go in with overwhelming force? Think of a reason. She must have a need to act quickly to solve the problem rather than simply wait around for help to arrive.

HOW FAR SHOULD I TAKE MY PROTAGONIST INTO THE STRUGGLE?

Take him to a place where readers are thinking, *I have no idea how he's going to get out of this situation/solve this crime/find the love of his life/stop the terrorists/save the human race from extinction.* Don't hold back.

QUICK FIX: Search for a way to make the situation more hopeless. It might require you to go back and foreshadow some sort of danger earlier in the story. If so, do it. This moment of darkness before the climax is one of the most crucial scenes in your story. All must appear lost or the climax will fall flat.

FINE-TUNING MY MANUSCRIPT

- Is the hero in trouble? If not, why would anyone want to read this?
- Have I believably isolated the protagonist for the climax by removing her support system or the ability to call for help? Is this the inevitable culmination of all that precedes it?
- Have I made him face his greatest fear? Confront his greatest question? Rise to the occasion? What would it take for him to abandon his pursuit? Could I use a "pressure to quit the quest" force in my story?
- How has she become disillusioned? In what areas of her life has she lost hope? What caused that? What has she lost faith in?
- Does the protagonist have a moment in which his resolve wavers or he wants to give up—but yet doesn't lose his status or the respect of readers?
- Have I made certain that the hero fights fair at the end, that she's at a disadvantage, and that she isn't rescued by someone else? Have I removed coincidence, problem solvers, or tools that appear right when she needs them?
- How can I make things worse? Have I really taken my character to the brink, or could he descend even further into the abyss?

17

CLIMAX

The best is no longer yet to come.

It's finally here.

As viscerally engaging or gripping as your opening is, it won't be as thrilling as your climax. As great as those chase scenes were, they won't compare to what goes down here.

The climax is more than just the last event in a series of events, more than just the cessation of the action in your story. It is the conclusive or resultant event. It is the culmination of all that came before it.

Everything you've been promising is about to come together.

If the promises of the story don't all meet here, intertwine, and pay off, readers will very likely feel let down—or worse, betrayed.

> **If any other scene in your story is more gripping or emotionally resonant than your climax, you're telling the story in the wrong order.**

FIXING CLIMAX ISSUES

While genre conventions will influence the content of your book's climax, some principles apply across the board.

1. **THERE WILL APPEAR TO BE NO WAY OUT.** It's going to look like the protagonist will fail, but here's the secret: Somehow he'll pull the rug out from under evil (or, perhaps, in horror, evil will pull the rug out from under him). He's going to turn the tables by finding a solution readers didn't anticipate but will immediately

recognize as the right one, based on the context and the promises you've made.

2. **THIS IS THE MOST IMPORTANT SCENE FOR YOU TO RENDER.** This isn't the time to summarize things. It's not the scene that you jump over and then come back to later to fill readers in on what happened. Don't explain things. Let the scene play out, blow by blow. By now readers have invested a lot of time in this story. Don't let it be in vain. Say less at the climax. Show more.

3. **THE PROTAGONIST WILL SOLVE THE PROBLEM HERSELF.** Don't let someone else come to the rescue. Don't solve the climax through coincidence. Don't solve it through divine intervention. If you do so, readers will rightly feel cheated. If you have multiple protagonists or heroes, construct a cascading climax in which each of them contributes in a meaningful way to the story's resolution, with the greatest challenge or sacrifice coming last.

4. **"PLAN A" WILL FAIL.** So will "Plan B." And each will cost your protagonist something. Readers don't want easy solutions. If the protagonist's first idea works, readers will not be thrilled.

5. **THE PROTAGONIST'S ACUMEN OR COURAGE WILL BE REVEALED.** Have her solve things (1) through perseverance, (2) through quick thinking or savviness, (3) by applying skills she has discovered or refined through the story, (4) by putting into practice a lesson or insight she has learned, (5) by facing a challenge or difficulty that she would not have been prepared or courageous enough to face at the start of the story, or (6) through inner resolve or strength of character.

6. **HIS UNIQUENESS WILL BE SIGNIFICANT.** Is the protagonist a sagacious detective who's always one step ahead? Is he a sharpshooter? Does he always carry a Swiss Army Knife? Consider ways in which he might use his special skills or emblem in the climax. (Or, if readers are expecting him to use that asset, take it away and let him rely solely on his wits. That'll work too.)

7. **THE SCENE WILL MAKE CONTEXTUAL SENSE.** Plant the seed for the solution early in the story. Here is where it flowers. This is not where it's planted.

8. **THE CLIMAX MUST COST THE PROTAGONIST SOMETHING, OR IT WILL MEAN NOTHING.** In narrative worlds, we measure the value of something by how much pain or suffering the character endures when it's lost. Let her make a courageous choice under pressure or offer something precious to save someone else. It might ultimately mean giving up her life in a symbolic (or even a literal) way.

WHAT'S THE SECRET TO A GREAT CLIMAX?

A masterful climax depends on the scene that precedes it and the promises that lead up to it. The climax will only be satisfying if the protagonist truly is in dire straights and has no conceivable way to solve his dilemma—but then manages to do so with a choice that results in a satisfying but surprising turn of events.

QUICK FIX: Don't edit your climax in isolation. Print out the preceding twenty pages (or two hundred) and let the context shape the way this crucial scene plays out. Keep the promises you've made earlier, and make sure things remain believable and logical all the way to the end. Remember that the climax reaches a moment after which no more escalation makes contextual sense. If you can think of a better ending, your readers will likely be able to as well.

FINE-TUNING MY MANUSCRIPT

- Is the climax the most exciting, tense, emotionally resonant, and fulfilling scene of the story? If not, how can I develop more escalation, sharpen promises, and then keep those promises in more believable and less contrived ways?
- Does the protagonist succumb to the forces of antagonism, or does she vanquish them? If she succumbs (that is, gives in to the darkness or is destroyed by it), do I foreshadow this so that it's inevitable? If she's victorious at the end, is it in a way that's unexpected but will make complete sense to readers?

- Does the protagonist face his greatest fear or meet his greatest challenge? If not, why not?
- Does he use his wits, resolve, persistence, or previously untapped inner strength in this final confrontation with his nemesis?
- Does it feel like the solution was too easy or too convoluted? Does it have too may twists? Is it too convenient or coincidental? What will I do about that?
- Does the outcome of the climax depend on the protagonist making a hard-won choice, or on a chance occurrence or an "act of God"?

18

EPIPHANIES

An epiphany is a transformative realization that alters the trajectory of someone's life.

It might lead to a spiritual awakening, a fresh perspective, or a new understanding of what really matters. The protagonist could experience a change of heart or deep remorse or true repentance. Sometimes he'll uncover a mystery or discover an important lesson about himself or about how to treat others.

Maybe he'll learn how much good he's able to accomplish.

Maybe he'll discover how much evil he's truly capable of.

Whatever the insight is, it'll affect him in a way that's evidenced by a choice he makes.

Your story is a way of observing life through the lens of meaningful moral decisions. Readers will evaluate whether it's telling the truth about human nature or not. Trite clichés and preachiness won't cut it—that's not what they're hoping for.

Sometimes epiphanies will come immediately *before* the climax and give the character the resolve or insight to rise to the challenge. Other times, they might follow immediately *on the heels* of the climax and reveal what the character has learned as a result of facing it.

> **Epiphanies must be earned. Every lesson worth learning comes with a scar.**

FIXING EPIPHANY ISSUES

Here are four ways to undermine the effect of your character's epiphany. Avoid them all.

1. He Hasn't Suffered His Way Toward Change

Just like people in real life, story characters learn important lessons the hard way. Pain is the greatest teacher. Growth is costly.

The more important the lesson, the more crucial it is for your protagonist to learn it in The School of Hard Knocks rather than The School of Easy Insights (that is, being told the answer and believing it, applying it, and living happily ever after).

Another character (typically a mentor or someone in a position of low status) might tell your protagonist the solution earlier in the story, but he will reject it.

Why?

Because accepting it would mean he's learning truth the easy way, and that's not what fiction is here to show.

But why not?

Because real life isn't like this, so that kind of story wouldn't ring true to readers. We don't typically embrace lessons and immediately put them into practice. We flail. We fall. We fail.

In fact, if the character *does* accept the advice and applies it right off the bat, readers will instinctively know that it's *not* the answer he was looking for. They'll assume that it's going to lead to more trouble and that the deeper epiphany lies somewhere at the other end of an impending painful experience.

2. The Epiphany Is Coincidental

Discoveries can be *serendipitous* (a character discovers something that she hadn't set out to find), but avoid *coincidental* ones (a character conveniently discovers exactly what she needs at just the right moment).

The most effective epiphanies don't come out of nowhere but rather emerge naturally from the context and the promises that undergird the story. Giving your character sudden insights without something to cause them will weaken your story and annoy your readers. You may need to foreshadow the epiphany to make it more inevitable. If so, do it.

3. The Lesson Comes from an Authority Figure

Mom gives her daughter useful dating advice. The pastor instructs his congregation on how to live victoriously. Your protagonist's breakthrough finally comes from the wise guru at that self-help seminar.

None of these lessons are satisfying because none of them are earned. (Not to mention that plots like these come across as preachy and predictable.)

If you absolutely must have another character share a lesson with the protagonist, that character will have learned the lesson the hard way himself—and have the scars (emotional, psychological, relational) to prove it. It's also best if the advice doesn't come from someone in a position of authority or high social status. Make the advice-giver a beaten-down and weathered observer of life, not someone who claims to have all the answers.

4. The Epiphany Is Drawn from a Positive Example

To show a virtue, don't tell a story about how well things work out if people would only put The Five Simple Steps to Happier Living into practice. Instead, to exemplify a virtue, tell a story that reveals the consequences of its opposite.

If your virtue is forgiveness, show the consequences of holding a grudge. If it's a story about the importance of listening to others, show the consequences of ignoring others or of making assumptions. (This is a staple of humor, which often taps into miscommunication, and of romantic comedies, which often utilize misunderstanding between the sexes.)

HOW CAN I SHOW MY CHARACTER'S PERSONAL DEVELOPMENT?

If your character comes to a new understanding of life, she needs to suffer her way toward it. Insights shouldn't simply be handed out by advice-givers or authority figures. The deeper the revelation about life, the greater the pain that precedes it.

> **QUICK FIX:** Allow any epiphanies to grow from conflict and choice rather than from a character seeking advice from someone else. Show your character's hard-won revelations by allowing him to make a choice that his suffering earned him the courage to pursue. Think of situations you can use to teach the lesson the hard way—and then test his new conviction in (or right after) the climax.

FINE-TUNING MY MANUSCRIPT

- Does the protagonist make a choice that leads to the epiphany or the climax, or am I depending on coincidence, chance, or an answer-giver to bring closure to the story?
- The epiphany might *equip the character to meet* the physical challenge of the story or *result from it* as he realizes what he's capable of. Which happens in my story?
- Does the main character experience a moment of clarity? Since readers want to see the protagonist learn something about herself, what she's capable of doing, or who she's capable of becoming, have I brought this out in the story?
- Do the revelations happen at the right moments? If readers deduce the solution to a mystery before the detective, they'll feel that he is dim-witted and less than heroic. Will that happen in my story?
- How well have I shown the main character facing his greatest challenge (or his greatest fear) and exhibiting wit and grit (or skill and will) to confront or battle the forces of antagonism? To what degree is this scene rendered rather than summarized? How can I improve that?

19

TRANSFORMATION

Think of times of transition in your life—getting married, having a child, going through a divorce, moving to a new home. Getting hired. Getting fired. Starting over.

Life is a series of doors opening and closing.

Transitions engender transformations. Things have changed and will never be the same again. Unveiling those transformations is what storytelling is all about.

A story without a transformation of some sort will feel incomplete no matter how many pages it spans. Readers want to witness how the protagonist's circumstances, understanding, or relationships are transformed.

So, explore how this character or his situation is no longer the same, because all the doors leading back to the old life are locked for good.

But new doors and new vistas lie ahead.

> Readers won't buy it if you depict (1) change
> without struggle, (2) change without choice,
> or (3) change without cost.

FIXING TRANSFORMATION ISSUES

You'll sometimes hear authors or editors talk about a *story arc* or a *character arc*. These terms simply refer to where the transformation occurs: externally or internally. While it's helpful to understand these concepts, not every story (or protagonist) has a complete arc, and the change is not limited to these two areas.

The greatest change (or arc) will occur in the realm of the greatest struggle, whether that's internal, external, or interpersonal.

Most of the time, one struggle will be paramount to the story you're telling. This is the struggle you've spent the most time exploring, fastened the most promises to, and focused the most attention on—and it's the one in which readers will expect to see the biggest transformation.

- Is the protagonist on an inner journey of self-discovery? Then the *character's nature or understanding* will be transformed.
- Is he battling external forces of evil? Then the *situation* will be transformed.
- Is he striving to start or repair a relationship? Then this *relationship* will be transformed.

Either the protagonist's circumstances, attitude, or perspective will change—otherwise the story is pointless. A *dynamic* character is changed by the outcome, even if the external situation isn't much different; a *static* character changes the outcome, even if his internal condition isn't much different. At the start of a story, the protagonist will have a personal definition of success or happiness. Some stories will challenge him to change that view, while others will challenge him to change himself or his surroundings.

When thinking of transformations, it's helpful to keep in mind the three realms of struggles and the promises and payoff each contains with regard to your story.

1. Internal Struggles (Character Arcs)

If you've shown that the central struggle is internal, then readers will expect the most transformation to occur in the character's inner life. At the end of the story, the rest of the world might go on as usual, but this character has been changed forever.

By the way, iconic characters don't change with each story. James Bond, Miss Marple, Tarzan, Jack Reacher, Batman, Sherlock Holmes—these characters aren't altered or internally transformed during each subsequent adventure.

In fact, that's why readers keep looking for the next story about that character—not to see him change, but to see him act. The stories reveal what he's like, but they don't cataclysmically alter his nature or perspective.

2. External Struggles (Story Arcs)

In stories that are primarily about tackling an external problem—catching a kidnapper, stopping a terrorist, saving the world—the story arc will often be quite clear.

Examine the depth of the promises you've made regarding the importance of solving this problem. At the end of the story, show situational change that is commensurate with those promises.

3. Interpersonal Struggles (Relational Arcs)

In a sense, these are both internal and external struggles. Here the relationships change. She might find true love, or she might realize that she doesn't need anyone else to feel complete. In either case, the state of her relationships will be affected.

• • •

The depth of the revelation will be determined by the intimacy or enormity of the struggle. Once again, lessons that come cheaply will feel cheap to readers: The bigger the insight, the greater the suffering that will precede it.

HOW SHOULD I SHOW THE TRANSFORMATION?

It'll depend on the type of story you're telling, but to show external change, focus on what's different in or about the world now that the character's pursuit is over. To show inner or interpersonal change, give him an opportunity to respond to a situation that he wouldn't have been prepared to tackle before the story began. Don't tell readers that he's *thinking* differently, show them that he's *acting* differently.

QUICK FIX: Study the overt and implied promises in your story. What does the protagonist want? What is she pursuing? In which realm are her struggles the deepest or most profound? Analyze each realm of struggle and clearly delineate how the story has affected the pursuit in that realm. Make sure that the primary struggle throughout the story is the one in which the most change occurs at the end of the story.

FINE-TUNING MY MANUSCRIPT

- Does the character undergo enough trial and suffering to justify this amount of transformation in this story? If not, where do I need to squeeze him more?
- What's altered at the end of the story compared to the beginning? What remains the same?
- How is my protagonist different? Will this transformation seem natural, considering the journey she has been on?
- What are readers coming to this story for? A hero they can believe in? An everyman character they can identify with? How does my storytelling voice support and/or affect my readers' expectations?
- How has the protagonist's view of herself, others, or her world changed? Does she still believe the same things will make her happy? Does she still desire the same things out of life?
- What aspects of the protagonist's inner character or true priorities have been revealed? How is he more prepared for his next adventure? What is the new direction his life will take?

20

RESURRECTIONS

A serpent has slithered into paradise and whispered lies to God's children.

Their choices have brought death, destruction, suffering.

And now—the death of God himself.

It's Friday. Jesus has been buried in the tomb.

But the story is not yet over.

A new day is about to dawn on Sunday morning.

Perhaps the most famous resurrection story of all is the one concerning Jesus of Nazareth. While Christians believe this to be a literal resurrection, in fiction, most of the time the protagonist's death and resurrection are symbolic.

Her "death" might come in the form of a shattered dream, a lost love, a prison sentence. She might be knocked unconscious or slip into a coma.

A "resurrection" comes when she emerges from the crisis (the "grave") and finds redemption, new life, or new hope.

Often, after the final climax, in which the protagonist appears to have no chance for survival, readers witness a form of mythic resurrection as she rises to fight for justice again or to battle evil another day.

Death and rebirth are powerful images that speak to our deepest longings for meaning and for a way to live on into the future.

The moment of darkness that precedes the climax might be so dark, so hopeless, that it will take the "life" of the protagonist. But that's not the end of the story ...

FIXING RESURRECTION ISSUES

Before the resurrection, someone or something must die—either literally or symbolically. Sometimes it isn't the main character who dies; sometimes it's a relationship or an abstract idea, like justice or hope.

Since your character is experiencing such a demanding test before coming through on the other side, it does make sense that when he reemerges it'll seem like he has "died" and then "conquered death."

Out of death can come new life.

The death of a dream can mean embracing a new destiny. The death of a marriage can be the start of a new relationship.

But as soon as the resurrection becomes blatant, it loses its effect. So, look for subtler, more understated ways to illustrate it.

RESURRECTION	HOW TO SHOW IT
Emblem	An object (a music box, military dog tags, a wedding ring, etc.) that was significant to the dead character is reintroduced at the end of the story to represent new life or to show that the character is moving on.
Photo	A photograph or video with the person who has "died" reemerges. (Often, this technique feels inauthentic and unsatisfactory if the person is literally dead.)
Journal	A diary, blog, or social media site is received, discovered, or reviewed.
Emergence	Someone goes under and comes back up (gets buried alive and is then rescued, gets baptized, wakes from a coma, etc.)
Birth/Pregnancy	Oh no, he's dead—but guess what? His wife/lover/one-night-stand/fiancée is pregnant! (This new life represents the man's "resurrection.")
Passageway	Someone steps off an elevator, exits a doorway, or walks out into the city, signifying new life, repentance, or a new perspective.
Voice-Over	The narrator or protagonist gives us her words or insights from beyond the grave.

Fertility	A symbol of new life unfolds: a flower greets the day, the fruit hangs ripe on the vine, the sun dawns in the sky.
Dream	The smiling image of a dead son or wife or Jedi appears and offers reassurance to the remaining characters that things are going to be okay.
Actual Resurrection	The kiss of his lover on his forehead brings him back to life.

If one of these images works organically within your story, feel free to insert it—but don't feel the need to. Resurrections are most effective when they don't draw attention to themselves.

Redemptive stories will end with the resurrection of hope: All seems lost, but it's not. It has returned, often in a different form. In contrast, horror stories will end with the resurrection of evil: The virus the doctors thought they had wiped out lives on—in the cough of that guy getting on the airplane. Or the killer is caught, but he has passed the torch, so to speak, to his young protégé.

A horror ending is actually like a reverse resurrection. Just as the story appears to end with hope, suddenly it takes a final plunge into despair. The story moves from resurrection to death—usually a worse death than the character could have ever imagined before the story began.

WHAT KIND OF ENDING DO READERS WANT?

Most of all they want an honest one. Readers prefer a natural and logical ending that's in sync with the story preceding it to an ending in which everyone unrealistically ends up happy or riding off into the sunset. Readers want the ending to make sense, to be believable, and, for most genres, to be redemptive. If the ending is *too* happy, it'll feel contrived. On the other hand, if it's too hopeless, it'll be depressing.

QUICK FIX: To avoid stories that leave readers disappointed, foreshadow that things might not work out well for everyone in the end. To avoid contrived endings, let the story play out honestly. Make sure the mood of the ending matches the mood promised by the story's opening scenes.

TROUBLESHOOTING YOUR NOVEL

FINE-TUNING MY MANUSCRIPT

- If appropriate for my story, could I circle back to an image or emblem at the end that would signify rebirth, redemption, or new life?
- Have I shown transformation of a situation, character, or relationship, perhaps through a new perspective, insight, renewed courage, or freedom?
- Do my climax and its aftermath make sense? Are the events believable—or does the solution come out of nowhere?
- Does the end feel artificial? Is it in concert with the rest of the story? Does it contain emotional resonance that will satisfy readers?
- Did I promise the tone of the ending by the style and voice of my storytelling before the story reached the climax?

21

CLOSURE

The closing is the final note of the song.

It will emerge naturally from all of the other notes and carry the melody to a satisfying conclusion. It's the one you want readers to walk away hearing, the final impression you want to give them.

Let it be the most resonant note of all.

The closing wraps up the story in an elegant way and pulls together events that have, until now, seemed unrelated.

When you include two storylines that appear to parallel each other, you're making a promise that they'll eventually intersect.

If they haven't yet, they will at the story's close.

Readers will feel let down if they can guess how the story will end or how it will get to the end. They'll also be unhappy if the closure feels inauthentic, inorganic to the story, contrived, or if it isn't the culmination of the character's pursuit or doesn't provide satisfying resolution.

> **The ending doesn't need to be tidy,**
> **but it does need to be honest.**

FIXING CLOSURE ISSUES

Apart from stories in the horror genre, readers typically want evil to be vanquished, love to triumph, choices to matter, and justice to prevail. If evil wins or love is defeated or the character's choices prove meaningless, readers might find the story depressing or even feel that it doesn't accurately portray reality.

Q: "Does my story need a happy ending?"

A: No. But a redemptive ending is usually preferable. Readers prefer endings that feel true to the story over syrupy-sweet ones in which everyone lives happily ever after. If happiness comes (and it probably will, at least in some form), it will come at a great cost.

Q: "Do I need a final twist?"

A: Readers always love a twist, so if you can include a final pivot or reveal at the very end, go for it. Just make sure it's organic to the story.

Q: "What about an epilogue?"

A: Don't let things get tiresome or try to explain too much at the end. Kill your story while it's still kicking.

Q: "Should I include a teaser at the end?"

A: Teasers make new promises or insert a new disruption that'll be significant to the next story in the series. If your book is part of a series, readers will probably enjoy a teaser. It should grow naturally from the story and come after the major resolutions have occurred. Don't include one that might annoy readers or make them feel like they need to read the next book to figure out what's really going on. Every book should stand on its own and not require another book to explain it.

Q: "Does the character need to change?"

A: Not necessarily, not in a fundamental way. However, if the story centers on his internal struggles, yes. Show the natural state of affairs for the story's characters. Show how they've developed and where they're going. Ask how (in a literal or figurative sense) the protagonist is moving in, moving out, moving up, or moving on. Let readers see that—or at least hint that things are going to be different for the protagonist from now on.

Q: "Can I leave any questions hanging in the air?"

A: If your reader will be more thrilled by uncertainty, sure. If they'll be more satisfied by closure, wrap things up. At this point in the story, readers have invested a significant amount of time and emotion, and they deserve an ending that gratifies them. Err on the side of providing closure instead of ending with ambiguity or making them feel stupid.

Q: "What about symbolic endings?"

A: Don't try to be too symbolic, and don't let your symbolism become more important than believability or causality. You don't want readers thinking, *Oh, I see what he's doing. That fog represents how the guy couldn't make decisions and how he was always in a fog. My high school English teacher would have been so proud.* As soon as readers begin dwelling on the presence of symbolism, they're no longer engaged in the story.

DO I NEED TO TIE UP ALL THE LOOSE ENDS?

No, but you need to keep all your promises. Not every story closes up in a way that's clean and tidy.

Even though some stories end with a dramatic plunge, the introduction of new conflict, or an open door for a sequel, generally readers don't like being left with unresolved questions about the story's resolution.

QUICK FIX: Page through your manuscript and identify the primary characters' pursuits, desires, or quests. Write them down. Next, look for locations, clues, or promises you've portrayed as significant. Either make sure they're all fulfilled or recast the story so readers won't expect them to be.

FINE-TUNING MY MANUSCRIPT

• Does the story ring true? Does it end in a way that's inevitable (that is, honest to what led up to it)?

- Is the moral dilemma resolved? Has the protagonist arrived at a place where he comes to terms with his problem or takes a definitive step toward doing so?
- If I've included a teaser, does it leave readers wanting more, or has it annoyed them because things aren't really over after all?
- Have I trimmed off as much as I can after the climax?
- Can I include a final reveal or twist that would add more meaning to the entire book or to one of the significant storylines? What would I need to foreshadow to make that happen?
- Have all the promises that matter been fulfilled? Is the payoff worth the anticipation? If not, how can I alter either the promises or the payoff to fix this?

PART II

CHARACTERIZATION

22

ATTITUDE

Fire or ice, take your pick.

Readers do not want to spend time with apathetic characters.

On fire? Yes. Ice cold? Sure, at least for a while.

Lukewarm? Not a chance.

In real life, apathy fizzles out conversations, turns people off, and ruins relationships. In fiction, an apathetic protagonist rings the death knell to reader engagement. The less a character cares about life, the less readers will care about that character.

Just as with real people, a fictional character's attitude will be affected by his setting, the people he's with, and the other issues in his life. There'll be things that distract him, worry him, or annoy him. He'll have goals and frustration. Temptations. Envy. Petty jealousies. Grudges. All of these factors (and more) have the potential to impact his attitude—in every scene.

Characters with a unique set of attitudes might be polarizing or they might be endearing—but either way they'll be fascinating to readers.

People with an attitude are instantly intriguing.

Having your character show an attitude toward something or someone is one of the fastest ways to make him interesting.

FIXING ATTITUDE ISSUES

Strive to capture your protagonist's unique way of seeing the world and responding to it. Does she hate pink puffy slippers? Do chipper people make her jittery? Is he advocating for chimpanzees to have the same rights as human beings?

Sometimes you can let your character love something that most people hate, or hate something that most people love:

> "You don't like dogs?"
>
> "Nope. Not at all."
>
> "But dogs are man's best friend!"
>
> "Yeah, well, I have a policy—any time my best friend starts sniffing my butt or eating his own vomit, it's time to find a new best friend."
>
> "Um. I never thought of it quite like that."

Let your character feel *something* toward issues. Don't let him be wishy-washy. He's going to take a stand, even if there are negative consequences for doing so. If he's easygoing in some areas of life, let him be driven to extremes in others. What does he rebel against? Who would he give his life to save?

Your protagonist can be opinionated but not judgmental.

Sarcastic but not smarmy.

And never whiny.

Never, never whiny.

Readers don't enjoy the company of someone who's moping around all the time; however, allowing your character to grumble once in a while can make her endearing:

> "Good luck. You have about as much chance of getting into that college as you do of finding a furniture store that's not going out of business."

Ask yourself:

- Is he a morning person or an anti-morning person?
- How does she feel about the metric system? Bacon? People who baby talk to their pets?
- What is her nemesis piece of clothing? Vehicle? Vegetable?
- What are his pet peeves?

TROUBLESHOOTING YOUR NOVEL

- What benign thing is she boycotting? What insignificant thing does she celebrate?

Consider the areas of her life where she conforms and those where she does not. Look for contrasts that reveal depth or ignite interest. Maybe she conforms in fashion but not in religion. Or she's conventional in her career but not in her hobbies. Or maybe she acquiesces and drinks any type of coffee but will only use that one particular brand of toilet paper and carries some with her wherever she goes.

What does she notice that others don't? For instance:

> "In every picture you see of Eve in the Garden of Eden, her hair is draped oh-so-conveniently in front of her boobs, but, I mean, what if she would've been poofing her hair when the picture was taken?"
>
> "I don't think it's an actual photograph."
>
> She went on, unfazed. "Or how about this: Can you imagine how different our impression of Paradise would be if Eve would've been bald? I suppose at least the story would be a little more interesting to junior high boys."
>
> "Point taken."

Since stories are about the pursuit of happiness and aren't just accounts of sustained states of bliss, if you show a character with too much optimism and an overly positive attitude, or someone who has all the answers, she can quickly annoy readers.

Perhaps give her a tragedy and let her struggle to remain optimistic, or have her show passion about life by noticing something special about another person, finding a new purpose for a worthless object, or seeing beauty in something other people would consider mundane.

To reveal a character's attitude toward himself or toward others, have him view himself through the other person's eyes:

> "Yeah, if he were to describe me, he'd probably say I'm too old for this sort of thing."

In this way, readers can see the character's perception of himself, of the other person, and of how that other person sees him.

WHAT MAKES A CHARACTER INTRIGUING?

Engaging characters have attributes that readers admire or respect. He might be passionate, courageous, adventurous, free-spirited, or fun loving. He might stand up for what he believes in or go "all in" when the cards are stacked against him. He's interesting to be around. There's more to him than meets the eye.

QUICK FIX: While honoring genre conventions, avoid clichés regarding your characters. Give your protagonist an attitude about a hot-button issue and a passion for a virtue your readers consider honorable, such as courage, self-sacrifice, compassion, or advocacy for the oppressed. Strive for contrasts, attitude, and self-deprecation rather than arrogance.

FINE-TUNING MY MANUSCRIPT

- Without overdoing it, have I allowed this character to express his uniqueness?
- Where have I gone too far and made him annoying? How will I tweak that?
- Does my protagonist have a broad consistency through the book, even as his attitude is affected by what's happening in each scene?
- In what ways does she go with the flow? How does she swim upstream? How will that impact her relationships with those closest to her?
- Which of my protagonist's attributes might turn off readers? How can I change those to make her more endearing?
- How will her attitude about the setting and her interaction with it affect the direction of the story?

23

INTENTIONALITY

If you were trying to understand what makes me tick, or if you wanted to figure out what I value most, the best way wouldn't be to have me describe myself, or even to have someone else describe me.

No. If you wanted to get to know me—I mean *really* get to know me—the best way would be to watch me when things don't go my way. How do I act when I face friction, deadlines, setbacks, failure? That's the true measure of character.

What am I like when I don't get what I want?

Don't ask me.

Don't even ask the people around me.

Watch how I respond.

• • •

Characterization is always depicted most clearly and quickly when your character is trying to overcome an obstacle that's keeping him from getting what he wants. Stick some roadblocks in his way and force him to handle them. Give him a moral dilemma and watch him try to solve it.

Until a character takes action in pursuit of a goal (or away from a pursuer), we have only the precursor to a story. We've set the stage for the tale, but it hasn't yet begun.

How does he deal with tragedy? Fight oppression? Rescue the innocent? Deal with (or avoid) his fear?

This is what lies at the heart of character.

> You control when readers ask, "Why?" They
> control how long they'll put up with having to
> ask it. Clarifying a character's intention
> grounds readers and gives feet to her desires.

FIXING INTENTIONALITY ISSUES

Intention is simply a goal-directed task. Motivation is the reason that leads the person to desire it.

Intention rather than motivation drives every story, affects every scene. The motive might not be evident or even relevant. For example, why does the killer kill: Genetics? Upbringing? Environmental cues? To what degree is evil hardwired into our brains, and how much of it comes from free will? What compels us to act?

While the motivation might be interesting to know, it often makes little difference to the scenes in your book. The fact that he's about to kill this girl right now and the protagonist has to stop him matters far more than the psychological factors that led the criminal to have these violent urges.

Many authors make the mistake of trying to delve into the character's past but neglect clarifying intention in the present scene. Why is the character here? What does he want? Only when readers know what the characters are trying to accomplish or overcome will they know what the scene is truly about.

Stop thinking in terms of the information you want a scene to convey. Instead, focus on how the character chooses to overcome obstacles.

When developing setbacks, don't just look for a multiplicity of things that could go wrong. Instead, choose ones that will impair that particular character's quest or get in the way of him reaching a specific goal in this specific scene.

Is he trying to get a promotion? Seduce the woman next to him at the bar? Convert his friend to a different religion? Punish his dad for what he did to him in the past?

Whatever his goal, make it clear to readers. Perhaps have another character ask him straight out what he wants:

> "What are you hoping to get out of this?"

> "Why would you even show up here today? What do you want?"

> "What are you trying to do?"

> "How can I help you?"

> "I see you have a gun. So, that's it, huh? You've come here to shoot me?"

You can also reveal intention by having a character simply state why she's in the scene. Try to construct scenes with mutually exclusive goals. In other words, one character is trying to accomplish something that won't be attainable if the other characters in the scene get what they want:

> "I'm here to kill you."
> "Good luck. I'm pretty good with a knife."

When you're working on a scene, the question isn't "If I were this character, what would I do?" but "How would this character most naturally respond?"

Stick your intriguing character in a difficult situation and see what he does.

Try this: Interview your protagonist. Tell her, "I may not have understood you before. What do you want to accomplish by the end of this book? What should I include or change to better show that to readers?"

It might feel a little weird at first, but give it a shot. Write down her reply. Take it to heart.

And let it affect the trajectory of your story.

CAN I INCLUDE A SCENE JUST FOR CHARACTERIZATION?

Allowing characters to face a setback or deal with a difficult situation is the best way to show characterization. If a scene has no setbacks, it probably doesn't belong in your story. If the character succeeds without a setback or without failing, readers will assume that the story is essentially about something else. This easily accomplished task might be a way of layering in a subplot, it might be subtext, but it's not the true heart of the story.

QUICK FIX: Cut or recast all the scenes that lack conflict but that you inserted so readers would "see what your character is like." Search for ways to reveal rather than describe those core characteristics. Force the character to choose, to act, to respond. Include revelatory actions that show his true colors or inner strength. Struggles do this better than anything else. Close the vice around him and see how he reacts.

FINE-TUNING MY MANUSCRIPT

- Did I keep in mind the difference between intention (what the character wants) and motivation (why he wants it)? In order to center readers on what matters in this scene, have I kept the focus on specifying his intention rather than examining his motivation?
- How can my character's desire be turned against her? In other words, how can her deepest passion become her most dreaded enemy?
- Does my protagonist understand his true problem? Is he using something else as a shield to avoid addressing the deeper emotional or psychological issues in his life?
- Have I stepped far enough out of the way to let the character's true self emerge?

24

DILEMMAS

Your protagonist is a priest. What beliefs does he have about God? Does he fear the wrath of God or revel in the love of God? How can you press the limits of his beliefs?

He's an atheist. What's keeping him from believing in God—the problem of evil? The desire to justify his actions without accountability? How can you force him to rethink his views?

Put your character's convictions to the test. Look for ways to pit his priorities against each other.

He cares about something, is passionate about something.

Good.

Now look for something else that he believes in just as strongly and make him choose between the two—compromising what he values or losing something precious in the process.

> Let moral dilemmas rather than
> moral lessons drive your story.

FIXING DILEMMA ISSUES

If a character has to choose between two harmless or even two desirable options, there's no real dilemma since something good will result from whatever he chooses and nothing is essentially at stake. Dilemmas only occur when a character has to choose between two painful outcomes.

To develop dilemmas, accentuate convictions. If your character doesn't want to do the right thing or doesn't care about doing the right thing, he won't be in an ethical bind.

The moral dilemma might involve choosing what's right, what's honorable, or what will cause the least amount of pain to others.

Find ways to turn dual desires into dueling desires: She doesn't just desire happiness, she also desires freedom and can't see how she can have both at the same time. And indeed, she can't. Not in this story. So, what will she do?

That's where the tension comes in.

That's where the story will take off.

1. **STIR THE POT.** Force your character into a corner. Let her convictions stand in opposition to each other.

2. **EXPLORE THE BOUNDS OF DUTY.** If no one else is assuring that justice is carried out, will your protagonist step up and carry it out herself? Is taking justice into our own hands ever justified? Does that matter to her? What matters more—doing what's right and going to prison for it, or safely allowing evil to occur and doing nothing about it?

3. **GET HIM TO MAKE PROMISES HE CAN'T KEEP.** He vows to his fiancée that he'll make it to the wedding rehearsal, but then his boss tells him he needs to attend a meeting that night or he'll lose his job.

4. **VENTURE INTO GRAY AREAS.** What's the difference between honesty and openness? How do we know how much openness is appropriate with friends or work associates? What happens when we step over that line?

5. **EXAMINE RELATIVE IMPORTANCE.** After a shooting, a friend is bleeding to death. What does your protagonist do? Placate him, tell him that he's going to be okay, or tell him the truth—that he's dying? What's more important, hope or truth? Avoid questions with yes or no answers. Instead, look for those "either-ors."

6. **REMOVE EASY CHOICES.** Chase the shooter (and save potential future victims) or stay with the wounded person (to save this one victim)?

7. **MAKE HIM BETRAY ONE IDEAL TO UPHOLD ANOTHER ONE.** Ask, "Will he give up (honor, honesty, justice, etc.) in order to save/protect (truth, freedom, innocent life, etc.)?"

8. **DIVE INTO ETHICAL DILEMMAS.** If abortion is the taking of innocent life, how ethical would it be to let it continue without intervening? How much intervention would be justified?

9. **PUT LIVES IN THE BALANCE.** "Kill a stranger or watch your son get murdered. Choose which is going to happen. You have ten seconds." Remember, your character must make a decision or the story won't go anywhere. Force her to re-evaluate her priorities and go against her values. Push your character into a place where he has to choose, abandon, or betray.

Create moral quandaries for your character that allow for unexpected results. Raise the stakes.

When you force her into an ethical corner, search for a way for her to uphold both values while solving the problem in a way that readers won't see coming. Find this, and you'll be on the right path.

HOW CAN I STICK MY CHARACTER BETWEEN A ROCK AND A HARD PLACE?

Give him two equally strong desires about something important, and then make him choose between them. If the desires aren't equal, he won't have much of a dilemma. If the issues aren't important, readers won't care. If the stakes aren't high enough, the choice won't matter.

QUICK FIX: You cannot have a dilemma without strong beliefs. To reveal his priorities to readers, show the two things that matter most to your protagonist through an action that he takes or a sacrifice that he makes prior to the introduction of the moral dilemma.

FINE-TUNING MY MANUSCRIPT

- What does my protagonist believe about violence? Does it solve problems or create more? What would justify him punching his wife in the face? Shoving her down the stairs? Shooting her point-blank in the head?
- Let the events of the story become (1) a mirror to reveal the character to herself, (2) a window to new perspectives, or (3) a doorway to change. Which of those three is primary in this story? Which could I accentuate more?
- Does this choice require him to leave a prison (literal or metaphorical) or enter one? How does it end up doing both?
- How can I sink my protagonist into a moral morass—one that he'll struggle to get out of but will end up sinking deeper into? What steps does he take? How does each one backfire? What action does that lead him to make that is logical, unexpected, necessary, and justified by the circumstances?

25

BELIEVABILITY

I enjoy "found footage" movies.

Well, at least up to a point.

That shaky-cam feel, the actors no one has ever heard of, and the documentary-style filmmaking all add to the slight uncertainty about whether this movie just might be true after all. Could it possibly have happened? I mean, I know it didn't, but maybe ... just maybe ...

And then (almost always right at the climax), it happens: The illusion gets shattered.

The person carrying the camera inexplicably decides to film his own death or manages to keep everything in focus while he's running at full speed away from the axe-wielding maniac. Or, sometimes, there's a camera view or angle that doesn't make sense—the videographer couldn't possibly be filming things from that vantage point.

I suppose the filmmakers assume that at this point in the story, viewers are so carried along by the tension that they won't notice. But I do notice, and I don't want to—because I want to believe.

But the director's choice has intruded on the story and made that impossible.

• • •

Never forget that your readers want to believe the story you're telling—not *that* it happened, but that it *could*.

As soon as you include something that would not or could not occur in the narrative world you've created, the illusion is shattered.

Every unbelievable moment in your story is a nail in the coffin of your readers' engagement.

Readers of fiction don't care that much if something is plausible or if it's probable or possible, or even if it might've actually happened in real life.

No.

It just needs to be believable.

The events in your book can be ludicrous, but they cannot _seem_ ludicrous.

FIXING BELIEVABILITY ISSUES

If something seems unbelievable to my readers, it's my fault.

I've created this narrative world. I've set up the rules. Now I have to play by them.

When something unbelievable happens in a story, it's often because the author has inserted an event or a reaction that doesn't logically flow or that seems "out of character."

But why would a novelist do that?

Maybe he just doesn't know any better, but most of the time I think breaches in believability happen when an author imposes an agenda on a character or a scene because he's letting his preconceptions about what he thinks _should_ happen interfere with what naturally _would_ happen.

He might be trying to set things up for a twist. Or he's including an event because it was in his outline. Or he's fictionalizing reality and inserting something that really happened (perhaps telling himself that authenticity equals believability).

In the end, the reason doesn't matter. Believability is crucial. Don't let your initial ideas about the story's direction become more of a guiding force than the natural progression of events, given this character in this situation.

Stop writing with the end in mind and start asking how this character would most naturally respond in this moment. Then, take a look at the bigger sweep of the story and see if it's really heading in the right direction after all.

As we explored earlier, in fiction, things happen for a reason. They're caused by what precedes them. Choices determine outcomes. Reactions reveal characterization.

- **IN ACTION:** What causes this character to make this choice? What consequences result?
- **IN DIALOGUE:** Why would she respond this way? Does her response make sense based on what just happened or what was just said?
- **IN REFLECTION:** Why is he thinking these things? How will those thoughts affect his emotions, his desires, his choices?
- **IN DESCRIPTION:** Why does she notice those particular things? How will her observations or perspective serve the story as a whole and lead to more revelations about her inner life or her pursuit?

The character must always react with the most reasonable response. If it doesn't seem believable to readers, it's often because you haven't given them enough information. If you write in that way, their trust in your storytelling skills will need to carry them through that section of the story until they get the answers they're waiting for. So, confirm that they have the information they need or the trust that will keep them reading.

Point out the incongruities.

As long as readers feel like there's a reason for this event—even if they don't know what it is yet—they'll stick with the story. So, if something happens for no apparent reason, have a character notice it, perhaps by acknowledging that it seemed to come out of nowhere or that she couldn't figure out what was up:

> I couldn't quite understand why he'd left the door unlocked, but I figured he had his reasons. I pulled out my gun and stepped forward.

Remember:

1. If you fail to show the consequence, you fail to maintain believability.
2. Events without a cause, or choices without an intention, undermine believability.

3. The better you know your main character, the more you'll be able to make the story believable—and the more believable you make the story, the better your readers will get to know your main character.
4. Try this test to see if something is believable: Step into your readers' shoes. You're at the point where the hero is being chased, and one bad thing after another happens to him. Would you be thinking, *Yeah, right!* (you don't buy it, it's too unbelievable) or *Oh, crap!* (you buy it, you're worried)? If you would respond in the second way, the scene works.

HOW BELIEVABLE DOES MY STORY NEED TO BE?

Every scene needs to be believable within that story's world. Every action, every choice, every snippet of dialogue must ring true to readers.

QUICK FIX: To make things more believable, (1) have characters notice the things that don't quite seem to fit so that readers know something more is going on and will continue reading, (2) use foreshadowing to remove coincidences, and (3) keep things logical within the framework of the story world you've created.

FINE-TUNING MY MANUSCRIPT

- Is everything believable when it occurs, and not just in retrospect (for example, after a twist)?
- How can I reshape the story to make sure that the events happen for reasons that grow from the context and not the eventual destination?
- If something inexplicable happens, have I pointed it out to readers and included a good reason for why it isn't believable at that moment?
- What would this character most naturally do in this situation? Is her response true to who she is? If not, why is she doing it?
- Is every aspect of my story believable? If there are glitches in believability, how can I foreshadow, fix causality errors, or alter the scene's direction to remove them?

26

DIMENSIONALITY

Writers will often talk about "fleshing out" a character, but it isn't flesh that readers need to see, it's what lies down closer to the bone.

Too many stories are littered with lifeless character corpses, with heroes who don't inspire us, with villains who don't unsettle us.

If things are exactly as they appear—your character has no contradictions, he's completely evil or optimistic or gloomy or demented—he won't remain interesting for long.

Here's the secret that great writers know: Readers will stick with an intriguing character longer than they'll stick with a likable one.

In a sense, dimensionality is a combination of all the chapters in Part II. It involves status and quirkiness, attitude and beliefs, individuality and uniqueness, and more.

Readers don't want flat, cardboard characters. They want ones that leap off the page as if they have a life of their own.

But how do we pull that off?

> Readers don't want to read about nice characters doing nice things. They want to read about conflicted characters doing difficult things.

FIXING DIMENSIONALITY ISSUES

To really get to know your character, stop asking what she's like or where she's from or what she does. Instead ask, "What does she regret? What does she desire? Where does she hurt?"

Your character's backstory is his résumé of pain—not simply the places he's worked or gone to school, but the scars he carries and how they continue to affect him. Those elements, not the superficial activities of his past, will lead you (and your readers) to the true essence of your character.

Plumb the depths. Look beneath the surface. Assume that things in her life are not what they appear to be—that there are layers of emotion and defenses that need to be peeled away.

Then get to work removing them.

Let the setbacks sandblast her shiny exterior until her true self is revealed.

1. Turn His Inner Life Against Him

Consider your character's convictions, secrets, beliefs, and desires. Then look for ways to pit them against each other and show the relational, emotional, and psychological fallout.

2. Let the True Character Emerge

Show readers all that she can become, but remember that transformations must make sense, remaining believable, logical, and supported by the context. So, if your 250-page story is about how the protagonist was transformed from a mousy, sexually repressed librarian into a self-actualized vixen who hunts down drug lords, you have your work cut out for you.

3. Ask Follow-Up Questions

What is my character searching for that he's not aware of? Where is he hurting that he hasn't addressed? What wrongs has he done that he won't admit?

Explore disillusionment with your protagonist regarding current or past loves. Where did his expectations end up unfulfilled? What does that reveal about him? What does it reveal about his understanding of others?

As you explore your character, move past the obvious into the realm of the struggle or the potential resolution.

- What burdens is he carrying? What's keeping him from setting them down? How would doing so hurt someone else?
- What wounds linger in her heart? What will it take to heal them? How will she take that first step?
- What dreams is he pursuing? Which ones is he putting off? What would change that?
- What is her fear covering? What setback could I use to scrape it away? How would she respond?
- What is his depression masking? How can I remove it? How will he fight me as I do?

4. Root Around Through the Darkness

Since dimensionality depends on what's roiling beneath the surface, what emotion does your character work the hardest to repress? What's lurking down there under her calm exterior?

Choose one of these five emotions: rage, grief, depression, fear, or joy. Your character is repressing it. Think of the power that this repressed emotion has on her life, on the way she sees the world, or on her emotional state. What's keeping that emotion in check? What will cause it to break loose? What will happen when it does?

HOW DO I CREATE A THREE-DIMENSIONAL CHARACTER?

Don't stifle your characters. As you develop them, as you add more depth to them, continue to let them act, choose, respond. There isn't a foolproof formula, but there is a process, and the first step includes listening to the character and letting him express himself freely on the page.

QUICK FIX: Show multiple layers of dominance and submission, reveal vulnerabilities as well as strengths, and search for ways to let him spread his wings and whisper (or shout) his uniqueness to the world.

FINE-TUNING MY MANUSCRIPT

- Does my story have internal, external, and interpersonal struggles that all intertwine to form or reveal a complex character?
- Does the protagonist show different degrees of status in different social contexts? (For more on status, see chapter thirty-three.)
- Have I dipped far enough into the dark streams of desire running beneath the surface of my protagonist's life? What dynamics have I been missing until now?
- Does this character have a magnetism to her? Unplumbed depths? Realms of personality that are still undiscovered? How can I let her reveal those to readers?
- When she's beaten down by her circumstances, what exceptional qualities can she exhibit? Persistence? Cleverness? How can I believably show this, especially in the climax?

27

PROTAGONISTS

We like spending time with certain types of people—others, not so much. They irritate us or make us feel like we're never good enough. They don't affirm us, they're not interesting, or maybe they're conceited and everything is always about them.

What if I offered you this deal: Spend the next ten hours alone with one of those people who annoys you—but feel free to simply walk away at any time. You never have to see him or talk to him again. And here's the greatest part: There's no obligation to stay, you won't hurt anyone's feelings, and you can choose to go on a walk with your best friend, or sleep with your lover, or play with your children instead.

What would you do?

It seems pretty ridiculous, doesn't it? But when readers pick up your novel, that's the deal you're offering them. They can either spend time alone with your fictional characters or invest in developing the relationships with the real-life people they love.

Too many authors don't take this into account when creating their protagonists.

Step back from everything you've heard or read about the importance of readers relating to the main character, or empathizing with him, or sympathizing with him, and simply ask, "Would my readers really want to hang out with a person like this? What's the attraction?"

Hero or not, the main character needs to be extraordinary in some way. As Donald Maass says in his book *Writing 21st Century Fiction*, "Everyman and Everywoman protagonists need to show us a hint of why they're not just like us, but that they're exceptional ... What heroic protagonists need to show us is that they're human."

The protagonist is your story's central character. She's not necessarily the most noble or heroic person in the book, but since she is the main character, she's the one readers will probably spend the most time with.

Because of that, she should be the one they *want* to spend the most time with.

....

Protagonists might not be the most endearing characters, but they should be the most intriguing ones.

....

FIXING PROTAGONIST ISSUES

The hardest aspect of creating engaging characters isn't developing scenes that reveal what they're like, it's discovering characters that your readers *will want to watch being revealed* for two hundred or five hundred or a thousand pages.

So, what characteristics make people in real life intriguing?

Typically, we like being around people who are passionate but not obsessed, dedicated but not workaholics, confident but not cocky.

Attractive people are hopeful, not depressed all the time.

They know how to disagree without being argumentative.

They forgive and don't keep reminding us of the times we hurt them.

We like spending time with good listeners, not those who interrupt us, change the subject, try to one-up us all the time, or nitpick what we say.

Adrenaline junkies and thrill seekers intrigue us, even if we're not super-adventurous ourselves.

Clingy, needy people turn us off.

Spontaneous, childlike, witty people are fun to be around. They make us smile. People who are cool under pressure help us feel safe. Unbalanced, neurotic people do not.

Charisma isn't easy to define, but we know it when we see it, and we're drawn to those who have it.

Greed, jealousy, selfishness—these things grow old pretty quickly.

We like people who are courageous in the face of danger and who don't back down from doing the right thing—even when it's unpopular.

Active, fit, carefree people are attractive, but people who are always showing off their scars, talking about themselves, or gossiping about others are not.

Someone who's a little rough around the edges can be lovable, but not someone who's rude and demeaning.

We like rogues.

We don't like buffoons.

It's flattering when someone flirts with us. That's always nice.

Maybe she has an air of mystery about her. Hmm. Or intrigue. Yes, we want to know more.

Maybe he's flawed but generous, or has an unshakable moral code or a special skill that sets him apart. Whatever it is, you enjoy his company and you miss him when he's not around.

• • •

Alright.

Now think: How does your protagonist measure up? Consider those traits and attributes listed above and evaluate them in regard to how your main character comes across on the page—will he attract readers or repel them? Will they take the deal and walk away to spend time with people in real life, or will they choose to hang out with your protagonist for the next ten hours instead?

Strive to create protagonists that readers find compelling and impossible to turn away from.

HOW CAN I MAKE MY PROTAGONIST MORE HEROIC?

Heroes inspire us to be better. They don't make us feel dirty or drain us of life. Give your hero opportunities to sacrifice, to make the tough decisions no one else is willing to make, and to act on noble convictions.

QUICK FIX: A hero isn't a hero until he takes action. Until his ideals are tested, they're simply aspirations. So, put him through the fire and see who comes out on the other side. Make him the underdog when he fights evil. Let him be outmatched, and show him overcome the obstacles through ingenuity, persistence, or depth of resolve rather than through superior physical strength.

FINE-TUNING MY MANUSCRIPT

- How is my protagonist intriguing, beguiling, or mysterious? What subtle changes will make him more engaging and memorable?
- Why won't readers want to spend time with her? What will annoy them or turn them off?
- In what way is he extraordinary and yet relatable? How can I make him more of both?
- What is it about her that both attracts readers and establishes her as someone *worth feeling attracted to*?
- What sort of role model is he? Is he someone I'd want my children to aspire to be like and in whose footsteps I'd want them to follow? Would his values and virtues inspire them to become better people? If I wouldn't want my children to be around him, why am I offering him to the world?
- Some stories reveal the character to herself, others reveal the character to readers. Most stories, at least to some degree, do both. What about my story? How will those unfolding revelations affect my protagonist's pursuit and my readers' engagement?

28

ANTAGONISM

A story might not have a "bad guy."

Your characters could be trying to survive together on a deserted island after a shipwreck, or they might be trapped on a disabled spaceship that's running out of air, or they could be stuck in a flooding cellar during a hurricane.

In those cases, the abandonment, the isolation, and the rising water would be the forces of antagonism that your character is facing.

Although a novel doesn't need a villain, it will need a *versus*: the character versus his perceptions of himself (he believes he is a failure), the limitations of his situation (he's disabled and must learn to walk again), a spiritual force (a ghost or demon), another person (a rival at work), or society, nature, a machine, a monster of some type, etc.

There's always a versus between the protagonist and something. When you know what that something is and how it's hindering him from reaching his goal, you'll know the central struggle of your story.

Don't think in terms of "about" but in terms of "against." So not, "What is my story about?" but "What's my protagonist fighting against?" Not "What is he doing?" but "What problem is he facing?"

If your novel has a human (or anthropomorphized) antagonist, think of your protagonist as the character whom readers will most want to succeed and the antagonist as the one they'll most want to fail.

Both the protagonist and the antagonist need to be as astute as, or more astute than, your readers. After all, if they think your protagonist is stupid they won't cheer for him, and if they think your antagonist is stupid they won't fear him.

113

> Stories are built on the bedrock of
> unmet desire. Forces of antagonism
> serve to hinder that desire from being met.

FIXING ANTAGONISM ISSUES

Natural events (such as cancer or planet-destroying meteors or giant rampaging lizards) are often anthropomorphized in fiction—that is, we attribute human characteristics or human motivation to them.

Supernatural forces of antagonism are typically vanquished through some supernatural means—a special talisman, an ancient text, a secret ceremony, etc. The solution must be believable (within that narrative world) but will only become available to the protagonist at the climax—otherwise, why wouldn't he just use it earlier in the story?

Whatever forces of antagonism you include, use them to require the protagonist to use his greatest assets in ways he never would have dreamed of before the story began.

If he's brilliantly deductive, he'll be facing off with someone (or something) even smarter. If he's super-strong, his opponent will be stronger. If he's a crazy-good computer hacker, he'll finally meet his match.

Memorable villains are complex, morally justified in their own eyes, have high status, are bigger than life, and are unswervingly committed to their cause. Here's how to make yours more terrifying.

Limit His Time on the Page

Typically, the less time we spend in the villain's point of view, the more frightening he'll become. Why? Because mystery and secrets unsettle us.

Think of a monster movie. The director won't show the entire killer mega octopus when he first comes on the scene. Audiences are given glimpses—just a tentacle or two—to make the big reveal more powerful at the climax.

Do the same with your villains.

Show How Unbalanced She Is

Someone who might snap at any moment, who might just as soon kill you as kiss you (or do both at the same time) is terrifying.

Remember Kathy Bates in *Misery*? Beneath the veneer of kindness and self-control, pure evil was writhing and squirming and searching for a way to get out.

For a villain, eccentricity doesn't necessarily equal threat. It's okay to give her an unusual habit, but oddness by itself won't make her frightening.

Unpredictability will.

Make Him Callous Rather than Sadistic

To a truly heartless person, others are simply objects to be used, no different than cattle to be slaughtered. A villain is more unnerving when he doesn't revel in people's pain but simply doesn't care if others suffer.

Don't Let Him Be Self-Congratulatory

Eliminate places where he chortles, giggles, exults to himself or others about how evil or clever he is, tries to prove himself, or is in a hurry to accomplish his plan. Make him slow, calculating, and clever.

Make Sure She Doesn't View Herself as the Antagonist

No one sees her own actions as evil. So, when readers are in the villain's point of view, she won't do anything that she considers wicked or unthinkable. She'll only do what seems reasonable.

The more she considers herself evil, the more she'll seem like only a caricature of a villain.

Tell Readers His Justification

Try to bring readers to the point where they nod their heads and say, "Yeah, you know what—he's actually got a point." Put yourself in the villain's head:

"It's okay to steal this diamond because ..."

"It's okay to murder this baby because ..."

"It's okay to rape this woman because ..."

Give Her a Virtue

Perhaps she's patient. Or compassionate to children. Or only kills people while they're asleep. Making a character 100 percent evil is difficult to pull off and tough to make believable. Even the Devil dabbles in the truth sometimes.

Allow Him Free Rein

Let him act naturally and without restraint as he pursues his desires. Give him the wheel, and then hang on—because he might just drive you through some pretty dark territory.

HOW SHOULD THE HERO BATTLE THE VILLAIN?

Alone.

QUICK FIX: The hero will fight with courage and virtue, and often the villain will respond with treachery and deceit. As they face off, the antagonist might force the protagonist into a wrenching moral dilemma or put innocent lives at risk.

Your hero is constrained by morality and will respond in a way that readers respect. If you're telling a story that upholds the theme of virtue triumphing over vice, often the villain's downfall will result from his own pride, greed, or cowardice.

FINE-TUNING MY MANUSCRIPT

- Since no one sees himself as the villain, how does this villain perceive himself to be the hero? How does he rationalize his actions and justify his choices?
- How does my protagonist figuratively outlast the storm (perseverance) or outwit the villain (cleverness)?

- How does she overcome evil or the threat to her life at the very moment when it seems most likely that she'll succumb to or be destroyed by it? How can I make that pivotal moment more believable or poignant?
- If the villain has a change of heart, finds religion, or repents, will readers buy it? What would make a more intriguing story—if he did or if he didn't? How will that affect my story's current ending?

29

DESIRE

Your protagonist enters the back room of the bar.

The five men seated at the poker table look up from their cards and stare at him coolly. Finally, the hulking bar owner says, "So, what do you want?"

"I'm here to find Jodie. You know where she is, and you're going to tell me."

• • •

In the scene above, the protagonist clearly states what he wants. That's his *expressed* desire.

But is he telling the truth? Is that really why he's there? After all, maybe he went into that room to kill all those men, or maybe the search for Jodie is just a ruse he's using to lead him to the mafia boss that he's actually looking for.

There should be something he's got his sights on accomplishing before that scene is over. It's the reason he believes he's there. That's his *perceived* desire.

But he might have an even deeper reason guiding him, something he might not consciously be aware of. If so, that would be his *actual* desire.

When these three types of desire (expressed, perceived, and actual) are not in concert with each other, it gives you a chance to explore interesting dynamics within your character's understanding of himself or your readers' understanding of the character.

Without desire there is no pursuit.
Without pursuit there is no story.

FIXING DESIRE ISSUES

As readers move through your book, they'll be piecing clues together to try to discern what each character truly wants (based on the context and on his expressed and perceived desires).

Gifted storytellers take into account both the character's awareness of his desire and the readers' awareness of his desire. This interplay can contribute to irony, suspense, or character revelation. As you write, capitalize on what the reader is and isn't aware of—and what the character knows or doesn't know about his actual desire.

Expressed Desire

A character might express his desire through his thoughts, through his words, or through his actions. If readers don't have any idea what the character wants, they won't have any idea what the scene (or the story) is about.

Often, you can simply let characters state their goals. Look for opportunities for characters to ask and tell each other what they want. Shoot for *clarity*.

Perceived Desire

This is what the character believes she wants. It will impact every conscious decision she makes.

Examine the perceived desires of your protagonist:

- "I want someone to rescue me," or "I want to rescue someone."
- "I want to live a life of adventure," or "I want someone to invite me on an adventure."
- "I want to settle down," or "I want to get out and live life while I have the chance."
- "I want to be loved," or "I want to be respected."
- "I want to feel good," or "I want to be good."

When the character makes choices, those decisions will make sense to her *and* to readers. Subconsciously, she might want something different, but she will *think* she knows what she wants, and that's what will drive her to act. Shoot for *believability*.

Actual Desire

This is what the character truly wants. Allow your story to explore it. Actual desire will sometimes influence him to do things that he doesn't understand.

- The protagonist might believe that he wants to marry his girlfriend because he loves her, when he really subconsciously wants to control her.
- She might believe that she wants revenge, but in truth she wants to let go of the pain and move on.
- He might believe that he wants fame and fortune, but deep down he desires contentment more than anything else.

Often, readers will become aware of the character's actual desire by watching how he responds to setbacks. Here, you'll shoot for *revelatory choices.*

• • •

Mine the depths of your protagonist's psyche. Is he trying to meet a need, fill an emptiness in his life, overcome the pain of loss, or move on? Does he dwell on the past? Do his best to forget it? Obsess about his shortcomings? Remain oblivious to his strengths?

Examine areas of awareness and concealment. How much does she understand about her deepest longings, and how does she keep those truths hidden from others and from herself?

Let that awareness influence her journey through the story, and then, at the end, show how the pursuit has affected her understanding of herself and others.

Try this: Imagine that your protagonist is having a conversation with her closest friend. Eavesdrop. They're talking about life at the moment, their dreams, their struggles. Suddenly, your protagonist mentions what she *really* wants, and it surprises you. What is it?

DOES EVERY CHARACTER NEED AN OVERRIDING DESIRE?

Some minor characters will basically serve as set pieces to the story, but every point-of-view character will have a perceived desire.

QUICK FIX: If you don't let readers know your character's desires, they won't know why he's taking the actions that he is. You might be able to reveal the goal through the character's actions, but often it's simpler and more effective if you just tell them. Make it as specific and clear as possible. Analyze your characters' every conscious decision, and make sure it's in sync with what they believe they want out of the scene.

FINE-TUNING MY MANUSCRIPT

- What does he think he wants? What does he really want? What act/scene/event could cause him to realize that? How would that affect him?
- Tension only emerges when desire is both known to the readers and unfulfilled for the story characters. So, are my characters' unmet desires clear to readers? Does the reason their desires aren't being met make sense?
- Are readers aware of what the protagonist wants in every scene? Have I allowed her to either tell or show readers her intentions so they can worry about whether or not she fulfills them?
- Is this scene primarily a progression of events or a clash of desires? If there's no clash, could I improve the scene by adding one?
- Do characters have mutually exclusive objectives? If not, how can I clarify and sharpen their goals to develop more tension?
- In what ways is the protagonist in the dark about what he really wants or needs? What does he think he needs that he doesn't really need? What does he want, even though he knows it's not good for him?

30

LOVE

"So, considering your story, can you make it more about love?"

"It's not a love story."

"Doesn't matter."

"But I'm telling you, it's not a romance."

"I don't care."

"So, why do you want me to make it more about love?"

"Because I want people to read it."

• • •

There are obviously different kinds of love. There's familial love. Friendship love. Puppy love. Erotic love. Selfless, sacrificial love. Love of roller coasters. Love of hot dogs.

The desire to love and be loved is one of the most powerful yearnings we experience as human beings.

In fiction, the deepest kind of love is shown not through declarations of undying commitment but through actions that reflect attraction, affection, devotion, and sacrifice. If readers are going to believe that love is genuine, it must be evidenced by action.

Nearly every story can be improved by adding acts of devotion and sacrifice.

FIXING LOVE ISSUES

Those four spheres—attraction, affection, devotion, and sacrifice—overlap, and some are more prevalent in different types of relationships or different genres. However, we're in the business of finding concrete ways to show abstract ideas (such as love, justice, hope, and so on), so think carefully about each sphere in regard to the type and depth of love you want to show.

1. Attraction

As you shape attraction-motivated scenes, think of how playfulness, touch, eye contact, and innuendo exhibit themselves while people are flirting. Work those in. Consider proximity and personal space—what does it mean when we enter someone else's or we let them enter ours?

Subtext is often used to show that what the characters are doing in a scene isn't really what's foremost in their minds during the scene. Almost every flirting scene depends heavily on subtext.

2. Affection

People don't just want to *be* loved, they want to *feel* loved. Some people feel loved when you tell them you love them, and some need you to demonstrate it through acts of kindness, phone calls, texts, love notes, gifts, and so on.

Brainstorm specific acts that can show affection (whether that's romantic affection or another type). Remember, affection can certainly be physical, but it doesn't need to be. Also, this sphere provides ample opportunity for conflict and misunderstanding. For instance, when an act is misinterpreted or when one person feels unloved even though her partner is trying to express his love for her.

Affection taken far enough results in intimacy, which we'll cover in the next chapter.

3. Devotion

How loyal is your character? This question can be answered only when the loyalty is tested in the presence of temptation. Will she flirt with that other guy at the party? Will he remain faithful to his wife while he's stationed in South Korea? How long will he stay by his brother's side at the hospital?

To show devotion, force your character to face temptation and see how he responds.

4. Sacrifice

The greatest act of love is self-sacrifice—but it won't feel like a sacrifice to the one who's offering it on behalf of his beloved. Instead, it'll just seem like the natural response.

For readers to believe something is a true sacrifice, they need to believe that something of value is at stake. So, develop scenes that allow your character to commit, to suffer, or to forgive (which is itself a sacrifice, since forgiveness is the act of giving up your right to feel wronged).

Those who look at love as costing themselves something will hold back, and their love will shrivel. Those who look at self-sacrifice as a way to invest in others will end up with more love than they know what to do with.

Love that simply feels or vows or flatters is cheap and easy. Love that acts and commits and gives is worth something because it costs something. The question isn't so much, "What will the character do in the name of love?" but "What will he give up in the name of love?"

The sacrificing of self always raises the status of the one making the sacrifice.

• • •

Stories are made stronger when they focus on learning to receive love and extend it to others, but they're weakened when they focus on developing more self-love.

A character can certainly learn to respect himself through a story, but if the theme of your story is "You love others too much. You must love yourself more," it won't ring true to readers—because they already know that the biggest problems in our world don't come from the lack of selfishness but from too much of it.

Love leads to vulnerability but also to courage—the willingness to suffer for the beloved.

To allow your protagonist to show more love, don't look for more ways for her to say that she loves someone; instead ask yourself, "How can I provide her a chance to show more devotion or more sacrifice?"

If you never give your character an opportunity to sacrifice something she values for someone she values more, you're failing to take advantage of what might be your story's most emotionally resonant scene.

DO I NEED TO HAVE A LOVE STORY SUBPLOT?

Since the desire to love and be loved is so universal, love stories will resonate with most readers. However, every subplot needs to be essential to the development of the main plot and not just haphazardly inserted.

QUICK FIX: Look for ways to include meaningful acts of love. An act reaches the level of sacrifice when it begins to cause a change in the life of the one offering it. Giving leftover change to a homeless person isn't much of a sacrifice, but if that act requires you to miss a meal yourself, then it's become sacrificial. As soon as someone else becomes a means to an end, you've stopped loving him or her. Self-promotion of any kind is the opposite of love.

FINE-TUNING MY MANUSCRIPT

- What does love require of my protagonist in this scene?
- Who does my protagonist love more than herself? How can I add a scene that will show this love through an act of devotion or sacrifice?
- Are other people stepping-stones for my character? Are his relationships simply a means to an end? In what ways is he using people? How can I alter the story to raise his status and deepen his sacrifice?
- Have I included temptations to test the depths of characters' love and their loyalty to each other? How do they respond? How does that affect their relationship?
- In scenes of affection and attraction, have I resorted to clichés or shown the love in fresh, unique ways?

31

INTIMACY

Romance stories might focus on first loves, sexual adventurousness and liaisons, affairs (or their aftermath), meeting a soul mate, weathering difficult times as a couple, and so on.

Typically, the protagonist's pursuit in a romance story involves a longing for intimacy, for belonging, and, often, for sexual satisfaction.

Most people want to find a soul mate—that one special person who understands us, who accepts us as we are, who loves us, who completes us. The search for a soul mate allows for endless dramatic situations. For example:

- What would you give up to be with your soul mate?
- How do you know when you've found your soul mate?
- Is there more than one potential soul mate for every person?
- Can you trust destiny to bring you together, or do you have to pursue your soul mate? (If so, how?)
- What if you're already married to someone else when you meet your soul mate? Do you stay faithful to your spouse? Do you tell her about this other person? Where does that lead?
- Is there even such a thing as a soul mate?

When writing about romantic love, emphasize desire, tension, and attraction.

FIXING INTIMACY ISSUES

For some people, sex is the result of intimacy; for others, it's the pathway toward it.

Take note of how your protagonist views intimacy, how she expresses it, and the promises of commitment she takes away (or does not take away) from intimate encounters.

Intimacy is not necessarily sexual. Sometimes emotional affairs or relationships are the most intimate of all (and the most difficult to get over or move past). And regarding religious encounters, sometimes people have such deep spiritual intimacy with God that they describe the experience as ecstatic.

Romantic love is about romantic tension, not sexual fulfillment. Let the would-be lovers flirt with each other. Let them tease each other. Let them yearn for each other.

But keep them apart.

Why?

Because as soon as they become a couple (however your literary genre might define that), the sexual or romantic tension you've built is lost. You've introduced resolution. Of course, you can always add more tension afterward, but just like crying or screaming or punching a wall, sex releases the tension pent up inside your characters.

The key is finding a believable way to keep the lovers apart as the sexual tension builds. After all, if they're in love, why don't they just have sex, get married, run off together, etc.? What's holding them back?

Identifying those factors is crucial to developing the tension for your romance story.

Intimacy occurs when affection and commitment deepen to the extent where the two people no longer feel like two, but one. And, in one of the paradoxes of human relationships, the lovers feel both stronger and more susceptible as a result.

If the lovers do sleep together before the end of the book, one of four things will happen to escalate the tension:

1. The intimacy will put pressure on the relationship or change the expectations of the lovers and end up pushing them apart.
2. Outside forces will persecute them as a couple, and they'll need to rely on each other and their newfound intimacy to succeed, survive, or find happiness.
3. Another person will infiltrate their intimacy and either threaten one or both of them by separating them, killing one partner, or forcing her to sacrifice the relationship to save the life of her beloved.
4. Their relationship will be tested with escalating setbacks and will withstand and endure, bringing them even closer together.

Intimacy is sometimes expressed through sex, sometimes through abstinence.

For instance, if you know that your lover was abused in the past and suffers mental anguish during intercourse, you would abstain so that your partner wouldn't suffer. Or the character might be a virgin and be saving herself for marriage. In either case, the act of abstinence is a sacrifice.

Readers want to feel that their relationships are special and purposeful, not just random. In romance stories, lovers are often brought together through fate, destiny, or divine intervention. Because of that, coincidence plays a more significant role in romance than in many other genres.

Regarding the route to romance, generally women want to be pursued and men don't want to be rejected. If a woman isn't pursued or a man is rejected, that person will be disappointed. So, when you shape your romance stories, keep in mind issues of rejection, desirability, and bruised feelings.

Your character's romantic and sexual exploits reveal his values and priorities. Who he sleeps with, when he sleeps with her, and what kind of commitment that implies says a lot about his beliefs about sex and about long-term commitment vs. short-term pleasure.

DO I NEED TO INCLUDE A SEX SCENE?

Sex scenes release tension, so unless you introduce a new struggle or a different relational dynamic afterward, they can stall out your story.

QUICK FIX: Unless you're writing erotica, don't feel pressured to weave a sex scene into your novel. Be honest to the characters and to the story, and let that honesty determine whether you include one. If you do write a sex scene, remember that some readers come to fiction to peer into someone else's bedroom and watch what's happening—the kinkier the sex, the better—while others aren't into that at all. Know your readers, and decide accordingly.

FINE-TUNING MY MANUSCRIPT

- Do I have scenes that show the commitment my character has toward those he's intimate with? If not, would that help my story?
- Is a sex scene necessary? If I include one, am I using it to titillate readers? Is that what they're hoping to get from this story?
- How does my protagonist view intimacy? How will this shape her actions, choices, etc.?
- What kind of intimacy does he want, need, seek, or give? How does he go about this?
- How can I include more emotional intimacy? Where have I mistaken emotional wants for emotional needs? How will that make a difference to the story's direction or the characters' development?
- Where has there been too much release of tension or too much resolution? How can I insert new conflict or unmet desire?
- How can the intimacy or resiliency of the relationship be tested or put through the fire?

32

BACKSTORY

You board a bus full of people. Each of them has a reason to be here, just like you do. That reason—where they're going and what they're hoping will happen when they arrive—is what matters right now.

Their entire life history does not.

Backstory and history aren't the same thing.

History is all that has happened to those people on the bus before today. *Backstory* is that fraction of a fraction of a fraction of their history that's relevant to them being here, now, riding this specific bus to a specific bus stop for a specific reason.

You won't know your protagonist's backstory until you realize which details are significant to your book—and that probably won't happen until you've finished your first draft, since only then will you know which events from your character's history are truly relevant to this story.

So, focus on this bus, on this ride, as you explore your character's backstory.

> Backstory is not what happened in the past
> that affects this character, it's what happened
> in the past that affects this story.

FIXING BACKSTORY ISSUES

When it comes to backstory, you'll be tempted:

1. to include more history than you need.
2. to mine the past for a motive that explains the present.

3. to assume that readers are as interested in the character's history as you are.

Here's what to do instead.

Stop Looking at History and Backstory as the Same Thing

What's vital? What's necessary? That's what you'll include—not what's simply interesting.

Often, writers are encouraged to create detailed histories of the characters in their stories before beginning their novels. This, of course, puts the author in a bind—after he's done all that work, he'll naturally want to use it. After all, no one wants to feel like he has wasted his time. So, he'll look for opportunities to include details that might not be relevant.

If you've already written up a history of your characters, set it aside. If you haven't written one, don't.

A résumé is never as informative as a first date. Leave the résumé behind. Let the story reveal to you which events from the character's past matter, and then only bring those onto the page.

Think in Terms of the Goal Rather than the Motive

A character will always enter a scene *because of* something (the motivating factor), and he will always enter it *in order to do* something (the desire or goal that he has). Focus on that second reason rather than the first.

Everyone's life choices are influenced by a multitude of factors. Readers know that, so the more you try to identify one event to explain the rest, the less believable the story will become.

Where is she getting off the bus? What is she hoping to accomplish when she gets there? That's where you'll direct your readers' attention rather than all the decisions that led up to boarding the bus.

Remember that Readers Are Most Interested in the Story They're Reading, Not the One that Came Before

You might find it intriguing to know where the protagonist spent the summer when he was thirteen or who he kissed at junior prom, but readers are more interested in what he wants right now, how he's pursuing it, and his response when he doesn't get it.

If the other story is more interesting, then you're writing the wrong book.

• • •

Backstory is a promise of significance.

If you include a detailed backstory of a character and then kill her off, readers will feel cheated. The amount of backstory you include should be proportionate to the character's relevance to this story.

Three final traps to avoid:

1. THE SPECIAL OBJECT CAUSES HIM TO REMEMBER SCENE: He'll touch an old photograph and remember those days at the beach five years ago. But what caused him to touch that photo now? Why today? If you use this technique, you'll need to justify his action by connecting it causally to what precedes it. Don't just insert the photo touching moment out of nowhere.

2. THE GREAT CHAPTER TWO BACKSTORY DUMP: We looked at this in Part I. Sprinkle the backstory in little by little rather than all at once.

3. THE "REMEMBER WHEN WE USED TO …" ROUTINE: This is when characters tell each other things they're already aware of just so the author can get the information to readers:

> "You know, that two-by-four reminds me of when we were twelve and we built that tree house out by the pond."
> "Yeah, it took us all summer."
> "I know. And it was where we held our secret club meetings."
> "Right! The one where we didn't allow any girls."

Whenever you have characters say, "Remember when we ..." or when they tell each other things that they both know, you're showing your hand. Discerning readers will get annoyed. Instead, have characters tell each other what they don't know and only remember things when the context naturally leads them to do so.

As you write, be ready to revise the backstory you've included.

You won't know your characters as well as you need to before you write your story. You'll get to know them through the writing process. As they reveal themselves to you, you'll likely have to go back through the chapters you've completed and recast their responses to be more authentic to who they really are.

Sift, sift, sift, and discern. Filter backstory from history, and keep intention rather than rumination in the forefront of your character's mind.

HOW IMPORTANT IS BACKSTORY?

Backstory isn't as important as it's sometimes made out to be. Yes, it affects the trajectory of the character's quest, but it's the seasoning, not the main dish.

QUICK FIX: Cut the history that doesn't contribute to this story. Determine what's essential to your story and what isn't, and then bring in the pertinent details in an unobtrusive way— through glances at the past, not long narrative forays into it. Prioritize relevance and forward momentum over including minutia of a character's history.

FINE-TUNING MY MANUSCRIPT

- What vital details do readers need to know about where this character has been or what he has done before this story begins?
- Where have I included too much history? Where have I not included enough backstory?
- How have I failed to use naturally occurring events to weave in backstory, and relied on obtrusive scenes instead?

- Where do my characters describe things to experts or to people who should already know that information? Rather than simply detailing the information to readers, how will I show my characters discovering it during the scene?
- At this stage in my writing process, what aspects of backstory can I identify as nonessential? How is the true character emerging through all of this?
- Have I steered clear of the three traps of backstory, or fallen prey to them? What will I do about that?

33

STATUS

In one of my books, I had this exchange between a dad and his vegan teenage daughter:

> As a big fan of cheeseburgers, I'd been trying to come up with a good argument to convince her to expand her culinary interests to include animals. Finally, I said, "If God didn't want us to eat cows, he wouldn't have covered 'em with meat."
> "He covered you with meat."
> "Oh. Good point."

• • •

Who's calling the shots in that scene?

Who's trying to?

Who's in control, and who's vying for it?

These questions all relate to status, one of the most overlooked and yet essential aspects of characterization.

Status is the degree of submission or dominance characters have in relationship to other characters. If a person is domineering or subservient with everyone, that character won't be as interesting because he always has the same status.

On the other hand, if a character has differing degrees of status with his boss, his wife, his daughter, his colleagues at work, the villains he's tracking, and so on, he'll seem more believable and multidimensional because that's the way things are in real life.

> The more varied a character's status is
> across his spectrum of relationships, the
> more interesting that character becomes.

FIXING STATUS ISSUES

The words you choose to describe someone's actions carry a lot of weight in determining his status. Consider, for example, the words *quickly* and *hastily*.

To move *quickly* communicates control and purpose. To move *hastily* conveys a loss of control. You would lower your character's status by writing, "She hastily crossed the room." You would maintain her status or even raise it by writing, "She quickly crossed the room." Every action on every page, every verb you choose, can serve to maintain status or undermine it in the eyes of readers. A character might *chortle* or *laugh*. He might *beg for his life* or *suffer in silence*.

Developing a strong protagonist relies on status management.

We tend to be attracted to people with high status. We want to spend time with them. They exemplify the things we believe in and exhibit the characteristics we value.

High-status characters don't quiver, shake, or tremble in the face of danger. They might be afraid, but they don't let the fear get the best of them. Despite the peril they're facing, they're able to make courageous choices—especially when it comes to rescuing or helping others in need.

To be dismissive of someone else will lower your status. To listen, truly listen, will raise it.

The person who's more patient will claim higher status in a scene, as will the person with the most composure. On the other hand, the most nervous, unsure, needy, placating, or boastful person will have the lowest status.

Both criticism and praise bounce off those with high status. Their self-confidence doesn't depend on other people's perception of them.

TO *RAISE* A CHARACTER'S STATUS, slow him down and show his self-control, confidence, resolve, virtue, courage, and willingness to sacrifice for others. Add stillness.

Persistence, devotion, and sacrifice all raise status.

People with high status aren't concerned about their image. Integrity matters more than reputation. They treat people with honor and respect.

To be content with the status you have raises it. Striving for higher status actually lowers your status because it shows your neediness and desire for attention.

Someone who refrains from retaliation when she's taunted or threatened (fighting back, returning an insult, killing the person, etc.) will raise her status because of her self-restraint.

TO *LOWER* A CHARACTER'S STATUS, you can alter either her situation or her attitude.

Situationally, you could put her at a disadvantage, either in an unfamiliar environment or pitted against a superior force of antagonism. Or you might expose her vulnerabilities to someone who can take advantage of them. As far as attitude, make her proud, self-congratulatory, defensive, or needy; or have her insult, mock, or demean other people.

TO *BALANCE* THE STATUS BETWEEN CHARACTERS, add banter and show equality. When friends or lovers jibe each other, without either person trying to get the upper hand, readers recognize that they're at ease having equal status.

A few things to remember:

- Despite the tremendous odds a character might be facing, his poise can give him the highest status.
- You won't want your protagonist to make a decision that lowers her status beneath that of the antagonist. (For example, don't have her placate or acquiesce to the villain.)
- When you're in the point of view of a character, don't have him perceive himself as having high status. If you do, he'll seem arrogant, which will lower his status.

- Lowering a character's situational status will put readers on her side. For instance, if she is outnumbered in a fight, readers will tend to root for her—even if she isn't the hero.
- Your protagonist will be in his lowest situational status in the dark moment immediately preceding the climax. His choice will flip the tables on the antagonist.

CAN MY CHARACTER ALWAYS HAVE HIGH STATUS?

Yes, but varying his status can create depth. To portray dimensionality and generate more reader empathy, show your character experiencing different levels of status within different social contexts.

QUICK FIX: Look for places to reverse status expectations. A small child might offer advice to her parent, an employee might intimidate a boss, and a confident hero might be flabbergasted on how to respond to a love interest. A protagonist often has equal status with friends, buddies, and lovers; high status when facing danger; lower status with mentors.

FINE-TUNING MY MANUSCRIPT

- Does my protagonist exhibit believable dimensionality by showing different degrees of status in different situations or with different people?
- Where does he make choices that end up undermining his status? How have I described his actions in ways that lower his status too much?
- If there's a tier of bad guys, does the ringleader have the highest status? Does he exhibit the most ruthlessness, stillness, and self-control?
- Have I created opportunities to allow my protagonist to show different degrees of status within her various relationships and through the choices she makes?
- How can I use my character's choices in the face of danger to raise his status? What verbs do I need to change in order to do so?

34

STRUGGLES

Your protagonist wants to relax with a cup of tea, take a nap, chill out with her friends.

Don't let her.

Add stress. Distract her. Frustrate her. Agitate her.

As soon as she relaxes, reader interest wanes. Be on the lookout for ways to add more struggles, which will not only help to shape her character but will also reveal what she is truly like.

As I mentioned earlier, struggles occur in three realms: *within* characters (internal struggles), *between* characters (interpersonal struggles), and *around* characters (external struggles).

- **INTERNAL STRUGGLES** can be spiritual (questioning your faith), emotional (trying to accept the death of a loved one), psychological (dealing with depression), or existential (wondering if life has ultimate meaning).
- **INTERPERSONAL STRUGGLES** deal with the dynamics of relationships. These struggles might focus on restoring a fractured relationship (welcoming back an estranged family member), embarking on a new one (finding a more understanding lover), or ending an unhealthy one (leaving an abusive spouse).
- **EXTERNAL STRUGGLES** might be physical (trying to survive alone in the Arctic), professional (attempting to stop the burglar before he strikes again), cultural (battling the effects of prejudice), or political (working to overthrow an oppressive regime).

Depending on the genre of the story, one realm of struggle will typically be more central to the protagonist's pursuit, but they do overlap, and typically will all be present to some degree.

The more finely drawn the struggle, the more universal the truth. For example, if your character has trouble forgiving people in general, the story won't have nearly the impact it might have if it focuses on how he's struggling to forgive his sister for what she said to him at his dad's funeral.

Why?

Because abstract concepts—forgiveness, love, wonder—are too amorphous for us to identify with until we see concrete examples of them. Look for specific, intimate, relevant ways to home in on struggles that readers will identify with.

Deepen the struggle to heighten the interest.

FIXING ISSUES WITH STRUGGLES

Stories run aground when the struggles (1) don't escalate, (2) are too diffuse, (3) aren't clearly defined, (4) aren't promised, or (5) aren't paid off.

Ask yourself the following questions.

Is There Enough Time for This to Go Wrong and Then Be Resolved in a Book This Short?

Every struggle is a promise, and making big promises that you won't be able to keep is a guaranteed way to let your readers down. Don't introduce struggles that your book won't have the length or breadth to resolve.

Within every relationship lies the latent promise for some type of struggle. If you do introduce a struggle, readers will want it satisfactorily addressed.

Is This Struggle Introduced Early Enough?

Sometimes, in the hope of keeping readers' attention, authors will introduce a new storyline in the middle of the book. Often, this is simply because they don't trust their story or don't want to take the time to go back to the beginning and weave in events, promises, or foreshadowing to make this new set of obstacles inevitable. Take the time. Plant the seeds for the significant struggles early on in the story.

Is There an Opportunity for Divergent Responsibilities or Priorities?

He wants to win the woman's heart, but how can he both please his family, who doesn't approve of her, *and also* win her heart? The tension is magnified: loyalty to family vs. the desire to be free of them, and the tug of stepping out into the world while also respecting his roots. Moral dilemmas can provide your story with profound struggles.

Will This Difficulty Deepen the Protagonist's Central Struggle or Make It Too Diffuse?

Don't just pile on more problems. Make every struggle work for you. So, things keep getting worse, but is the struggle getting deeper? Does it provide opportunity for revelation?

When a character is forced to rise to an occasion, readers will see his resolve, resourcefulness, or inner fortitude. The scenes that best reveal characterization are those that do more than show things happening or people talking; they show struggles as the character tries to accomplish a specific goal. So, give him something to complete, achieve, or overcome rather than just something to explain.

What Is the Struggle Requiring of My Character?

Struggles will reveal aptitude; they will also require growth. They show what lies at the heart of a character and will also help to develop or shape that character. Explore both avenues of revelation and of transformation. Don't focus simply on who he is but also on who the struggle is requiring him to become.

WHAT IF MY PROTAGONIST DOESN'T STRUGGLE WITH ANYTHING?

Then she doesn't belong in the story. Get her out of the way and start writing about someone who desires and pursues something that matters to her and to your readers.

QUICK FIX: To create a struggle, insert an objective and an obstacle. This initiates pursuit, which is the backbone of your story. To deepen struggles, tap into the character's questions, wounds, beliefs, fears, desires, and vulnerabilities. Let readers know how much success matters, and make it harder and harder for her to accomplish it as the story progresses. Accentuate her desire. Raise the stakes. Give her a problem to solve, a moral dilemma to face, or a sacrifice to make.

FINE-TUNING MY MANUSCRIPT

- Have I developed a well-rounded, but also well-defined, set of struggles for my protagonist?
- Do the struggles escalate as the story progresses? If not, how can I sharpen them?
- Are the struggles appropriate for this story, or have they become too overreaching or generic?
- Typically, the way the protagonist solves the external struggle gives her some type of insight on how to solve the internal struggle. Did I allow for this?
- When having the character solve the climactic struggle, have I used the first idea that I came up with? If so, since many readers will likely think of this idea as well, what could I use instead?
- What does this struggle draw out of the character? What does it require him to do? What type of person does it lead him to become?

35

INCONGRUITIES

If you've been around literary types for any amount of time, you've probably heard a number of myths about storytelling. We've already touched on a few of them:

> **MYTH:** "Stories need three acts."
> **TRUTH:** The length of the story will determine the number of acts. Some stories have one, others three, or five, or seven, or more. Stories need origination, escalation, culmination, and resolution, no matter how many acts they might span.

> **MYTH:** "Stories are either 'plot driven' or 'character driven.'"
> **TRUTH:** All stories are tension driven. That tension might be internal, external, or interpersonal.

> **MYTH:** "A story needs rising action."
> **TRUTH:** A story needs tightening tension. This doesn't always come from more activity or action, but from precipitating more worry about dire things that are about to happen.

Finally, there's this one: "Your characters need to be consistent."
And the truth?
There's nothing more boring than a consistent character.

....

> **Characters will be consistently themselves,
> but not consistently the same.**

....

FIXING INCONGRUITY ISSUES

A character who's always happy would certainly be consistent. He'd also be incredibly boring.

It's the same for someone who's always grumpy or always frustrated or always benevolent. Readers don't want characters who, regardless of what else is going on in the scene, constantly act the same.

In fact, when your always-chipper character keeps showing up, readers will be on the lookout for a dent in her armor. They'll be thinking, *There's gotta be more to her than that.*

If there isn't, they'll quickly tire of her.

Or that guy who seems impatient all the time: When isn't he impatient—when he's holding his baby? When he's taking care of his kittens? When he goes on meditation retreats? That's what'll make him interesting—not the times he loses his patience but the instances when he does not.

Readers want characters to always act in concert with who they are. In other words, characters won't always have the same attitude or emotion (angry, loving, resolute, etc.), but they will always act in ways that naturally reflect their relationship to the other people in that scene.

Incongruities aren't inconsistencies. When a character is *inconsistent*, he won't be acting authentically within that context. So, if the emotionally needy and yet intellectually astute college student suddenly acts emotionally mature or fails to notice a clue that's obvious to readers, that inconsistency will jar them out of the story.

On the other hand, when he's *incongruous*, he won't be acting identically in every circumstance. Incongruities make characters both more believable and more empathetic because readers see those characters mirroring traits that they themselves have.

Respect genre conventions, but don't get into the habit of using cookie-cutter characters.

Memorable characters are more than just a combination of habits and hobbies, more than a bundle of preferences and foibles and needs. You can't just add a Dash of Quirks to a Cup of Desire, mix in a Unique Setting for fifty pages, chill for an hour, and then serve.

Instead, look for contrasts: When does your character lack confidence? When doesn't he have all the answers? What draws out his childlike nature or demonstrates his maturity?

Some psychologists identify nine different types of intelligence: naturalistic, musical, logical-mathematical, existential, interpersonal, bodily-kinesthetic, linguistic, intrapersonal, and spatial. Spend a little time reading up on these, and then explore the two extremes—the end of the continuum where your character is the most "intelligent," and the one where he's the least. Tap into this contrast and you'll have found a rich source of story material to mine.

Try adding more winsome incongruities to your major characters.

Have the characters whom you don't want readers to identify with or care about act the same in every situation regardless of the context. Do the opposite for the characters who play a major role in your book, or whom you're hoping to inveigle readers to want to be around.

Play with genre expectations.

Think of a stereotype in your book's genre. For example, the always-nice gay fashion consultant who lives next door. The hypocritical Southern preacher. The lonely divorcée who's searching for love. The overworked, alcoholic cop who takes justice into his own hands and (gasp!) has marital problems.

Now brainstorm ways to leverage that stereotype to your advantage. Either use it to create reader expectations that lead to a twist in which you turn things on their head, or overplay the stereotype to create a comical situation through exaggeration.

Utilize incongruities to deepen the characteristics of antagonists as well. What is it about the assassin that makes him attractive or even admirable? When he's not out killing people, what does he do that could show he's a morally complex person? Does he care for his elderly mother who has dementia? Run a pet rescue business? Volunteer at a homeless shelter?

Often, the confluence of contradictory characteristics draws readers in. For example, the stiff, stuffy accountant does magic shows at children's birthday parties on the weekends. Or the suburban soccer mom teaches skydiving lessons all day while her kids are in school.

WHY ARE INCONGRUITIES IMPORTANT?

People in real life are incongruous. They have hobbies you wouldn't expect, pastimes that don't seem in line with their personalities, surprising interests, and funky quirks. Incongruities occur within the space between expectation and actuality.

QUICK FIX: Because of their life experiences, readers will naturally assume things about the characters you bring into your story. Don't let those assumptions define your characterizations. Identify reader expectations regarding a character, then twist them in a believable way. Incongruities attract interest, so as we explored earlier, utilize them for your most important characters, but tone them down for characters with less important roles.

FINE-TUNING MY MANUSCRIPT

- Have I deepened the uniqueness of overly positive characters by denting their armor, and of negative characters by giving them polished spots?
- Where have I made the minor characters more interesting than the major ones? If so, how can I recalibrate things?
- Am I propagating stereotypes? How can I reverse roles or add depth to avoid that?
- Have I waited too long in the manuscript to show that this character isn't one-dimensional? Will readers trust me enough to stick with the story that long? If not, how can I show the incongruities earlier in a scene that naturally brings them out?

36

PHYSICALITY

Having read a lot of work by aspiring novelists, I've started to think that there must be a training class somewhere out there on how to write physical descriptions:

> "Alright, everyone. First, you must tell us about the color of your characters' eyes and hair. Then, for women, call attention to her cheekbones. And those cheekbones will always be high—the cheekbones of fictional women must never be low. Never. With men, mention their jaws. The jaws of heroic men must be 'strong' or 'lantern,' which means ... well, I have no idea what it means, but that's not the point. Say it with me now: 'Eyes, hair, cheekbones, jaw ... eyes, hair, cheekbones, jaw.' Good. We'll talk about bushy eyebrows tomorrow. That's enough for today. Class dismissed."

Truthfully, I can't ever remember meeting a man and admiring his jaw or being beguiled by the height of a woman's cheekbones.

We can do better than the "eyes, hair, cheekbones, jaw" writers. It's time to start thinking outside the box when describing the physical traits of our characters.

> **Trust readers to visualize your character— don't describe her so much. Draw attention to her uniqueness in unique ways.**

FIXING PHYSICALITY ISSUES

It's usually wise to lock in the age and gender of your protagonist early in the story. Physique? Maybe. If it's important. Ethnicity? Depends.

Only give readers what they need. Avoid clichés. Don't try to be overly symbolic. Consider drawing attention to the one defining characteristic or trait that makes this character special.

Here are six techniques that can help when portraying your character's physicality.

1. Have Characters Describe Each Other

Whenever you have one character describe another, readers learn about them both. So, if the male friend of the protagonist says, "Suzy has a Miami body," that tells readers about Suzy—but it also tells them about the man describing her in this way. What matters to him? How will that affect readers' impression of him?

Consider the impressions of the describer and the describee in each example below.

> "You'll know him right away. He has a cement-block head."

> "He looked about fifty but kept in shape. Trim. Wiry. Athletic."

> "It was a dog only a PETA member could love."

EXERCISE: Write a twenty-word description of your protagonist from the point of view of the person who knows him best.

2. Get the Character Moving

Think carefully about your verbs. To "saunter" is much different than to "stride." "Toying" with a curl of hair is different than "preening" it.

> He seemed to meander in a vague scribble across the parking lot.

> She walked as if every step she took set a trend.

> His movement was as thick and rolling as his gut.

EXERCISE: Describe your protagonist's style of walking from the point of view of someone he just met. Two sentences max.

3. Let One Character Remind Another of Something Else

> He was a bull of a man with a megaphone voice.

> Landra brought to mind a lynx—quiet, watchful, and sensitive.

> Tall, spindly and methodical, the guy was a human spider.

> With his flowing hair and bulging muscles, he made me think of Thor.

EXERCISE: Compare your three most important characters to an animal and then to a movie star. Could you use any of these descriptions in your book, perhaps in lieu of the "eyes, hair, cheekbones, jaw" descriptions you might currently have?

4. Be Selective in What You Describe

Whatever physical trait you draw attention to will take on added importance. If something in the character's appearance is significant and necessary—she's six feet tall, he has a prosthetic hand, she wears wire-rimmed glasses that end up being a clue to her identity as the killer later in the story—be sure to mention them. And do so the first time that character comes on the scene so readers immediately start picturing him accurately.

5. Words Matter—Choose Them Carefully

Is she sturdy, hefty, robust, corpulent, or buxom? It matters. Is his beard scraggly, thick and grungy, or old and wizened? Is her voice husky, smoky, sultry, breathy, or lustrous? Attend to the subtle difference between your adjectives.

6. Beware of Happy People

Does she have a plastic smile or a free and breezy one?

Since readers know that in stories things are not always what they appear to be, having characters laugh or grin all the time will actually undermine how much readers will believe that they truly are happy.

The more a character smiles, the less readers will trust him, or the more they'll think he's masking his true feelings.

To show happiness on the page, focus more on the character's contentment, appreciation of the little things in life, or how the natural world fills him with awe. In fiction, one of the best ways to show happiness is through moments of quiet celebration.

BUT WHAT IF I NEED TO DESCRIBE HAIR OR EYES?

Then go for it—but don't do it for each character.

QUICK FIX: Consider underscoring a character's attributes by the way you describe her: "Ethel's hair was a tangled, worrisome cloud hovering over her head." Also, rather than describing the color of someone's eyes, give readers a picture of the person by showing that her eyes have become something that eyes could never be, or that they are doing something eyes could never do. Are his eyes icicles? Are they daggers? Do they drill into people? Do they dare you to reply when he's speaking? Be evocative rather than simply descriptive.

FINE-TUNING MY MANUSCRIPT

- Do I portray vital physical characteristics as succinctly and clearly as possible while avoiding the most overdone types of descriptions?
- Where can I improve the verbs I'm using to render characters' actions?
- Can I opt for more accurate or evocative adjectives to describe their attributes?
- Since elaborating on a character's special skills is a promise that he'll use them, have I given him the chance to do so?
- Where have I overdescribed characters? How can I recast the descriptions to make them more concise and show more trust for my readers' imaginations?

37

CHOICES

Years ago I worked as an outdoor instructor. One day when we took a group of students out to float on inner tubes down a river, a kayaker paddled past us.

We were simply letting the river chart our course.

He was charting his own.

That image stuck with me when I became a writer: floating or paddling—what is my character doing in this scene?

Is your protagonist on an inner tube or in a kayak right now?

Passive characters aren't interesting; they just float aimlessly through your story. Readers will get bored pretty quickly if the protagonist gets bounced around by the river and never tries to paddle anywhere. They want to see kayakers fight the current as they maneuver their way downstream.

> Choices reveal priorities. What a character does—not what he says—reveals what truly matters to him.

FIXING ISSUES WITH CHOICES

Our first response to stimuli is sometimes instinctive. We say something we don't mean. We lose our temper. We wish we could take back what we said.

In those cases, feelings, rather than logic, are in the driver's seat.

Does she slap him in the face? Smash the phone? Take a baseball bat to the windshield? Spray-paint the word *slut* on her rival's garage door?

When a character makes a conscious choice, she's responding to what just happened in the hope of influencing what will happen next. It's purpose driven. She's paddling in a specific direction.

If an event doesn't affect her thoughts, emotions, or behavior, it'll seem like an artifice that you stuck into the story just to prop up your plot.

Thoughts, actions, and emotions can all cause each other.

PROGRESSION WITHIN THE CHARACTER	END RESULT
Reflect → Feel → Act	The way he feels leads him to act.
Reflect → Act → Feel	The way he acts affects how he feels.
Feel → Reflect → Act	His thoughts cause him to make a choice.
Feel → Act → Reflect	His actions lead him to a new understanding.
Act → Reflect → Feel	His thoughts end up affecting his feelings.
Act → Feel → Reflect	His feelings influence what he's thinking about.

Choices are the only way readers can gauge a character's progress though a story. Thought progressions can be interesting occasionally, but unless they lead to action, they'll soon cause narrative static and weigh down your story.

Every decision has implications and repercussions. Play them out.

Stop asking what a character is like, and instead ask what she chooses. Her actions under pressure, while she's pursuing what she desires, will show you all that you need to know about what she's truly like. As Dr. Martin Luther King Jr. noted, "The ultimate measure of a man is not where he stands in moments of comfort and convenience, but where he stands at times of challenge and controversy."

Choices are vital at every stage of the character's journey through the story, and they always reveal something.

He's a cop looking for a suspect. Does he step onto the hood of the car, scan the area, locate the killer, leap down, sprint through traffic to try to catch him—or does he stand aside, chatting on the police radio while someone else chases the suspect?

Which character would you rather read about?

Yeah.

The kayaker cop.

Not the inner tube one.

And so would your readers.

• • •

Regarding choices, remember that:

The Pursuit Begins with a Conscious Choice

Some writing instructors teach that stories need a "refusal of the call." For example, the protagonist is offered a job, given a noble task, called out of retirement, invited on an adventure, etc., but he says no until An Important External Event Changes His Mind.

This technique is overused. Readers know that the character is eventually going to say yes—otherwise there wouldn't be any story. Just let the guy accept the challenge and get on with it.

Choices in a Story Are Contingent

In real life, we might think about major decisions for a long time before finally deciding what we should do—and we might not be able to identify one specific event that led us to make that choice when we did. However, in fiction, readers will want to see the moments when your character makes important decisions. Also, they want to know the impetus that causes him to make that decision.

It doesn't help to write, "She thought and prayed about her decision for three months, carefully weighed the pros and cons, and then finally decided to join the Peace Corps."

Why did she decide? Why now? What precipitated that choice? That's the scene readers want to see. Give it to them. Otherwise, the choice will seem random, unbelievable, or coincidental.

Choices Reveal Priorities

Choices are revelatory in that they show readers what a character is really like and what really matters to him.

You can study aspirations apart from choices, but you cannot study morality apart from them. Stories are about more than dreams; they are about the steps a character takes to pursue them and the moral compass that guides him as he does.

Choices Determine the Story's Outcome

Readers will be most satisfied when they see the character make a choice at the end of the story that she would not, or could not, have made at the beginning. This choice often reveals a change in the character's priorities or perspective that was brought forth by dealing with or overcoming the story's primary struggle.

A crisis might initiate the story; a choice will end it.

• • •

Remove the easy choices. We want desperate measures. Nobody wants to read the account of someone who has to make easy decisions that lead to reasonable actions in order to solve inconsequential problems.

Instead, hand your character a paddle and stick her on the river at flood stage.

That's when the story will really take off.

WHY ARE CHOICES SO CRUCIAL?

If a character doesn't make meaningful choices, she's not involved in a meaningful pursuit. Even choosing not to respond to taunts (for example, she turns the other cheek) or pretending that an event doesn't affect her is a choice that carries significance and reveals important characteristics.

QUICK FIX: Put your character in situations where she needs to (1) make meaningful, relevant, and significant decisions; (2) act on her beliefs; (3) respond to escalating difficulties; and (4) pursue her goal despite more and more devastating or debilitating setbacks.

FINE-TUNING MY MANUSCRIPT

- Have I let my character's choices matter?
- Do his decisions inextricably relate to what has just occurred and cause what follows?
- How can I do a better job of sustaining believability and causality by showing a natural progression of responses that don't require an explanation for why they happened?
- Are the repercussions for decisions clear? If not, what changes do I need to make?   .
- How is my character moving downstream? Is she in a kayak or an inner tube? Is she fighting the current or simply being carried along by it? Is that what readers want?
- What rocks and obstacles can I place downstream from my character to force her to be creative and responsive in how she maneuvers down the river?

38

STAKES

You're playing a game of cards, and the stakes keep getting higher.

Are you all in or not?

The most intriguing and compelling characters aren't the ones who play it safe and hedge their bets, but the ones who gamble more than they can afford to lose. A person who never risks will never know the sting of loss. Some people might say he's better off because of that.

Your readers would not.

Let your character take risks—and sometimes, let him get burned.

The stakes are simply who gets hurt, in what way, and how deeply if the protagonist fails to accomplish his goal. Always consider the consequences: What disaster will befall him in this scene if he fails in his pursuit?

If nothing vital is at stake, why would it ultimately matter if he loses?

And here's the key: The stakes need to be high enough for readers to care but also believable enough for them to buy into what's happening.

Ask yourself if you have big enough stakes in your story and a big enough story for your stakes.

FIXING ISSUES WITH STAKES

Because of the narrative force of escalation, you'll continue to raise the stakes as the story progresses—not necessarily in terms of how many people are affected, but by how deeply the failure or loss impacts the main character.

So, while it would certainly raise the stakes to plant a bomb in the middle of a stadium filled with fifty thousand fans, it's not necessary to put that many people in danger. Depending on the story, that type of scenario might come across as completely unbelievable. But putting the life of the one person your character loves most on the line would make it personal and might be all the stakes you need.

The higher you raise the stakes, the more you strain credulity. This is one reason thrillers are often longer books—they have incredibly high stakes, so the writer needs to take the time to set up a world in which those stakes are not just believable but inevitable.

What's at stake in your story? Justice? A relationship? Someone's sanity or well-being?

Life itself can be at stake, the future of the planet can be at stake, and so can the destiny of the entire universe. (I'm not sure you can raise the stakes much higher than that. But if you can make it believable, go for it.)

Think in terms of "or else" and "if … then." For example, "We have to accomplish this *or else* [the terrible consequences will come to pass]." Or "*If* we don't accomplish this, *then* [the terrible consequences will come to pass]."

Clarify the stakes as specifically as possible:

- **SUSPENSE:** "If we don't find her by eight o'clock, they're going to kill her!"
- **COMING-OF-AGE:** "I swear, if my parents make me go to that stupid treatment center again, I'm gonna slit my wrists."
- **MYSTERY:** "Someone will be getting away with murder unless we solve this case."
- **ACTION:** "We need to get out of here, Colonel—this whole place is about to blow. In thirty seconds, anyone left in this building is going to be a corpse."
- **ROMANCE:** "If she doesn't find out that I love her, truly love her, she's going to marry the wrong person."
- **SPORTS:** "So, alright—we win this game, we move on. We lose, we go home. What's it gonna be? Into the arms of a cheerleader or back to the arms of your mama?"

- **LITERARY:** "You don't understand: My dad's a mullah. If I convert to Christianity, he'll disown me—my whole family will!"
- **FANTASY:** "The Kraken has been released. It'll destroy that entire underwater village unless we stop it."

The security or well-being of any aspect of the character's existence can be at stake. Ask, "What part of her would die (in a literal or a symbolic sense) if she fails?"

Defining the stakes will also likely help you define your premise, which is usually a combination of stakes plus dilemma. (However, don't pressure yourself to do this before you start writing your story. Often, the premise will only become clear to you as your story develops.)

The more specific the tasks, timing, and consequences, the sharper the story will be. These consequences might be:

- Emotional/Psychological

    - He has decided that unless he stops feeling depressed by his birthday, he's going to end his life.
    - If they don't find a cure for her dementia, she will ultimately lose touch with reality.

- Spiritual/Metaphysical

    - He must find salvation before the Devil returns to claim his soul at midnight.
    - When Morgan is stranded in the Arctic, she must come to grips with her beliefs about God and eternity before she freezes to death.

- Physical

    - The mob will break his fingers one by one unless he can come up with the money by Sunday.
    - If the chemo treatments aren't successful, she'll be dead in three months.

- Relational

  - His ex will get sole custody of the kids unless he can find a job in the next two weeks.
  - The love of her life will be gone forever unless she manages to get to the airport before his plane takes off.

- Material

  - If she can't come up with the mortgage payment by month's end, she'll lose the house.
  - The priceless jewel will be sold on the black market unless the detective can find the thieves before they make it out of the city.

- Societal

  - The banking system will collapse unless the hackers can be stopped by noon.
  - If the dragon isn't killed before the full moon arrives, the village will be destroyed.

Since your protagonist is multidimensional, with various relationships and struggles, there'll likely be stakes in different areas of his life. All those storylines need to find some sort of closure and be satisfactorily resolved by the story's end.

WHAT ARE THE MOST COMMON PROBLEMS WITH RAISING THE STAKES?

Authors tend to err in three ways: (1) making the stakes too small, (2) making the stakes too big, and (3) not making the stakes clear to readers.

QUICK FIX: Evaluate your story's genre, and then look for ways to raise the stakes as high as possible while also keeping them believable. Clearly state the consequences of failure. Don't beat around the bush. Increase empathy, make the peril more impending, and widen (or intensify) the possible impact.

FINE-TUNING MY MANUSCRIPT

- Does the protagonist's pursuit really matter? To whom? How much? Who'll suffer if she fails? How much will they suffer? Is that something readers will care about?
- Have I unequivocally communicated the stakes?
- Will readers realize why this scene is significant to the protagonist's journey through the story? If not, how can I more specifically delineate what is at stake?
- Are the stakes high enough? Are there realistic ways that I can increase them?
- Are the stakes believable? Do I need to edit the beginning of the story to create a world in which building up to those stakes makes sense and even seems inevitable?

39

INDIVIDUALITY

As long as you keep your characters on a short leash, you'll have a safe, quaint, manageable little story.

But that's not what I want for you.

If I could, I would slip in during the night, cut all those leashes, and watch each of your characters scurry into the darkness, or shake off the dust and rise on their own two feet and start actually living, choosing, pursuing, failing, falling, or howling at the moon or blowing kisses at the stars.

That's when your story will really start thrumming with life.

So here, let me hand you the knife.

You can take care of those leashes yourself.

• • •

The more a character distinguishes himself from others, the more significant readers will assume he is. Individuality is a promise. Uniqueness will match importance. The most important characters in your story should be the most intriguing ones.

Don't just think of the trait that makes the character unique; think of how it affects the scene or his relationships with other characters. In the chart below, notice how the character's attribute affects the other characters in the scene.

TRAIT OR ABILITY	REACTION OF ANOTHER CHARACTER
Special Skills	"I had no idea that you could ..."
Emblems	"Do you always carry that _____ with you?"

Hobbies or Preferences	"Huh, I would never have pegged you as someone who likes _____."
Physical Tics	"Do you always _____ when you're nervous?"
Secrets or Former Career	"What?! Really? You used to be a _____?"
Wounds or Scars	"So, then we have that in common. We both lost _____."

Don't tell readers that a character is quirky—they won't believe you. Instead, show them the quirkiness as part of the natural extension of who that character is.

> **Let your characters respond without restraint. Don't hem them in.**

FIXING INDIVIDUALITY ISSUES

You'll cut the leash off your characters when you start noticing, *really* noticing, those special things about them:

1. **HER AWKWARD PHYSICAL HABITS:** She never looks you in the eye, she tends to invade your personal space, or she checks her text messages constantly.

2. **HIS ENDEARING QUALITIES, CELEBRATION, OR WONDER:** He plays hopscotch at least once a day, no matter where he is in the world.

3. **HER MEANINGFUL QUIRKS:** As a way of honoring her dad's memory, she's worn one sock inside out ever since she was ten, after she accidentally did it on the day of his funeral.

   - What does she dislike that everyone else likes? (Cats? Silk? Chocolate?)
   - What trend does she refuse to become a part of? (Gluten-free? Kale? Smart watches?)
   - What is she afraid of that most people don't fear? (Styrofoam? Pudding? Sporks?)

- What does she find endearing or delightful that most people find annoying? (Yapping dogs? Being put on hold? Beets?)
- What odd habits does she have? (Yogurt addiction? Burps too loudly? Does housework naked?)
- What animal best symbolizes what she's like? (A lone raven? A powerful lion? A playful otter? A charging rhino?)

4. **THAT ONE THING HE DOES OLD SCHOOL:** He only uses a flip phone, still listens to cassette tapes in his car, or only reads library books—and never from an e-reader.

5. **THE UNIQUENESS OF HER CLOTHES/STYLE/WARDROBE:** What does she wear that you wouldn't expect? Why: Comfort? Style? To impress? To save time? To save money? What's unusual about his outfit? For example, if he's an FBI agent who doesn't wear a tie, why doesn't he?

6. **HIS WOUNDS AND EXTRAORDINARY ABILITIES:** The wound helps readers empathize with him; the extraordinary ability leads them to admire him.

7. **HOW OBSERVANT SHE IS AND HOW SHE NOTICES TRUTHS OTHER PEOPLE MISS:**

- "The best way to get little kids to try something new is to tell 'em they'll like it, but the best way to get teens to try it is to tell 'em they won't."
- "Why do they call it a space walk anyway? Why not a space float? I mean, if that's walking, I wish I could walk to work every day."
- "Anytime someone says, 'To make a long story short …' it's already too late."

8. **HIS CURIOSITY AND UNIQUE PERSPECTIVE:** Let him ask, "Did you ever notice how …?" Or "Did you ever wonder why …?"

9. **THAT INCONGRUITY IN HER BELIEF SYSTEM:** She believes in heaven but not in God. How does that affect her choices?

If too many characters have the same characteristics, readers will think you haven't really done your work as a writer. Also, if characters play the same role, it'll seem redundant. Often, characters can be conflated. Too many disgruntled cops? Mentors? Brothers and sisters who just serve to get in the way? Eliminate some of them, or maybe combine them all into one.

Every character in your story is an individual. The server at the restaurant isn't just a woman in her thirties—she's a specific woman of a particular age and ethnicity doing her job with a certain attitude, aptitude, and uniqueness. Problems come when you place more narrative weight on someone than her uniqueness can uphold.

The protagonist isn't a caricature. He's not merely an allegorical representation of the controlling idea or the overriding theme in your story. He's not here to represent anything. He's here to be himself.

Give him free rein. No more leashes. Cut your characters loose.

HOW CAN I ADD MORE QUIRKS?

Start by observing other people, noting the things they do without thinking, the habits that seem to control them, the incongruities between their hobbies or interests and their career choice. Consider what television show your character watches that readers wouldn't expect him to watch. Now justify why he watches it.

QUICK FIX: Search online for "100 weird quirks," and you'll find more ideas than you could ever use. But don't get carried away. One or two quirks per character is enough. The more you add, the more diluted each one becomes.

FINE-TUNING MY MANUSCRIPT

- Have I given my character a memorable quirk, idiosyncrasy, habit, or interest that will make her unique?
- Is her uniqueness in proportion to her significance? Have I made the characters who bear the majority of the narrative's weight fascinating enough to do so?
- By including these quirks, am I making promises that aren't being fulfilled?

- Are the characters who pepper the background distracting from the story? (That is, are they too interesting?)
- How is this character extraordinary? What is he better at than anyone else? How is he alone equipped to resolve this story's struggles?
- On the other end of the spectrum, how is he just like you and me? What makes him normal and relatable?

40

RELATIONSHIPS

Everyone lives within a web of relationships, and just like with a spider's web, if you tug on one thread, the others connected to it will be affected.

When tragedy strikes, or misfortune comes, or a marriage dissolves, it'll impact family members, friends, co-workers. All those threads. All those tremors.

At the beginning of your story, the main character will have a variety of relational threads emanating from his life. Then, as the novel progresses, some of these will be plucked, some will be snapped, and, most likely, some new threads will be spun.

Our interactions with and feelings about parents, children, siblings, spouses, friends—all those whose lives intersect with ours—raise questions of trust, dependency, responsibility, and morality, and often force us to make difficult choices that affect many people.

Because of this, relationships offer endless opportunities for tension. As you uncover your story, you'll be exploring these threads, seeing which ones are necessary, which aren't, and how, as the tension and setbacks brush against the web, it'll look different at the end of the book from how it looks at the beginning.

> Every character in your story is enmeshed in a web of relationships. It'll be altered by the story's end (even if the only relationship that's altered is your protagonist's relationship with himself).

FIXING RELATIONSHIP ISSUES

When your story opens, the main character will have a tumultuous collection of misunderstandings and anger and loss and grief and terror and joy that make up his life, that come from the relationships he has.

As you consider his relationships, think in terms of his perspective concerning others, their view of him, and how the differing goals in each social encounter affect the movement of the story.

Since relationships are dynamic, during your story secondary relationships might become primary ones and vice versa. Keep your finger on the pulse of your narrative to monitor how the relationships are changing and how that's affecting the mood and choices of your protagonist.

Backstory will naturally accent and shade the development of the scenes. Keep in mind that the genesis for every storyline is hidden within the interrelationships that already exist as the story opens. Tap into them to deepen your tale.

When you evaluate each aspect of your protagonist's relationships, don't simply look at where they are now, but where they are heading and how they are changing.

How Is Your Protagonist's Relationship with Herself Evolving?

One day, when my daughter was four years old, she came up to me with a big smile and announced, "I love me!" On the other end of the spectrum, when my grandmother was ten, her stepmother told her that she was ugly and, even to the day when my grandma moved into the nursing home, she shied away from being photographed because she didn't believe anyone would want to look at her picture.

What does your character think of herself? "I love me!" or "I hate me!"? What does she tell herself about herself? What's the soundtrack that's playing in the back of her mind?

You're no good. No one likes you.

You can do this. You know you can.

He'll never love you for who you are. You have to change.

Life is so short. Seize the day. Seize it!

Does she emotionally beat herself up? What effect does being so hard (or easy) on herself have? How might it change? What would cause that to happen?

Sometimes readers will realize that a character is heading off an emotional or existential cliff long before she does. They'll worry. That's good, as long as there's narrative payoff in the end.

How Are Her Primary Relationships in Flux?

Stability is an illusion.

Life is many things, but it is not static. And when we slip into a rut or get caught up in our routines, the world continues swirling around us, taking us with it the whole time.

We are all on trajectories: trajectories in our work, in our health, in our relationships, in our resolve, in our sense of spiritual peace. We are moving, we are in flux.

People are always coming and going in our lives. Friends. Family members. Lovers.

Probe the protagonist's relationships with those closest to him. Is he married? Does he have children? What about his work associates, his college buddies, his online relationships?

In every relationship there's a level of *actual intimacy* and *perceived intimacy* that each person has. Examine how this character views the relationship and how he believes others view it. Plumb the depths of those perceptions and impressions for tension, misunderstanding, and grudges.

Typically, when a character is in a scene with the protagonist, it's for one of five narrative purposes: (1) to help him, (2) to hinder him, (3) to reveal his characteristics or personality, (4) to unearth the moral dilemma, or (5) to ask the story's central question. Identify the character's primary role in the scene you're working on, and sharpen it to strengthen the story.

How Are His Secondary Relationships Affecting His Primary Ones?

Secondary relationships might become primary ones, and the relationships that are strong at the start of the story might diminish. As you write, monitor how the relationships are changing and how that's affecting the mood and choices of your protagonist.

How are the goals of those on the periphery altering the state of mind of those in the center ring?

• • •

Pluck at the web.

Watch it vibrate.

And invite the spider to spin new threads that lead your story to places you never even anticipated.

> ### WHAT IS THE TRAJECTORY OF THE PROTAGONIST'S RELATIONSHIPS?
>
> All relationships are fluid and transitory. We suffer when we try to cling to ones that should be over, or when we pine for ones that'll never develop.
>
> **QUICK FIX:** Avoid being overly committed to your original ideas. Explore different relationships as you move through different drafts. Each relationship will have its own pathway through time.
>
> - History: This might include wounds, moments of forgiveness, lingering resentment, and shared memories.
> - Present: Look at what's happening right now between these characters. What are the dynamics of power and submission, the characters' feelings toward each other, and the trajectory of those feelings?

- Future: Examine where things are heading and where the characters want them to go. This might include mutual (or mutually exclusive) goals.

FINE-TUNING MY MANUSCRIPT

- How will the change in one relationship send vibrations across the other relationships in the story?
- Regarding close relationships, whose tears has my protagonist kissed away? Whose tears has he caused?
- Who would he call at 3 A.M. to help him in his time of need? What does that tell me about him and about who needs to be in this story?
- Since stories from other settings, times, and places (historical, fantasy, or science fiction) have different social constraints and expectations about relationships, have I kept in mind how people would naturally interact in that setting? How would they establish relationships? What cultural norms would they have? Have I shown those in my story?
- How are the protagonist's relationships changing throughout the story? If I were to track them, which are on a positive trajectory? Which are on a negative one? How will that affect the closure of my novel?
- Who are the three most important people in my character's life at the beginning of the story? What about at the end? Is there a natural progression of events that will make that transformation inevitable?

41

BELIEFS

Why do you set an alarm? What beliefs does that simple act reveal?

After all, if you believed you were going to die tonight, you wouldn't set an alarm for the morning. Setting that alarm is a small act, yet it's one born of hope that tomorrow will come, that you'll be alive, and that it'll matter if you get out of bed.

It shows faith and bears evidence of your beliefs about yourself and about the future.

In fiction, just as in real life, beliefs affect behavior and behavior reveals beliefs.

Our beliefs shape us.

Our worldview affects every facet of our lives.

If your protagonist claims that he believes something, but his actions contradict that, readers will be more apt to trust what he does than what he claims.

A belief means nothing until an action is taken.

FIXING ISSUES WITH BELIEFS

Take a careful look at your character's beliefs. To identify them, test them. He'll act on them, he'll put them into practice, or else he's showing that he values something else more than the things he claims are important.

Pretend that you're inventing a new religion that takes into account your character's belief system, spirituality, and priorities. Ask the following questions, and then, after each one, ask yourself, "How is this belief expressed in my character's actions or choices?"

- Is there a God? If so, what is he or she like?
- What role does fate or destiny play in life?
- Do angels and demons exist?
- What is the meaning of life?
- Is there life after death?
- Do heaven and hell exist? If so, how does a person get to heaven? What would condemn him to hell?
- Do our choices have any lasting significance?
- Why do bad things happen to good people?
- Why is there evil and suffering in the world? Does it have an origin? Does it serve a purpose?
- Did people evolve, or were they created? A combination of both? What implications does that have for understanding human nature?
- Are people basically good, basically evil, or born as clean slates?
- What plays a bigger role in defining who we are—nature or nurture? What evidence is there for that conclusion?

A character might not always live up to his moral aspirations. Sometimes his weaknesses will get the best of him. In real life, temptation hounds all of us. At times, we do what we know we shouldn't. Sometimes we act without thinking. We say things we regret. We hurt those we love.

This will happen to your protagonist as well.

Dig into the implications of his moral meltdowns. The actions he takes in their aftermath will reveal his highest priorities.

For example, the committed family man ends up sleeping with his co-worker on a business trip after they've both had too much to drink. Okay—so what happens next?

His actions here, at this point, reveal more about his priorities than his compromising choice did. Does he confess to his wife the truth and risk losing her and hurting the children, or does he keep his one-night stand a secret in order to protect them? Does he quit his job so he won't be tempted in that way with that woman again?

What does he do? What does that *cause*?

His willingness to go through a months-long journey toward reconciliation speaks louder about what matters to him than his night of indiscretion. Wanting to have sex proves he's an animal. Owning up to the implications of his infidelity proves he's a man.

Think in terms of passions, priorities, and addictions. Every one of these can be an asset or a liability. Where does her zeal lead her in the wrong direction?

If we're passionate about the wrong things, we'll lose our way. If we prioritize the wrong things, we'll hurt those closest to us. If we're addicted to the wrong things (i.e., vices rather than virtues such as joy, love, hope, thanksgiving), we'll end up destroying ourselves and will probably take others with us over the cliff.

Sometimes our beliefs are a result of our upbringing; sometimes we develop them despite our upbringing. The origin of your character's beliefs matters less in this story than the effect they have on his decisions right now.

Readers are more interested in what your character does because of his beliefs than what he claims to believe. Examining beliefs is best done through the lens of actions. Keeping that in mind, look closely at your character's guilt and shame—the choices that caused them and the consequences they have.

Guilt

ANALYSIS: Does she carry around a burden of guilt? (Most people do.) If she doesn't, why not? If she does, what's the cause of the guilt?

EXPLORATION: When she feels guilty, what does she do? How does she try to quiet her guilt so she doesn't have to think about it? Does she compare herself to others so she doesn't seem so bad? Does she seek forgiveness? If so, what actions does she take to receive that forgiveness—apologies, prayers, kind deeds, repayment?

Shame

ANALYSIS: What actions from his past cause him the most shame? What does that tell you about what he considers virtuous? Is he harder on other people or on himself? What effect does that have on his peace of mind and his relationships?

EXPLORATION: What does he do with his shame? Does he mentally relive his mistakes over and over? How does this affect his demeanor and his friendships?

WHY DO MY CHARACTER'S BELIEFS MATTER?

Your character's beliefs will affect every choice he makes—and it isn't just existential or religious beliefs that matter. Every character believes that something will bring her relief or happiness in some form. She might be wrong about the pathway, but she will be committed to the journey.

QUICK FIX: Explore how your character would define success. Write a paragraph to yourself from your character that starts with this sentence: "You never knew this before, but this is what would make me feel the most fulfilled …"

FINE-TUNING MY MANUSCRIPT

- Have I let my own beliefs creep into my story? How will this help it? How will it hurt it? What will I do about that?
- How is my protagonist's obsession serving his best interests? How is it destroying him? How do his actions bear this out?
- How can I pit two strongly held beliefs against each other to create inner struggles for this character?
- Where do her allegiances lie? What is one way I can make those visible through choices and dilemmas?
- How do guilt and shame affect this character's life and sense of peace? What steps does he take to manage them?

42

VULNERABILITY

There's a fable about the day Lion asked the other animals to line up: the smartest on his right side, the strongest on his left. Everyone else took their place, but Monkey kept scurrying back and forth between the two sides. When Lion asked him why, Monkey said, "What do you want me to do—cut myself in half?"

• • •

Monkey's answer reveals a lot about how he views himself.

What does your protagonist think of himself? How is this perception healthy? How is it harmful? How does he think other people perceive him?

Characters who are self-aware enough to know their weaknesses will fare far better in facing their struggles than those who are unaware of their vulnerabilities.

To know your vice is to know yourself.

Vulnerabilities might come from disillusionment, fear, or pride, but vulnerability doesn't result only from vices or weaknesses. Strengths can become weaknesses when taken to the extreme. (This observation is nothing new. Aristotle explored this dynamic 2,400 years ago in his writings on virtues or "means.")

Vulnerability can also result from love.

In *The Divine Drama*, Kurt D. Bruner writes:

> No matter how powerful, brave, or noble a hero may
> be, he becomes vulnerable to defeat when he loves another
> ... Capture his child and threaten harm if demands aren't
> met ... Steal away the affection of the one he seeks to save,

undermining his resolve by turning the quest into a pointless pursuit. Through one means or another, the object of a hero's love can become the key to a villain's victory.

The greatest vulnerability comes not from lack of ability but from depth of love. The more you care, the more you can be hurt.

FIXING VULNERABILITY ISSUES

To be human is to be vulnerable.

The less vulnerable a character is, the less readers will empathize with him. They'll be glad to admire him from a distance, but reader identification requires character vulnerability.

Characters who can suffer are easier for readers to identify with. Superheroes who can bruise? Sure. Superheroes who cannot? Not so much.

The more impenetrable someone's armor is, the less fascinating her struggles will seem. After all, if she cannot lose, if she cannot suffer, the stakes are low—and the lower the stakes, the less interesting the story.

Keep the following points in mind as you examine the vulnerability of your characters.

Typically, a Character Is the Most Vulnerable in the Moment Right Before the Climax

That's when his choice and sacrifice matter the most.

While love of others can be a vulnerability for the protagonist, love of self can be a weakness for the antagonist. Explore how you can reveal this dynamic clearly in the moments leading up to your climax.

Readers are Drawn to Mistake-Makers and Pain-Bearers

David Corbett, in his book *The Art of Character*, writes, "Vulnerability creates a kind of undertow, pulling us toward a character who is wounded or imperfect, and that attractive force is far more important than whether the character is 'likable.'"

You'll want to make your protagonist vulnerable but not cowardly, weak willed, or overly needy. To reveal vulnerability, show him struggling with a decision, tackling a challenging task that he doesn't seem equipped for, or trying to maintain a relationship that's slipping away.

Temptation Tests How Much We Actually Tell Ourselves the Truth

Here's how temptation works: Beforehand, we're promised pleasure without consequence.

We feel that morality should make an exception for us on this one occasion, that we have a right to do this thing, that we're justified, maybe even obligated to do it. *Nothing bad will happen*, we think. *No one will know. It's not that big of a deal. And besides, it's nothing compared with what some people do.*

Then, while we're acting out, we push aside thoughts of morality or of right and wrong. They become almost unreal to us. We're not *trying* to hurt anyone—no, of course not.

Finally, after the act (or maybe after we get caught) comes the shame. That inner voice: *How could you have done that? You're a bad person. A failure. You'll never be forgiven. You deserve to go to hell!*

So, temptation typically goes through three stages: justification, rationalization, and shame.

We convince ourselves that it really isn't so bad beforehand and, afterward, that it's impossible to be forgiven. And so we don't tell ourselves the truth in either direction—either before or after the act. We become practiced liars whose lies cause us to avoid both responsibility and forgiveness—two of the most vital things we can ever experience.

When you tempt your protagonist, move him through those stages:

- **BEFOREHAND:** He isn't telling himself the truth about what will happen. What's he telling himself instead? He knows this act will hurt people, but how is he justifying it?

- **DURING THE ACT:** He's in denial as he does it. What's that inner voice saying? How is he shutting out the voice of truth?
- **AFTERWARD:** He's not accepting responsibility for it. What will cause him to own up to it? Is pride the problem? Fear? What could lead him toward hope and forgiveness?

WHY DOES TEMPTATION MATTER SO MUCH?

How and when we're tempted reveals a lot about our vulnerabilities, shows how much we're telling ourselves the truth, and tests our moral resolve and our devotion to others and to our ideals.

QUICK FIX: Does your character prepare for times of temptation? If so, how? If not, why not—does she secretly want to give in? Tempt your character to betray her convictions. She will be most vulnerable when she's alone, hungry, in a unique setting, or tired. Tempt her then. What temptations are the most alluring to her? What comforting lies does she tell herself throughout the process?

FINE-TUNING MY MANUSCRIPT

- How have I successfully shown the ways in which my protagonist can be the most deeply hurt or compromised? Where can I do a better job of letting the forces of antagonism turn my character's vulnerabilities against him?
- Where is she vulnerable? What is she hiding? What's she afraid of losing? Of finding? Of revealing to others?
- How can I twist things one last time at the climax and let him use his apparent vulnerability (blindness, deafness, missing a limb, etc.) as an asset?
- Does my protagonist have some sort of special ability or superpower? What can I do to show her humanity and vulnerability?
- When it comes to temptation, where does he toe the line? Where does he draw it? When does it seem easiest for him not to?
- Can I use the vulnerabilities of the cast of characters as a whole to show the overwhelming power of the forces of antagonism?

43

RESISTANCE

One day, as I was talking with my dad in his garage, he nodded toward the looming stacks of decades' worth of accumulated debris from living in the same house for forty years. Then he sighed. "If I die, you're going to have to get rid of this stuff."

"What do you mean, 'if'?" I said.

• • •

Denial results from resistance to accept something at face value. Most of us live in denial of our mortality, of the destructive consequences of our own selfishness, and of the human suffering going on out of sight around the bend or on the other side of the world.

It's so much easier to bury our heads in the sand—or maybe it's not easier per se, but it does at least seem like it'll be less painful. Whereas vulnerabilities are often the result of unconscious choices, resistance is the result of conscious ones.

The more we live in denial, the more we construct our happiness on a fragile artifice. On the other hand, the more we tell ourselves the truth, the stronger our foundation will be when the storms roll in.

And they will.

In a world like ours they are never far away.

Difficult times have a way of dismantling our denial.
Let the story do that to your protagonist.

FIXING RESISTANCE ISSUES

Stories are about bringing on the storms and watching how they affect the protagonist.

We all resist change. Sometimes we avoid problems, sometimes we ignore them. We know we need to change, but we don't like to hear that. We see in others the flaws we ignore in ourselves. We try to change others rather than change ourselves.

Sometimes we try to heal ourselves by hurting others. We lash out, we insult, we put people down. We hold onto our pain and swing it around and end up wounding those closest to us.

As you mine areas of resistance, carefully consider the actions your character takes and the feelings that result. Analyze the timing, the questions, the context, and the source of resistance at that moment.

TIME	QUESTION	GOAL	ANALYSIS	FEELING
Past	"Why is this happening?"	Searching for motive	Does his resistance come from memories of painful experiences?	Regret
Present	"What will I do now?"	Determining action	What steps is he taking to try to regain balance in his life? What do those steps reveal about the source of resistance?	Fear
Future	"What is going to happen next?"	Anticipating consequences	Does resistance come from anxiety about what the change would mean for the future?	Worry

Often, resistance comes in the form of fear (of failure, rejection, or disapproval), but it can also come from lack of momentum. In those cases, we hold back from embracing change simply because it seems like too much work.

The couch is so comfortable, and those running shoes by the door just seem so far out of reach.

Maybe one more episode in the binge-watching marathon.

But just one.

Look at your character's central struggle to see where the most resistance and excuses reside.

People get into ruts. They let patterns hem them in and habits stifle them. They stay in relationships that don't nurture them, in jobs that don't fulfill them, in belief systems that hold them back from reaching their potential, all because the thought of change is intimidating or psychologically paralyzing.

If change were easy, we would all be doing it willingly, gladly, and without therapists, depression meds, or kindly, empathetic bartenders.

For example, to confess is a lot easier than to repent. If you repent, it doesn't just mean you're sorry; it means you change. If you're still enjoying the rewards of your vice, you haven't repented.

So, if you're a drug dealer and you buy a house with the money you made, and then you give up selling drugs but keep the house, you haven't repented yet.

A change of heart will result in a changed life.

Resistance to change is a core element in developing any character.

We do all we can to avoid the silence and the pain that forces us to really examine our hearts and get to know ourselves. To cling to the old ways, to live life through the rearview mirror, often feels like the safest place to be, but that's only because it's the blindest place to be.

Life is less a series of small victories leading to major ones than it is a series of watching our dreams crumble and then picking up the pieces and moving on—hopefully toward more meaningful dreams in the future.

The question is not if we will die but when.

And how we will choose to live until then.

HOW CAN I PRESS MY PROTAGONIST TOWARD CHANGE?

Make her look the truth in the eye. She's mortal—how can you make her face that? She's not a good wife—force her to admit that. She's wasting her potential—allow her to realize that and make a choice that leads her life in a new direction.

QUICK FIX: Build into your story moments of heartache, of poignancy, of suspicion. Explore areas of resistance: Is she guided by her inner child or by her inner adult—that overly cautious analyzer, that play-it-safe, hedge-your-bets actuary of emotion and risk? What effect is that having on her life and her relationships? What will it take to listen to that childlike voice of wonder once again?

FINE-TUNING MY MANUSCRIPT

- My character is clinging to something—a belief, an excuse, a way of thinking—that's going to be revealed in the story. What is it? How will it be put to the test?
- In what way is she trying to prove herself, justify her job, her affair, her addiction?
- What will it take to impel him to overcome his resistance to change? Will change be forced upon him? Will he come to embrace it? If so, why today?
- What realities about life is she unwilling to accept? How does that get her into trouble?
- What does his frustration reveal about his goals? What doubts undermine his hope? What shame sabotages his joy?
- She's trying to juggle too much. What will she end up dropping? How will that affect her relationships?
- How can I justify his reasons for resistance? In other words, how will he resist without seeming like a coward? How can I show him both resisting change and pursuing it at the same time?

44

BLIND SPOTS

In my novel *Every Crooked Path*, the protagonist takes a moment to reflect on human nature:

> I've seen it over and over. People turn to affairs when their marriages are crumbling, to drinking when they're depressed. They work extra hours to assuage their guilt for not being there enough for their kids. They buy clothes and cars and houses and gadgets to fill their empty hearts, even though they know those games of distraction and diversion will never work in the long run, but will only leave them more hollowed out.
>
> Human nature hasn't changed much in the millennia of our existence. We are just as lost as ever, trying desperately to get back up the hill by running headlong into the valley. We willingly avoid the things we know we need, and desperately embrace the things we know will destroy us.
>
> What lies at the heart of human nature? The quest for happiness along the roads we already know lead to pain instead.

Everyone's heart has layer upon layer of contradictions, fears, beliefs, shame, hope, joy, and longing.

We want to both fit in and stand out, to disappear and to shine, to leave a legacy after we die and—of course—not to die at all.

And so we put on our masks. We hide our pain under well-practiced smiles in well-practiced ways.

And sometimes the most elaborate and enduring masks are the ones we use to hide ourselves.

From ourselves.

> Often, the parts of our lives where we're the blindest are the parts other people see the most clearly.

FIXING BLIND SPOT ISSUES

When I was studying acting, our teacher, Tony Montanaro, who was one of the world's most acclaimed mimes at the time, showed us how he portrayed a drunk man in one of his shows. It was astonishing. Then Tony told us, "You don't act drunk. That's the key. You become someone for whom being drunk is natural, and then you try to act sober. No one who's drunk acts drunk. It's the same for anything. Don't act angry. Don't pretend to be shy."

Good advice for actors.

Good advice for authors.

So, as you write, don't ask:

- "How can I show how angry this guy is?" but rather "How can I show how this guy is trying not to look angry?"
- "How can I show how shy she is?" but rather "How can I show her trying to hide her shyness?"

Psychologists have a saying: "There's something about you that I don't like about me." Sometimes we project onto other people the attributes we hate most about ourselves. We quickly notice those traits in others but refuse to see them when we look in the mirror because it's too painful.

It's true what they say: The truth does hurt.

But it does so in a way that, ultimately, heals.

Some writing instructors teach that your protagonist should have a "fatal flaw." While that advice can be helpful in some cases, most of the time a character's flaws are not that dramatic, and not everyone has a fatal flaw. Think instead of turning her strength against her, of taking her safety net away, or of exploiting her where she feels the safest.

Rather than asking what the fatal flaw is, ask what her blind spot is. For example:

- a glaring moral lapse or psychological drawback that she doesn't notice
- a passion that can boomerang back and become a vulnerability
- a crutch she's clinging to
- a belief she doesn't think she can live without
- a person or relationship she feels is indispensable
- a physical limitation or condition that hinders her from pursuing the kind of life she would like to live
- an unhealthy appetite for something good (food, sex, love, truth, happiness) or for something destructive (booze, drugs, cutting, controlling others)
- an obsession that becomes overwhelming
- a habit that undercuts her dreams
- an opinion that gets her into trouble
- thoughts that lead her astray
- an emotion that ends up controlling her
- a memory that terrifies her
- a secret that limits her
- a trait that defines her
- a dream that inhibits her
- a quirk that becomes a preoccupation
- a weakness that becomes an asset
- an embarrassing physical trait
- a desire that seems good but is really bad
- a desire that seems bad but is really good

Let the blind spots be visible to readers but not to the character. Then consider having another character point them out to him—but don't use an authority figure (a pastor, teacher, professor, etc.) but rather the last person your protagonist wants to hear advice from.

Does she accept the input or reject it?

How does that affect the trajectory of the story?

Remove the masks. Reveal the blind spots. Don't let your character continue to hide from himself.

HOW CAN I BEST GET TO KNOW MY CHARACTER'S BLIND SPOTS?

Look at him through the eyes of the other characters around him. Each of those characters will have an impression of him: He's impatient, he's careless, he's a workaholic, his heart is heavy, he used to be so much fun before the accident, etc.

QUICK FIX: Write a letter to the protagonist from his friend, lover, or close relative, starting with this sentence: "I'm not sure how to tell you this, but I care about you and I need to let you know that you ..." This one small exercise can open up all sorts of new insights concerning who your character really is and what your story should really be about.

FINE-TUNING MY MANUSCRIPT

- How has my protagonist lost his way? Is he drifting, or is he running as hard as he can from the direction he knows he should go? What is that place? What will it take for him to turn around?
- What delusions is this character under? In what way has she finally found clarity?
- What does he fear the most? Which wound needs to be healed most? What problem or dilemma needs to be solved?
- Which relationships could be restored or initiated?
- How do the struggles with blind spots reveal what she's like and capable of? How do they develop or shape her personality?

PART III
NARRATIVE
TECHNIQUES

45

ATMOSPHERE

In the novel *The Silent Wife* by A.S.A. Harrison, a woman drugs her husband and starts to suspect that she might have killed him. At first she avoids going into the bedroom, but finally she ventures in.

> She enters like a wary animal, all nose and ears in the lurking gloom. The stagnant air has a sour note that fondles the back of her throat, forcing into her mind the appalling thought that he might have survived the pills and alcohol but choked to death on his vomit.

In this excerpt, the atmosphere is accentuated through phrases such as "a wary animal," "lurking gloom," "stagnant air," "a sour note," "the appalling thought," and that closing image of someone choking to death on vomit.

However, in the middle of all this, the author has chosen to say that the stagnant, sour air "fondles" the back of her throat.

Fondles? Really?

That word carries a connotation that obliterates the mood. Just that one poor choice makes the scene almost seem comical, like a parody of a dark moment in the story rather than one readers are supposed to take seriously.

This is a common problem. Writers have been taught to use "vivid verbs," but they haven't been taught how vital it is to keep them all atmosphere specific.

....

Every word you choose can either support or undermine the atmosphere of the scene you're rendering.

....

FIXING ATMOSPHERE ISSUES

On a date with your lover, one word can ruin the mood of the entire evening. The same can happen in your novel's scenes if you're not careful.

Keep the Atmosphere of Your Story Broadly Consistent

Atmosphere, like so many other aspects of your story, is a promise. If your story starts out as *Jaws*, it shouldn't end as *Sharknado*.

Since readers are the least oriented to your story's world at the beginning of the novel, it's vital to establish the atmosphere in the opening pages. The sooner you lock in the atmosphere, the clearer readers will be about the promises you're making and the payoff they should anticipate.

Are you writing a humorous novel? Begin that way.

Is it serious and dark? Show readers that grittiness early on.

If you move the atmosphere from serious to funny, it'll undermine the value of what you've presented as serious earlier. If you shift from funny to serious, readers will wonder where the laughs have gone— they were expecting the story to get sillier, not more somber. In that case you would have de-escalated the humor rather than escalated it.

When Weeding out Mood-Affecting Words, Focus on Verbs and Adjectives

The dark clouds rumbled over the forest.

See how the nouns *clouds* and *forest* are neutral? By themselves, they don't necessarily create a positive or a negative mood. Instead, the atmosphere is created by the adjective *dark* and the verb *rumbled*.

Now, someone might write, "The dark clouds played over the forest," or "The dark clouds danced over the forest," but this would create dissonance in the mood, which never serves readers since they won't know if the scene is supposed to be negative and foreboding (from the dark clouds) or positive and celebratory (because the clouds are playing or dancing). Be clear. Uphold the mood.

While it's certainly true that many verbs are neutral—*run, jump, dive, lift*—those aren't the verbs writers are typically encouraged to use. Instead, they're told to choose "strong verbs." So, they go with ones like *vacillate, massage, annihilate, encourage.*

Or *fondle.*

And each one has a positive or negative feel.

Consider these examples:

> **EXAMPLE 1:** The cottony clouds languished in the sky.
> **ATMOSPHERIC DISSONANCE:** *Cottony* has a positive connotation that contradicts *languishing,* which has a negative one.

> **EXAMPLE 2:** She flitted across the room and slumped into the chair, which seemed to swallow her whole.
> **ATMOSPHERIC DISSONANCE:** To *flit* is to move in a carefree manner, but the word *slumped* and the phrase *swallow her whole* are negative.

Think about your word's connotation within that context. Avoid using bright words in a dark scene or vice versa. So, for atmospheric consonance you could write:

> **EXAMPLE 1 REVISED:** The slate-gray clouds languished in the sky.

> **EXAMPLE 2 REVISED:** She dragged her feet across the room and slumped into the chair, which seemed to swallow her whole.

Identify what type of atmosphere or mood you're trying to convey in this scene. Then choose your words carefully so that every one of them contributes to rather than detracts from it.

Pay Attention to Senses

When thinking about upholding the atmosphere, pay particular attention to how you portray your character experiencing his senses. Did the smells greet him or encircle him? Was it an odor or a stench?

Did he hear the susurrus stream gurgle by, or did the water hiss and boil as it sluiced down the gorge?

Accentuate the mood through sensory impressions.

Stay in the Viewpoint of the Character

You might write, "He'd chosen a sensible cardigan." But would *he* describe his sweater as "a sensible cardigan," or is that how *you* would describe it? If he wouldn't, then using that phrase will feel authorial and intrusive.

When writing from a character's point of view, opt for the words he would choose.

> ### CAN THE ATMOSPHERE CHANGE THROUGHOUT THE BOOK?
>
> To a certain extent, yes. Even a dark, gripping crime novel will likely have moments of comic relief, and even the most humorous story might have some serious, dramatic scenes. However, the baseline atmosphere of the story is a promise that's established early on, and if the story doesn't remain grounded in it, you'll jar readers.
>
> **QUICK FIX:** Examine your word choice—particularly your use of verbs and adjectives. Do they serve that scene? Do they uphold the atmosphere you're shooting for? In a broader sense, does this scene sustain the mood of the story? Recast any scenes that might weaken the story as a whole.

FINE-TUNING MY MANUSCRIPT

- Does this scene contain any mood-shattering words (especially adjectives and verbs)? What alternate words might carry more strength while retaining contextual consistency?
- In one word or short phrase, how would I describe the atmosphere of this scene? Is that appropriate for this moment in the story? Does that mood contribute to, or detract from, the overall effect of the story on readers?

- How can I better sustain the atmosphere through clearer, more succinct, more evocative words?
- Are the mood and tone appropriate for this genre? Do I undermine any scenes by trying to add humor where it wouldn't naturally occur?
- How can I shade this scene, word by word, toward the levity, darkness, tautness, or romance I'm trying to create? Does the novel retain the feel I'm shooting for and that I've promised by its opening?

46

PACE

If we were to watch a movie or television show together, we would both be viewing the same images—the ones the director chose for us to see—and they would pass in front of us at the same rate.

However, when people read, both the rate of the images and the images themselves are different for every reader.

If one million people read your book, there'll be one million different versions of your story out there since each person pictures things slightly differently. Also, some people read fast. Others go slowly. Some skim. Some labor over every word. Understanding the dynamics of your readers' experience is important to shaping and managing how you pace and lay out your story.

We'll cover how to create images in the chapters on description and detail. For now, let's think about the rate at which the images move past your readers.

In a novel, pace is more related to your readers' engagement with your story than how fast or slow events occur within the story itself.

If readers think things are too slow, they'll get bored.

If they think things are too fast, they'll get confused.

So, strive to keep readers oriented to and engaged with the story through the formatting, pace of revelations, and payoff of promises.

As we discussed in Part I, as a story progresses, characters will seek something, fail to get it in the way they had hoped, re-evaluate, and then proceed in a new direction. Because of this pattern, a novel's pace will settle into a rhythm of disruption, setbacks, processing, and renewed pursuit.

These beats of tension and resolution, as well as how you format the novel, will affect your readers' perception of the story's pace.

> In a novel, pace is not so much how fast things are happening but how fast readers perceive them to be happening.

FIXING PACE ISSUES

Paragraph and section breaks affect how your readers process the text.

Do you want to create a breathless chase scene?

The length of your paragraphs can help facilitate that.

They'll be shorter.

Your sentences will be quick.

Abrupt.

Succinct.

And perhaps even interspersed with sentence fragments.

On the other hand, if you want to write an atmospheric build to your climax, include longer, immersive paragraphs that create a more measured mood for your readers. If you have blocky paragraphs and long, complex sentences, readers will have to give more attention to each word and will process the story's progression more slowly. So, to slow down the pace, use convoluted sentences, long paragraphs, and unfamiliar words.

Ask yourself not just how quickly you want the story to move but how quickly you want readers to picture it moving.

Readers will fly through one-line paragraphs.

Their eyes can just scroll down the page.

It's easy to read.

Fast.

White space on the page facilitates a snappier pace.

Often, that means writing for "eye grab," which is how much text readers can take in at once. When people read, their eyes don't necessarily capture one word at a time, so writing one-line paragraphs can be very effective in creating a tense atmosphere or in moving a story along:

> Dust.
> Rubble.
> Charred bodies.

Here, the eye grab works.

The pace is quick, the flow makes sense.

When using this technique, stay true to the mood and the narrator's voice. In the following example, the incongruity between the terse mood of the first three lines and the somewhat languid and reflective nature of the last one makes this passage seem inauthentic and undermines the consistency of the voice:

> Dust.
> Rubble.
> Charred bodies.
> The explosion had not been discerning.

However, you might write:

> Dust.
> Rubble.
> Charred bodies.
> Everyone in the room was dead.

Continue escalating the setbacks, and respect the conventions of your genre. Don't move along *slow, slow, slow, slow—FAST, slow, slow, sl—FAST.* Don't jar your readers. Build steadily, trust them, and do all you can to format the story in a manner that facilitates the pace you're shooting for.

HOW DOES DIALOGUE AFFECT PACE?

It almost always increases it. The experience of reading dialogue is much different than the experience of reading exposition—it appeals more to auditory parts of the brain than visual processing ones. Also, the amount of white space on the page can create what feels to readers like a faster pace, even if less action is occurring.

QUICK FIX: When you think of pace, consider the paragraph length, the formatting, the complexity of the sentences, and the confluence of the voice and genre of your novel. Use dialogue to break up daunting blocks of text, but make sure to sync it with the movement of that section of the story.

FINE-TUNING MY MANUSCRIPT

- Since structurally complex sentences slow readers down and punchy dialogue helps them read faster, are my sentences shorter and is dialogue used appropriately as the story builds toward its climactic scenes? Does the pace of the storytelling escalate, with shorter chapters and paragraphs to help ratchet up the tension?
- Is my story penduluming too much from action to reflection to action again? How can I bring more overall cohesion to the movement of the story by better managing the pace and balancing out my readers' experience?
- Does the format enhance or undermine the story's deepening tension?
- Does the content of this scene merge well with the voice and the mood? Am I using paragraph breaks to my advantage? If not, how can I rethink their progression to facilitate the pace I'm looking for?

47

FLOW

Sometimes after a fierce rain or a heavy snowfall, the normally dry streambed along the edge of our property fills with water.

Since it skirts through the woods, it naturally collects leaves and sticks. When they get caught in the current, they snag and bunch up at the mouth of the culvert running beneath a nearby road.

When that happens, it's my job to clear them out so the stream can flow unrestricted again—before it floods our neighbor's yard.

Removing the obstructions so the water can go where it's supposed to helps contravene all sorts of problems.

When writing, it's your job to remove any distractions that might get in the way of your readers' engagement or jar them out of the story.

Yank out the sticks.

Dig away the leaves.

Do whatever it takes to keep the water flowing.

....

How well your story flows depends on how well you channel your readers' attention, keep your promises, and remove distractions.

....

FIXING FLOW ISSUES

You are your book's first reader.

If you get bored reading some scenes, other readers will likely get bored there too. If you can't picture a scene, or don't care about what happens in it, or find yourself skimming over dull sections to get to the good stuff, the same thing will probably happen when others read it.

Readers stop being engaged when they get confused, bored, annoyed, or offended.

If they don't understand what's going on, don't see things getting more interesting, don't care or are bothered or offended by the story, chances are pretty good they won't stick with your book all the way to the end.

Remove the debris, and keep your readers immersed in your story.

To Cut Down on Confusion, Remove Plot Flaws

Sometimes a fictional detective will act in inexplicable ways as he solves the case before readers do. They trust that eventually they'll find out the reasons why he was pursuing those unusual avenues of investigation. Most of the time, unless you're writing in that genre, you won't want readers to be asking why the character is acting like he is.

Many plot flaws or glitches are expectation related: What readers would naturally expect, given the context, doesn't happen. Either (1) something that should happen doesn't, (2) something that shouldn't happen does, (3) something happens for no reason, or (4) it takes too long for the character to respond to what is happening.

Evaluate every one of your scenes with those four things in mind.

As we've explored earlier, it's important to clarify the character's intention before he acts and then to move the scene forward, naturally, from cause to effect. Ask yourself if this sentence, event, choice, or action requires explanation. If it does, you can probably improve the scene by reordering the events.

For example, show the revelation or discoveries after the events that precipitate them rather than telling readers what the character learned and then explaining how he learned it.

Make sure that choices make sense, characters act believably, and inexplicable events don't disorient your readers.

To Eliminate Boredom, Add More Promises and More Escalation

Adding action isn't the key to fixing boring sections of your manuscript. Relentless action can be just as boring as tedious description.

If readers are bored, either you haven't made big enough promises, readers have forgotten or don't care what they are, or you're not keeping those promises when readers want them kept.

So, escalate the action you have, remove repetition, remind readers why this pursuit matters, and make bold and clear promises regarding the jeopardy the character is in.

To Stop Annoying Readers, Stop Insulting Them

Don't jar readers, manipulate them, or make them feel stupid. Respect them.

Including "twists" that are only surprises, having characters act in ways that don't make sense, writing predictable scenes, telling mediocre stories, or including clichéd or stereotypical characters will often make readers feel cheated or deceived.

Anytime you suspect that something might be too gimmicky or contrived, it probably is. Cut it.

To Avoid Offending Readers, Stop Giving Them What They Don't Want

Some readers are offended by profanity; some aren't. Some accept graphic violence or sex scenes; some don't. Remember that swearing shows a lack of self-control and often lowers your character's status in readers' eyes. If you use cursing, use it sparingly and to effect.

How much or how little objectionable or controversial content you include is, of course, up to you. I will say, however, that over the years I've had many readers thank me for not including gratuitous sex and unnecessary profanity in my novels. No one has asked me for more sex scenes. No one has asked me to use the *F* word more.

Take that for what you will.

• • •

Keep the story flowing by getting rid of those distractions, plot flaws, and scenes that are confusing, make the wrong types of promises, or clog up the different storylines with irrelevant information.

WHAT WILL DISRUPT MY STORY'S FLOW?

Anything that doesn't contribute to the logical progression of the story will put you on the wrong track. Jumping back and forth through time, inserting nonessential flashbacks, and shifting through different characters' thoughts in the same paragraph will all disorient readers.

QUICK FIX: Since clichés, alliteration, and symbolism can easily become distractions, weed them out. Don't play literary games. If you flip the narration or viewpoint between different characters, make sure that the timing of their storylines syncs and that it remains clear whose point of view you've switched to.

FINE-TUNING MY MANUSCRIPT

- Letting a story's structure "show through" can be distracting to readers. Does my story have three clearly partitioned acts? If so, how can I reweave the storylines so I don't have such a cookie-cutter book?
- Have I unintentionally included alliteration, overt symbolism, or other literary gimmicks that will be noticeable and annoying to my readers?
- Have I created distractions by introducing characters or storylines and then letting them hang in the air, unfulfilled or unresolved? How can I make sure that all the characters who appear in each scene are contributing in some way?
- What other barriers or branches that might be needlessly clogging up the story do I need to remove?
- Where have I insulted readers? What changes do I need to make to trust or respect them more?

48

SUSPENSE

Your protagonist is about to open her bedroom closet door.

Does this scene have suspense? If readers know that a killer is hiding in the closet and the protagonist doesn't, yes.

Does it have mystery? If readers think that the closet might contain a clue, but that no danger awaits her, yes.

Does it have horror? If readers know that she's about to discover a decapitated body when she opens the door—oh, yes.

The same event can evoke concern, curiosity, or dread based on what readers know and expect—and what they don't.

In writing circles, there seems to be a common misconception that we create suspense by withholding information. In truth, it's just the opposite. We create suspense by *revealing* information. We create *mystery* by withholding it.

Ambiguity confuses readers; it doesn't put them in suspense. And, as *New York Times* best-selling author Steve Berry says, "When you confuse your reader, you lose your reader."

When producing suspense, consider the orientation of both your readers and your characters: Who is aware of what? For example, in the scene above, what is the character expecting to find in the closet? What are readers expecting? Anticipation relies on how much information you've revealed to the readers about the threat and the stakes.

Stories can appeal to curiosity ("How will this end?") or concern ("Are the characters going to be okay?"). The first engages intellect; the second, emotion.

FIXING SUSPENSE ISSUES

Think of suspense as building worry or apprehension. What factors need to be present for your character to worry about someone? What would build apprehension for him as he's walking into a deserted warehouse?

Tap into your own understanding of, and experiences with, worry and apprehension to get ideas for developing those feelings in your fiction.

In order for readers to worry, they need to be aware of the danger that's threatening a character that they care about. The more specific and imminent the threat, and the more reader empathy and concern you have, the more apprehension you'll elicit.

A character doesn't need to be afraid for readers to be afraid, but a character *does* need to be facing peril of some kind for readers to be concerned.

Allow readers to see danger that the character isn't aware of, or let the protagonist realize that danger is coming closer and that he needs to escape it.

Stopping in the middle of an exciting action sequence, switching to another, less tense storyline or point of view, and then returning to the suspenseful scene will only annoy readers. It certainly won't add to the suspense.

To create and sustain suspense, use these three techniques:

- **ENGENDER CONCERN FOR THE CHARACTER'S WELL-BEING.** If readers don't care, they won't worry. Give the character a wound or a vulnerability in order to create empathy or sympathy and invite readers to desire what's best for her.
- **SHOW AN IMPENDING THREAT.** If readers don't know what the danger is or what the stakes are, they won't be worried. Let the threat to the character's well-being (physical, psychological, or relational) be imminent, devastating, intimate (against someone who matters to him), or universal (against a large number of people).

  Reveal, don't conceal. Readers need to have information about the threat, or they won't know what to worry about.

- **HEIGHTEN THE PERIL.** Readers will be in more suspense as the peril approaches in proximity in relation to time (a countdown), space, or a convergence of storylines.

  Keep escalating the threat. If you continually hint at danger but never bring it any closer, readers will get annoyed.

• • •

Usually, apprehension is built through the anticipation of something going wrong or of things getting worse. The payoff comes when the character meets the threat and has to respond in a believable way.

Often, images that readers imagine will be more frightening than any you could come up with, so you may choose to "pan the camera" away from visceral or graphic scenes and show only the setup and the aftermath, but not the actual violence.

However, don't pan away from scenes of valor or sacrifice. Those are the payoff scenes that readers are anxiously anticipating and deserve to see.

HOW IS SUSPENSE DIFFERENT FROM MYSTERY?

Mystery concerns the past; suspense concerns the future. In a mystery, the characters try to solve a crime, piece together a riddle, or resolve a conflict. In suspense, they try to stop a crime or tragedy. Mystery appeals to readers' curiosity, suspense to their concern.

QUICK FIX: To build suspense, (1) let readers see the impending danger or disaster (often that the characters themselves are not aware of), (2) have characters tell readers their plans, (3) use countdowns to your advantage, and (4) sharpen apprehension by clarifying the consequences of failure and by heightening your readers' concern for the character.

FINE-TUNING MY MANUSCRIPT

- Am I relying on shock value or on tension to retain my readers' interest? How can I promise more danger, deliver on my promises, and cut back on cheap surprise?
- Is there the right amount of suspense, horror, and mystery in each scene for my genre? In other words, have I included problems that generate the right amount of curiosity or concern in readers' minds?
- Have I dealt with violence and graphic scenes appropriately, showing what readers want (or need) to see but relying more on their imagination than on grisly descriptions?
- To increase the tension and suspense, have I eliminated unnecessary action and instead included more promises about impending danger?
- Are the promises strong enough to carry readers through to the payoff? Have I fulfilled enough of the smaller promises and escalated tension enough to keep readers flipping pages? Is the payoff worthy of the readers' investment of time and emotion?

49

FLASHBACKS

A flashback isn't a glance in the rearview mirror.

It's more like stopping the car, letting it idle, getting out, walking around the park for a while, and then climbing back in and taking off.

So, here's the crucial question: Will readers want to walk around the park with you?

Often, they will not.

Flashbacks stop the forward momentum of the story, can easily distract readers from the core events of the story, and are often used simply to fill readers in on a portion of the character's backstory that the author wrote up while outlining the book and doesn't want to waste.

Entertainment value, curiosity, and concern tug readers through a story. A flashback rarely relies on concern (since readers already know the character survives or he wouldn't be in the present scene), so it must rely instead on fueling curiosity or the excellence and entertainment value of the prose.

To be worthy of inclusion, the flashback needs to delve so deeply into mystery or be so well written that it becomes indispensable to the story.

....

Appropriate flashbacks contain necessary context for the current scene. We don't include them because they're interesting but because they're essential.

....

FIXING FLASHBACK ISSUES

There are legitimate times to use flashbacks. Indeed, some stories that alternate chapter by chapter between the past and the present depend on them. (However, even acknowledging that, I have to admit that I've never read a past/present story in which the past story mattered enough to justify reading the flashbacks. I just skim them to get to the story that matters, the one where something is at stake.)

If your flashback propels the story forward, it might be just what you need. However, if it's simply there to clarify or explain something, it might not be necessary. If you've only included it for mood, backstory, or the revelation of motive, it can typically be dropped.

To determine whether or not to include a flashback, it's important to know your story. Often, that means making the decision about its inclusion after you've finished your first draft, not before you begin it.

Ask yourself:

- Is this flashback necessary for the forward movement of the story?
- Does it answer a long-held question or address a secret that will turn the story in a deeper, more tension-filled direction?
- Does it reveal something essential about the story or the characters that could not be communicated any other way?
- Will it entertain readers? Will they be more annoyed if I do include it or if I don't?
- Does this flashback answer a vital question (1) that readers are asking, (2) that they care about, and (3) that they want to read about right now, at this moment in the story?

Use flashbacks to add to the tension rather than relieve it, to answer lingering questions at crucial times, to show the interconnection of subplots, and to add to the mystery rather than solve it. Sometimes as you edit and reshuffle scenes, the flashback will become a prologue.

Here are some common problems with flashbacks:

- **NOTHING NEW IS REVEALED.** Readers already know the character is nice, mean, troubled, depressed, or a drunk. They don't need to hear about how he was that way last year too, or how he became that way. If the flashback simply shows readers what they already know, or if the story stands on its own without the flashback, cut it.

- **NOTHING IS AT STAKE.** The flashback doesn't add to the stakes, it just distracts from them. Flashbacks rarely add to the suspense. They might answer questions or address backstory secrets that are affecting the main plot, but most of the time, the peril is in the past. They include answers and resolution rather than escalation and tension. If that's the case with your flashback, cut it.
- **NOTHING IS VITAL TO THE CURRENT STORY.** If your flashback covers a parallel story, or one that's only tangentially connected to the main story, it's adding weight that will drag down the current story. Cut it.

CAN I HAVE MORE THAN ONE FLASHBACK?

You can include as many as your story demands, but that's the key: Unless the story requires the flashback, don't include it. It's a tool you won't need to use for every story, and most stories don't need it. Use it in the wrong way or at the wrong time and it'll detract from, rather than serve, the story.

QUICK FIX: Read your story without the flashback to see if it's really necessary. If you do include it, make it eminently clear to your readers when the flashback begins and ends. Also, don't ask more of it than it can provide. Build suspense in the present story, add intrigue through the flashback.

FINE-TUNING MY MANUSCRIPT

- Will readers just skim (or entirely skip) this flashback? How would that impact their understanding of the story?
- How can I transition into and out of my flashback to help readers grasp its importance?

- Will readers feel that the time reading it is well spent? If not, how can I recast the story to include the essential details from the flashback in another section of the story?
- Does the story stand on its own without this flashback? Is the flashback merely an excuse to include historical details that fill readers in, or does it actually propel the narrative forward?
- Am I forcing readers to wait in the car while I walk around the park? Will they still be there when I get back?

50

DIALOGUE

In the following exchange from my novel *Every Crooked Path*, FBI Special Agent Patrick Bowers is speaking with the fifteen-year-old daughter of the woman he's dating. The girl has discovered that there's a museum at the New York City FBI Field Office.

> "How did you know about that?" I asked her.
>
> "There's this crazy thing they invented called Google. You can look stuff up on it. You should check it out sometime."
>
> "Ah. Sarcasm, right?"
>
> "Um. No."
>
> "But that was?"
>
> "What do you think?"
>
> "Wait—was that?"
>
> She looked at me disparagingly.
>
> "Alright, I'll take you to the museum."
>
> She finished her carrot. "Excellent."
>
> "You're sure Central Park is out of the running?"
>
> "Fresh air makes me break out in hives."
>
> "And here I thought you were Miss Nature-Lover Girl."
>
> "You pretty much suck at this, don't you?"
>
> "At what?"
>
> "Communicating with a teenager."

Dialogue is one of the fastest ways to show characterization, status, and attitude—all at the same time. A few lines of dialogue can often reveal more about a character than an entire page of exposition or description.

> Trim your dialogue. Often, he who
> speaks the least says the most.

FIXING DIALOGUE ISSUES

Give your character an objective and an obstacle in each conversation: Perhaps she's nervous about giving away details that might make her look guilty of the crime—but the detective won't leave her alone. Notice the *but* in there. In every scene worth reading there's a *but*.

Explore what the characters are trying to accomplish. What's getting in the way? What are they hoping for, working toward, or attempting to overcome?

Insert a goal and a *but* into your sections of dialogue and you'll almost certainly improve them.

DIALOGUE PROBLEM	HOW TO FIX IT
Too Formal	Use contractions. Read the dialogue aloud. Don't just think about how it looks on the page, but evaluate how it sounds and how it makes you feel when you read it.
Too Complex	The more eloquent someone tries to sound, the less authentic he becomes. We suspect people have ulterior motives when they speak in complete, well-crafted sentences. Keep your sentences short. Punchy. Direct. Use fragments. The dialogue will sound more realistic and less contrived.
Too Explanatory	Don't ask, "What do I need my characters to say?" but "What do my characters need to overcome?" Give them goals beyond *your* goal of conveying information to readers.
Too Trivial	If characters discuss trivial matters, the scene needs to be driven forward by subtext, which is also one of the best ways of communicating emotion, longing, and desire.

Too Long	Condense. Communicate more by saying less.
Too Many Characters	Limit them—typically to two or three people per conversation.
Info Dump	Use dialogue to move the story forward, not to relive the past. Let tension (looking forward) rather than rumination (looking back) drive the story.
Lack of Clarity	Don't play "Can you guess who's talking?" Make sure it's crystal clear to readers who is speaking during each line of dialogue.
No Distractions	Insert misunderstanding and external distractions. Perhaps it's too loud in the room, other people are interrupting them, or the characters are inferring too much or implying too little. Can they communicate two things at once? Misjudge? Use sarcasm that carries a grain of truth?

Get Your Characters Moving, Acting, Responding

Action can be helpful, but don't just have characters walk around purposelessly. Only add action that will advance the story or enhance or enrich the scene.

Weed out conversations that occur during meals, unless there's intense, poignant, tension-producing subtext.

Structure Attributions Properly

You wouldn't write, "explained he," so don't write, "explained John." Instead write, "John explained." Unless there's an overwhelming contextual reason to reverse the order, speaker tags follow the name or personal pronoun of the speaker.

Fix the *as* and *-ing* Problem

Wherever you find the word *as* or a verb ending in *-ing* following a line of dialogue, you can usually improve it by recasting things:

> "Look at that," she said as she walked toward me.

Or:

> "Look at that," she said, walking toward me.

Could become:

> "Look at that." She walked toward me.

Or the following examples:

> "I don't really understand this," he said as he scratched his head.

Or:

> "I don't really understand this," he said, scratching his head.

Could be changed to:

> He scratched his head. "I don't really understand this."

Why is this even an issue? Because *as* and *-ing* are the default choice for far too many authors. You'll find these constructions in almost every dialogue exchange they write. It's a distracting and sophomoric way of writing that can easily be fixed.

Cut the BOGSAT Scenes

When I was interviewing the award-winning crime writer Hank Phillippi Ryan for my podcast, "The Story Blender," she mentioned BOGSAT scenes: Bunch of Guys Sitting Around Talking.

BOGSAT.

Great word.

I love it.

You'll find BOGSAT scenes all the time in the work of aspiring novelists (and even accomplished ones): People sit around and chat. They eat meals and chat. They meet for drinks. They have coffee. They drive around. They talk on the phone. Chat, chat, chat. Nothing is really at stake, nothing really matters, and nothing really changes.

Instead, give your characters a goal and let them face setbacks.

You're going to want as little BOGSAT as possible in your book. Search for it, and, wherever possible, slice it from the story.

HOW DO I MAKE MY DIALOGUE MORE REALISTIC?

All dialogue is contextual. The setting, the mood, the goals of the characters, and their attitudes toward each other all affect dialogue. Before writing your dialogue, evaluate what the characters would be thinking, then let their speech reflect their state of mind and their intentions in that scene.

QUICK FIX: Often, dialogue fails to show the distinctiveness of each character. As you evaluate your sections of dialogue, look for ways to bring each character's uniqueness out. Allow them to express their individuality in their responses—but don't get carried away. Use idioms judiciously. If the English guy says, "Cheerio," every time he shows up, it'll grow old fast.

FINE-TUNING MY MANUSCRIPT

- Where can I eliminate or recast speaker attributions to better convey the attitude of the characters in this scene?
- Where have I overused certain speaker tags? How can I reframe those sections of the exchange?
- Is the dialogue natural sounding? Are the sentences long, complex, stilted, and grammatically correct—or is the language abrupt, conversational, and informal, like actual conversations are?
- Does the dialogue ring contextually true for each character?
- Do I have any BOGSAT? How will I address that?
- Have I pared down the dialogue so I'm saying more by letting the characters say less? Do the characters give any speeches or diatribes that I need to edit or recast?

51

NARRATION

Narration (otherwise known as exposition) is how you render the actions your characters take.

Since much of narration comes from the point of view of a character, narration is closely tied to viewpoint. It's also closely tied to voice, which is your unique writing style.

When you're not relating a character's thoughts, rendering dialogue, or describing something, you'll be utilizing narration. This is how you'll move one conversation, situation, or promise to the next.

Narration is where readers see things occur—they don't hear dialogue or inner reflection, they don't just read a description of something, they watch the events happen. Think action, response, movement.

Readers have to be able to picture the action playing out.

For example, in fight scenes, they need to know distances—how far away is the guy with the knife? Could he really stab his opponent from there? What's the setting? How will that affect how they fight? (If the fight on the beach plays out the same as the one in the corporate boardroom on the sixtieth floor, then your scene probably isn't detailed or setting-specific enough.)

Whoever describes the action within the story is its narrator.

FIXING NARRATION ISSUES

Just as descriptions tend to be too long in manuscripts, narration tends to be too limited. Some authors shy away from showing their characters involved in conflict of any kind and opt instead to simply describe its precursor and aftermath.

That's the opposite of what readers are hoping for. Give them what they *do* want by keeping the following principles in mind.

Action Is Purposive and Directional

One of the biggest problems I see in the work of aspiring writers involves action without intention.

Things keep happening—often exciting, exhilarating things—but readers don't know *why* they're happening. So, although readers might be enthralled for a little while by the shock and awe, by the spectacle and movement, they'll soon get confused or straight-out bored.

To fix that, before the action sequence, clarify the purpose or goal of the character in that scene. Then allow the action to portray the pursuit in an engaging manner. Afterwards, show the characters' natural response to what just occurred.

Your story doesn't need to be action packed, but as we explored in chapter twenty-three, it does need to be *intention* packed. Analyze every paragraph, every interplay of cause and effect. Look at the story both sentence by sentence and scene by scene. Clarify the intention of the character and the implications her choices have.

Stop making things happen without a promise behind them or a payoff waiting out there before them.

A Change in Attitude or Perspective Doesn't Come out of Thin Air

If someone's heart races, why does it race? What causes that? Unless readers know if it's because of sexual attraction or nerves or fear or a heart attack, they won't know what the scene is really about.

If someone "wises up," something has to cause it. What makes him change his mind? What leads him to this decision? That's what readers need to see. Render those scenes.

Thoughts and Feelings Eventually Lead to a Choice, or Else They've Led Nowhere

Worry causes a character to act. So does pride. And greed. And lust. In a story, characters act; they don't simply feel. If they don't act, the story never moves forward.

Look for ways to physicalize your character's internal world through his choices. And remember that when he refrains from retaliation, you'll be showing his self-control, which will raise his status.

- He's tempted to punch the other guy in the face but holds back.
- She's pushed to the limit and is about to lash out at her son but catches herself at the last moment.

Although inner reflection might reveal what a character wants to be like, action shows what he's really like. In this way, action is revelatory.

Voice, Pace, and Context Determine the Amount of Narration

She stood with her feet angled in and her hands stuffed into her pockets. As she spoke, she lowered her eyes and quieted her voice as if anything above a whisper would break the fragile glass vase that was her heart.

Could that work for your story?

Maybe.

But before you decide to write something in that vein, evaluate if a whole paragraph of narration is necessary for this scene. Taking flow and context into consideration, it might be better to just write, "Her voice sounded as fragile and wounded as she looked."

Or take the expression of terror:

Her heart was beating rapidly in her chest. Her hands shook as the fear coursed through her veins. She could feel her chest tighten and her voice constrict as she opened her mouth and screamed for help.

Is all that necessary, or would, "Terrified, she screamed for help," do the trick?

By studying the context you'll be able to discern how much narration to include.

Characters Need Goals, Not Just Activity

Avoid those "scenes" in which a character who's taking a run/sipping a cup of tea/doing housework/sitting at the bar/walking the dog (or doing anything else that doesn't matter) ruminates about her past.

No sitting around mulling things over, no riding the subway reminiscing. Why? Because rarely in those scenes is anything at stake. With enough subtext, you might be able to keep them, otherwise cut them.

Also, don't drag out scenes that readers already know (or can anticipate) the conclusion of.

In Narration, Word Choice Is Essential to Maintaining the Atmosphere of the Story

- Was there a "drop of blood" or a "pornography of violence"?
- Does she "fish" through her purse for her phone, "search" through it, or "grope" through it?
- Does she "recoil" or "draw back" when he touches her?
- Does he "glance his flashlight beam across the wall," or does he "lance the darkness" with it?

Action Is Relative and Contextual

The amount of action in a novel is tied to its genre, the number of storylines it contains, and the time span it covers. Action doesn't necessarily help improve the pace, but lapsing into long stretches of nostalgia will certainly kill it. Also, if action sequences are too drawn out, their effect will be muted or drowned in minutia, and the pace will suffer.

Evaluate how your character is progressing through the story. Is it by means of coincidence, chance, and carefully following wise advice—or through obstacles, setbacks, and disregarding that advice? Opt for the latter three rather than the former. Go with obstacles instead of coincidences, contextually appropriate setbacks instead of chance occurrences, and let your protagonist disregard helpful advice rather than follow it—at least at first.

Then show, through narration, how those things occur and what they cause to happen next.

DO I NEED TO ADD MORE ACTION SEQUENCES?

When action doesn't encapsulate the intentional pursuit of a character, it's really just a distraction. Shoot for tension rather than simply action. Creating suspense will help. It relies on promises and engages readers more than action scenes that go on and on with lots of movement but little direction.

QUICK FIX: If your story is dragging, you'll be tempted to insert more events and excitement, but that might not be what you need. Instead, accentuate the promises, tighten the tension, heighten the suspense, and then use action as payoff.

FINE-TUNING MY MANUSCRIPT

- Have I effectively used narration to reveal, sustain, and render character intention in this scene?
- Has the narration become a way of fulfilling promises, or a distraction from them? Where can I fix this by reminding readers of the promises that propel this scene?
- Where have I failed to make the action sequences genre appropriate?

- In what ways have the character's actions undermined his status or the impression of him I'm trying to create? How can I fix that?
- Do the characters respond believably to every stimulus? If not, what changes need to be made?

52

DESCRIPTION

When we were young, we all learned that a noun is a "person, place, or thing."

True enough. Easy to remember. And nouns will be what we're describing in our stories, but in each case, ask if the description simply *informs* readers, or if it *affects* them. Does it *describe* something or *evoke* a feeling about it? Does it just help readers *to picture this scene*, or does it lead them *to feel something toward it*?

It might seem counterintuitive, but although descriptions deal with the five senses (what something looks, smells, tastes, feels, or sounds like), descriptions aren't primarily used to describe the physical characteristics of those things.

....

Descriptions are not here to describe; they are here to evoke. Stop describing so many things, and start affecting your readers on a more emotional level.

....

FIXING DESCRIPTION ISSUES

A person, place, or thing.

Let's look at each of them in turn.

Descriptions of Persons

When describing a character, be vivid, visual, and concise:

> His chiseled face was all creases and shadows, and he had only a thin slit for a mouth.

The guy was a human wrecking ball.

She had a fairy-tale princess face.

Use contrast. Use comparison. Really, anything that will create an immediate impression on readers.

Think of the connotation of the words you're using. Is her hair golden (bringing to mind royalty) or straw-colored (bringing to mind poverty)? These are the decisions you'll be making in every sentence of your book, and every one of them influences the mood, the scene, the story.

Stay in the voice of the narrator. Keep in mind the viewpoint of the character rendering the description. Also, be sensitive to the pace of the story and how the length of a description might affect (or be affected by) it.

Narration and description can merge seamlessly when introducing characters. Don't follow this specific formula for everyone, but you might note your protagonist's (1) clothing, (2) one physical characteristic, and (3) mannerisms or movement:

A beefy man with disheveled clothes and a thick handlebar mustache ambles out of the building to meet us.

Avoid long, meandering descriptions. Readers can get lost, and, paradoxically, the more you describe something, the harder it can be for readers to see it. If you spend a paragraph describing someone's eyebrows, readers aren't going to picture the man any better than if you wrote, "Mr. Unibrow walked up and heartily shook my hand."

Descriptions of Places

Rather than trying to describe a setting, focus on revealing as much as possible about your character (goal, state of mind, prejudices, age, etc.) by his impression of the setting or his attitude toward it.

Render the setting and situation through his eyes. This allows readers to both visualize that location and also understand how the character sees it. By doing that, you'll find you've described it in the most appropriate and efficient way, and also given insights about your character's personality:

> I can't believe how cramped the coffee house is, but still, the aroma of the roasting beans doesn't manage to overwhelm the body odor of the sweaty guy on the chair shoved up beside me.

Save the detailed descriptions for locations that are unfamiliar to your readers: the back streets of Mumbai, eighteenth-century Paris, a star cruiser from four hundred years in the future.

By the way, when you describe nature, do so in a way that readers can feel what you're feeling when you see it rather than just picture what you're picturing.

Descriptions of Things

When describing something that readers would be familiar with, call attention to facets or attributes they might never have noticed. Let them see what they often miss. For instance:

> A bowl of fruit and a sweating glass of orange juice are waiting for me on the table.

Read that sentence without the word *sweating*, and then read it again with it.

Adding that small detail brings vividness to the scene and communicates the idea that the glass has been there for a while. So, whoever set it out for the character has probably been waiting for him for a while as well. That fact may very well affect that person's mood in this scene. All of this is achieved by inserting that one word.

Most often, writers choose descriptions simply to tell readers what something smells like or feels like or what color it is, but very rarely do any of those things matter to the story.

A red sign? Who cares?

Oh, it's crimson, you say? Rose red? Blood red? Hmm ... now we might be getting somewhere.

Always look for ways to evoke rather than just describe.

Incidentally, when describing something that's unfamiliar, use comparisons. Let readers experience what they never have by relating it to what they have. For example:

> I'd never seen that kind of fish before. It had the body of a barracuda but the mouth of a catfish.

• • •

In descriptions, remember:

- Less is more.
- Point of view matters.
- Familiarity affects specificity.

Also, sometimes you need to clear the stage. For instance, if you have more than two or three people in the scene, it may be difficult to keep straight where they are and who's doing what. Readers don't want to keep track of fifteen people at the same time.

Even four can be tough to manage. Let's say you have four men in a sedan parked in front of a gas station at 4 A.M. Find an excuse to get two of them to leave. Maybe one guy says, "Hey, I'm gonna run in and grab some chips. Billy, why don't you come with me? Give your old man some company." They leave. Now you're set. You can now render a conversation between Billy and his father, or between the two men in the car.

HOW CAN I IMPROVE MY DESCRIPTIONS?

Make them more concise and evocative. Odds are, you've overdescribed what doesn't need describing and underdescribed what does. Remember that the goal isn't to help people see that noun, it's to help them *feel something about it*.

QUICK FIX: Trust your readers. Prudently appeal to senses other than just sight, and strive to have your characters use descriptions that will incarnate an emotional response in your readers. Look for distinctiveness, variety, and atmospheric words.

FINE-TUNING MY MANUSCRIPT

- Have I described inconsequential physical characteristics of the characters? If so, why?
- Where have I overdescribed things that readers are already familiar with?
- How much do readers need to know in order to picture this scene? Do they know this setting well? How will that affect how I describe it?
- How can I be more concise? How can I use fewer words to greater effect?
- Where can I sharpen my descriptions to make them more emotionally resonant and not so "on the nose"?

53

DETAILS

When my daughters were in preschool, they loved it when we finished a roll of paper towels. They would snag the empty cardboard tube and run around the house, staring through it as if it were a telescope.

Okay, I admit it: I did too.

Of course, the tube didn't magnify anything; it simply focused our attention on one thing at a time. Still, it was amazing how I started to notice things that I was already familiar with—to notice them in new ways.

In fiction, we call attention to something either by specificity (detail) or by magnitude (word count). If you invite readers to look through the tube at something, it's your way of letting them know that it counts, it matters, it's important in some way. And the longer you have them stare through that tube at it, the more important you're promising them it's going to be.

....

Every detail is a promise of significance.

....

FIXING DETAIL ISSUES

Details are either wings or extra weight. They'll either lift your story or burden it.

When considering which ones to include, ask:

- What's vital to the scene?
- What am I drawing attention to? From whose perspective? For what purpose?
- What's essential to creating the setting and mood?

- What promise would I be making if I mentioned this detail? How might it end up being a distraction from the story?
- Does this detail contribute to, distract from, undermine, or contradict the atmosphere?

THE DETAIL ...	HOW TO FIX IT
makes too much of a promise.	Think in terms of proportion. What will readers expect from this detail compared to what they actually get later on?
isn't evocative.	Stop trying to describe things. Look for ways to touch on, draw from, or tap into emotion.
isn't specific enough.	Don't try to do too much. Zero in on one aspect of whatever it is you're describing. Notice the one attribute or characteristic most people miss.
isn't true to the viewpoint.	Try to view things through this character's eyes, and use the words he would use.
undermines the atmosphere.	Choose words that have connotations in sync with the scene's mood.
doesn't fit the narrator's voice.	Always lean in the direction of honesty and be authentic to the voice of the story.
leaves the unfamiliar unclear.	Compare things to what the readers know, even if they've never seen that object or location.
overdescribes something familiar.	Pare back the description. Note what's unique, what makes this thing stand out from others like it.

Clarity comes through the judicious use of details.

Often, while you're working on the first draft of a story, you'll include details that you think are significant, but then in later revisions, you'll realize they're not. Cut them or change them. If you don't, readers will naturally make assumptions and see promises in them that you didn't intend and that you never kept.

For example, you might write:

> He had to duck as he passed through the doorway, and
> all of his lanky limbs seemed to move at a different speed
> as he walked.

That could certainly be an effective way of showing that someone is tall, slim, and uncoordinated. But is all of that necessary? Is it contextually appropriate? It becomes a promise about his significance to the story.

If this scene happens in a field where there's no doorway to duck under, and the man was standing rather than walking, how would you describe him?

Instead of just asking yourself, "How could I show how tall he is?" ask, "How does his importance affect the details I should include in his description?"

If he only says a few lines and then disappears from the story entirely, you might be better off just writing that he was "a stick-figure of a man" or "pushing seven feet tall."

A word of caution: When it comes to sensory details, writers tend to go in spurts.

Everything in the story will be moving along smoothly, then all of a sudden the refrigerator is humming, the smell of fresh bread is wafting through the air, the soft dough is squishing between the protagonist's fingers as she presses out more of it onto the breadboard. It's as if the writer suddenly remembers, "Oh, that's right. I'm supposed to appeal to the senses." So, he hits as many as he can in one paragraph.

Senses. Senses. Senses.

Then none for the next twenty pages.

Until he remembers again, and the character sees, hears, smells, tastes, and feels everything around her for another paragraph.

Yes, include some sensory details, but spread them out, keep them succinct, and don't overdo it.

HOW SPECIFIC DO I HAVE TO BE?

Be specific enough to make and to keep the promises that are significant to the story. Readers won't know what a "little boy" or a "big hill" is. What are they supposed to picture? Is a "little boy" two years old? Five? Is a "big hill" ten feet high or five thousand feet high?

QUICK FIX: Carefully evaluate the details: how they're rendered (to retain the voice), how evocative they are (rather than just descriptive), and what cues they'll give readers about what's important to this story. When you invite readers to stare through the cardboard tube, make sure that what you ask them to look at matters.

FINE-TUNING MY MANUSCRIPT

- Do my details about characters, locations, and objects evoke the emotion I'm shooting for?
- Where can I tweak the details to improve my descriptions?
- How can I do a better job of bringing out the uniqueness of this common object?
- Do my details uphold the mood, feeling, or image I want readers to experience at this moment in the story?
- Have I used specificity to highlight what matters in this scene? Do I make implicit promises? Do I fulfill them when readers want them fulfilled?
- Have I dealt with the shortcomings listed in the chart included in this chapter? If not, what changes do I need to make?

54

THEMES

I'm about to tell you something that's either going to ruffle your feathers or make you very, very happy.

Here it is: Your story does not need a theme.

In fact, the more clearly you can define the theme, the shallower your story will likely be. If you can summarize your novel in a catchphrase, your story is probably too small, too limited, too one-dimensional.

A theme statement isn't so much an idea you're trying to explore as a lesson you're trying to teach: "All you need is love." "A true friendship is worth the cost." "Don't worry; be happy."

But our stories aren't there to give advice but rather to make observations. Choices have consequences, and the sum total of these consequences in your story will make an observation about life and morality. Every story exists within a moral universe, so every story will make these observations. Regarding your story, ask yourself:

- Which virtues or vices are celebrated?
- Which virtues or vices are muted?
- Which virtues or vices are rendered truthfully?

For example, what does evil look like in your novel? Is it tame? Is it tantalizing? Is it disturbing? What ethic lies at the heart of your narrative: one that calls us to become better people, or one that invites us to peer longingly into the darkness?

These are all issues you'll have to wrestle with as you work on your book.

....

**If you have any theme at all for your story, it should be:
"This is what's true about human nature."**

....

FIXING THEME ISSUES

Rather than start with a lesson you want to teach, start with a moral dilemma or a question you'd like to explore.

In his screenwriting book, *The Moral Premise*, Stanley D. Williams notes:

> Adventure films frequently explore the conflict of secrecy vs. discovery. Coming-of-age films frequently explore the values of self-expression vs. conformity. Historical dramas are often about the clash of tradition vs. revolution. Science fiction often sets up a conflict between technology and humanity.

Notice how, in each example, there's conflict—two ideas vying against each other. This happens in novels just as it does in film, and it's what you're going to shoot for: not a lesson dressed up as a story but an exploration of the human condition through conflict.

Look for opposing forces or concepts. Choose contention, trials, and difficulties rather than fortune cookie sayings, bumper sticker slogans, or theme statements.

CLICHÉ	WHY THE CLICHÉ ISN'T ENOUGH	INSTEAD ASK …
"Follow your heart."	Hitler followed his heart …	When is your heart the worst thing you can follow? In what ways do our hearts lead us astray? What would be a stronger moral compass than our hearts?

"Be true to yourself."	Pedophiles are true to themselves …	What should you choose—being true to yourself or helping others be true to themselves? In what ways are people "false" to themselves? Is that such a bad thing?
"Pursue your dreams."	Serial killers pursue their dreams …	When your dreams harm others, what should you do? How should we balance pursuing our dreams with paying the bills? When is it worth giving up your dreams? When isn't it?

Show that the cliché is never enough.

In fact, I want you to refute it.

Through your novel, reveal that the shallow, trite answer that sounded so good at the beginning of the story isn't really the truth after all. Yes, it seemed like the theme was going to be "Follow your heart," but then the protagonist realizes how destructive a message this is and uncovers a deeper truth: Our world doesn't need people who follow their hearts but people who follow something greater than their hearts.

The question isn't *if* we'll deal with evil in our books, it's *how* we will. The portrayal of evil isn't what desensitizes people to violence, but the manner in which it's portrayed might. Is evil winked at, leapt over, or made to look intriguing? Or is it rendered for what it is—the destructive poison that doesn't just lurk around us but also within us?

In our postmodern, multicultural world, where everyone is trying to be sensitive to others' feelings and politically correct in what they say, it seems like people are afraid to affirm virtue.

They talk about "values" instead of "virtues."

"What are your values?" they'll ask, rather than "What virtues are you pursuing?"

Virtue is what matters most, not what you value. After all, what if someone values insulting other people? Demeaning them? Pouring toxins into the atmosphere? Raping two-year-olds? What if someone values one ethnic group over another and values genocide?

Rather than thinking of lessons you want to teach, think of moral decisions that need to be made. This will lead you away from didactic stories and lessons, and toward observations that ring true to readers.

Being able to identify a story's theme might have been important to your high school English teacher, but it's not important to most readers of marketable fiction. (In fact, many of us hated probing for themes in high school, and we hate it now because it diminishes stories and turns them into mere lessons.)

Don't try to make a point, just strive to render the truth of what we, as humans, are like, and the questions and struggles we face. Look for places where the bones of your theme poke through—then amputate them.

The more you beat your book's message against your readers' heads or try to ram your cliché down their throats, the less impact you're going to have.

Expand your story. Examine the truth, the paradoxes, the deeper morality of virtues and vices. Instead of trying to get a message across, explore life through the matrix of meaningful dilemmas.

If you do that, you just might touch readers in the places in their lives and hearts where it matters most.

HOW SHOULD I DEAL WITH EVIL?

Violence, when responsibly portrayed, serves an important role by confronting us with the truth about evil and human nature, exploring the consequences of immoral choices, and calling us to live responsibly in an all-too-often morally starved world. Moral ambiguity isn't the same as moral complexity. Moral ambiguity claims that no one can know right from wrong. Moral complexity acknowledges that we all act in ways that are both right and wrong.

FINE-TUNING MY MANUSCRIPT

- How does my story portray evil? Is it glamorized, or is it vilified? Does it win in the end, or does virtue triumph? What does the story celebrate?
- Would the Devil pay to have this book published? Why do I say that? Would God? Why or why not?
- Where have I capitulated to build my story around a cliché or axiom rather than a dilemma? How can I redirect the story away from being a lesson?
- Am I promoting moral ambiguity, amorality, or morality in the way that my story is shaped and the consequences my characters face for their ethical choices?

55

SYMBOLISM

When I heard that the famous painter Thomas Kinkade hid the letter *N* in many of his paintings as a way of honoring his wife, Nanette, I began to look for the *N*s.

Then I learned that he wrote the number of *N*s in the lower right corner of his paintings so people could determine if they'd located them all.

Now I can't shut it off.

I'm on an endless *N* hunt whenever I see a Thomas Kinkade painting.

The same thing happens when I notice the symbolism in a story. Rather than enjoy the artistry of the storytelling, from that point on I find myself symbol hunting—even if I don't want to.

Don't let that happen in your book.

• • •

The *N*s in Kinkade's work weren't inevitable and didn't grow naturally from the world of the painting. They were imposed on it for reasons that had nothing to do with art.

Just as Kinkade did with his *N*s, writers often let symbols or other literary devices impinge on the inevitability or believability of their stories.

For instance, while trying to show how the hero and villain are mirror images of each other, you have them stare at each other through a window, or into a mirror at the same time, or you have them "mirror" the actions of each other in the way they get dressed, treat others, or handle their weapons.

As soon as readers notice all this mirroring, they'll get distracted just like I did with the paintings. Your readers will start looking for mirrors or glass or reflections everywhere in your story—even if they don't want to. In that case, you would've done precisely the *opposite* of your job. You were supposed to be drawing them into your story, and now you've got them playing *Where's Waldo?* instead.

Strive to lead readers on a journey where they don't notice any of those things but are swept away into another world. Don't invite them to become distracted or lure them onto a literary equivalent of an *N* hunt.

Stop trying to be so symbolic. Just tell your story.

Most readers don't come to your book to hunt for symbolism. Don't let them find any.

FIXING SYMBOLISM ISSUES

Ray Bradbury wrote, "I never consciously place symbolism in my writing. That would be a self-conscious exercise, and self-consciousness is defeating to any creative act."

Whenever you're tempted to insert things—for whatever reason—that aren't believable, contextual, and logical, resist, resist, resist.

Readers won't get distracted by things making sense, but they will get distracted as soon as they notice your symbolism or your literary games, gimmicks, themes, and devices.

Readers don't typically care about whether the lily that keeps showing up in your scenes represents "the brevity of life" or "hope reborn" or "purity of soul." They just want to be enthralled by an emotionally engaging, entertaining story.

When using symbolism, you risk having your most astute readers get distracted from the story and end up the least satisfied. Why on earth would you even chance that?

Don't invite readers on an *N* hunt. And don't have characters stand for things (like science, religion, or some aspect of society).

Incidentally, readers do like to see the tables turned on the villain so he gets what he justly deserves. Often, this ends up being a form of poetic justice as his emblem or weapon is turned against him.

For example, the evil witch uses her wand to cast a spell in the direction of the main character, who whips out the mirror she gave him earlier and deflects the spell back at her. Or the gold that the greedy pirate stuffed into his pockets is what causes him to sink to the bottom of the sea.

Why is this plot convention of reversal of fortune so common?

First, it absolves the protagonist of accountability for the villain's death—it was simply self-defense, or it was the villain's fault. Second, it meshes with our natural instincts that justice should prevail.

However, readers don't want to predict exactly when or how this justice will be meted out. So, be careful with all of this. Trying too hard to include poetic justice and the symbolism it so often includes can be a pitfall:

> "Right, I see. So, he just *happened* to step into the very same bear trap he set up earlier. Gotcha."

> "Oh, let me guess—that terrorist who invented the virus is gonna get infected at the end of the story and die from it. Man, that'll be an amazing plot twist. Super satisfying."

If you use poetic justice, make sure that it grows naturally from the context and isn't the result of an unbelievable coincidence or a choice imposed on the story. Rather, let it be the natural result of believable choices made within the story.

WHAT IF I END UP BEING TOO SUBTLE WITH MY IMAGERY?

It's impossible to be too subtle in your use of symbolism, theme, and so on. In fact, if you drop it all entirely, readers aren't going to complain.

QUICK FIX: Clearly show your characters' desire and intention—these are not matters to be subtle about. Opt for subtlety

TROUBLESHOOTING YOUR NOVEL

in descriptions and with any imagery that finds its way into your book. Nuance won't turn readers off. Being too obvious, blunt, heavy-handed, or over-the-top will.

FINE-TUNING MY MANUSCRIPT

- Where will my use of symbolism and literary devices be noticeable to astute readers?
- Does my story include a moral dilemma for the main character? Does he make a difficult choice or personal sacrifice that resolves his final encounter with the forces of antagonism?
- Where am I being tempted to entice my readers onto an *N* hunt? How will I change things so that doesn't happen?
- Is there a sense of poetic justice? Is it too symbolic? How can I handle this in a more organic way?
- Have I managed to use the choice of the antagonist to absolve the protagonist of guilt for the villain's demise?
- What statement about virtue or vice is being made by the fate of the antagonist and protagonist? Is that really the impression that I want readers to walk away with?

56

TRANSITIONS

Transitions between settings, scenes, chapters, and point-of-view characters are four of the most common areas where authors disorient readers. You never want to confuse and frustrate the people reading your book or leave them thinking:

> So, where are all those characters now? I can't picture this at all.

> Who's there with that guy? How many people are in the room?

> Did it switch to another point of view?

> What's going on here?!

When you jar readers, you lose them. "I don't get it," really means "I'm no longer in this story." So, keep your readers oriented by helping them follow along when the story transitions from one scene to the next. Answer their natural questions:

- When is this happening?
- Where is it happening?
- Who is it happening to?

Remember, setting is both spatial and temporal. Things happen in a specific time at a specific place. In essence, it's *when* a character is *where* he is. And since stories rarely take place entirely in one location and often include gaps in time, there'll almost always be transitions from one setting to another.

**Make transitions clear, distinct, and straightforward.
Use them to serve your readers.**

FIXING TRANSITION ISSUES

The best transitions are invisible: They occur off the page. For example, end one chapter with the characters hopping onto their motorcycles; open the next with them arriving at the hotel.

Here are some practical methods for clarifying and smoothing out your transitions.

Point-of-View Transitions

Flipping from one point of view to another often causes readers momentary confusion as they try to figure out who's talking or whose head they're supposed to be in for that section of the story.

So, lock in the viewpoint character in the first line:

> Missy knew she was about to die.

> When Andrew glanced at the floor, he saw the shattered glass.

> Back when she found out she was pregnant, Brineesha wasn't an alcoholic.

Catch readers up on what the characters have been doing since the last time we saw them. Based on what just happened, what would each character be thinking, planning, working on, hoping for, or afraid of?

When you switch viewpoint, give some sort of textual indication (a chapter break, fleuron, or an extra hard return) to indicate a point-of-view flip. Make the switch clear by (1) the formatting, (2) the verb tense, (3) the name references, and (4) the voice.

Transitions of Time

Make sure readers know what time it is.

Plain and simple.

Before the time transition, have characters state their plans. For example, you might write, "I'll see you at the ballgame at five," or "I'm going to bed. I'll call you in the morning." This will clue readers in that a period of time has passed when the characters reappear.

By the way, you don't have to be specific down to the second. The more precise you are in denoting the time, the more readers will assume that the exact time you noted must be important. If it turns out to be inconsequential, they'll get annoyed.

Transitions of Location

Make sure readers can see the new location. Orient them just like you did in your novel's opening pages.

Avoid using the same type of transition over and over again. A common transition ploy is the trusty phone call: He's sent to the crime scene. Then, just as he finishes examining the body, his wife calls—gotta head home. Then, at the house, his buddy calls to meet for drinks.

Are characters always opening doors or driving up to buildings to start scenes, and then walking out those doors and driving away at the end of the scene? If so, brainstorm other openings and closings that aren't so repetitious in transitioning to a new location.

Chapter or Section Endings

Use them to propel the story forward, not slow it down. When you close a chapter, dive in. Don't plop down by the pool.

Before starting a new chapter, show the decision, the forward thrust of the story; don't end with those annoying "cliff-hangers." You know how it goes:

> The phone rang, and I went over to answer it.
> *End chapter.*
>
> The serum was in the drawer. I knew what I had to do.
> *End chapter.*

Then the first line of the next chapter answers everything—telling who was on the phone or what the character did with the serum. You'll annoy readers with those antics. Instead, answer their questions before you end the chapter:

> The phone rang, and I went over to answer it.
> "Hello?"
> "This is Andy. I'm the one who has your daughter. Right now, I'm on the street corner outside your apartment, and if you want to save her, you'll be out here within the next twenty seconds. Otherwise, I'm walking away and you'll never see her again."
> *End chapter.*

> The serum was in the drawer. I knew what I had to do.
> I pulled it out, injected it into my leg, and waited for the pain to go away.
> Only then did I realize I'd grabbed the wrong vial.
> *End chapter.*

Instead of thinking of chapter endings as places to pause or take a break, think of them as opportunities to reveal something significant enough to compel readers to turn the page and keep reading.

WHAT'S THE KEY TO GOOD TRANSITIONS?

Always keep readers grounded in the scene's setting, the viewpoint, and the character's goal. Whenever your story jumps through space or time, or from one point of view to another, it'll take readers a few seconds to reorient. Do all you can to help them do so quickly and smoothly.

QUICK FIX: Page through your manuscript, noting every time you move from one location to another, show the passage of time, or flip to another point of view. Then tap into the same techniques you used to start your novel for orienting your readers to the setting and the characters' intentions.

FINE-TUNING MY MANUSCRIPT

- Have I used formatting to my advantage to keep transitions unobtrusive?
- Do the chapter lengths serve or interrupt the flow? Do they have a broad consistency in length that grows naturally from the story's genre and pace?
- Have I included legitimate reasons for the characters to move from one scene to the next, and have I used transitions of time to the advantage of the story?
- Do my characters open and close doors or answer the phone too much? Are people constantly arriving or approaching each other?
- Do my chapter and section endings serve to propel the story forward, or do they include too much coincidence, closure, resolution, or too many gimmicky cliff-hangers?

57

FORESHADOWING

On December 23, 1938, fishermen in South Africa caught a fish that scientists thought had been extinct for 66 million years.

The coelacanth.

When I read about that, I thought of how the species had been alive the whole time, all those millennia, and no one realized it.

Maybe it's just because I'm a novelist, but it reminded me of how foreshadowing works: It happens right in front of readers, but they don't notice it until finally, at just the right moment, you let the fulfillment swim into their nets.

When the coelacanth was caught, scientists had to rethink what they knew about the fish's history. When something that was foreshadowed is revealed, readers go through the same process of re-evaluating earlier events in the story.

The fossil takes on new meaning when the fish appears.

....

To foreshadow is to make a promise that readers won't realize was made until the moment it's finally kept.

....

FIXING FORESHADOWING ISSUES

When you make overt narrative promises, readers are aware of them and look forward to them being fulfilled. However, when you foreshadow, readers don't notice at the time but are later pleased and surprised when the foreshadowed event occurs.

So, with foreshadowing, readers look back to see significance they hadn't noticed. With promise making, they look forward to something they anticipate will be significant.

Promises and foreshadowing can let readers down in different ways. Readers will be disappointed if you make promises and don't keep them; they'll also be disappointed if they notice that you're foreshadowing something.

If you don't keep your promises, they'll notice.

However, if you don't use what you've foreshadowed, they won't.

Foreshadowing can be used to make revelations and transformations more believable, show the inner logic of a story's progression, and provide insights to solving mysteries.

It can also be used as a setup for humorous misunderstanding between characters, and to retrospectively make plot twists and pivots more inevitable.

A fish swims deep beneath the surface until you bring it up in the net. But throughout the course of the story, it needs to remain unobtrusive and out of sight.

To embed foreshadowing in your book, make sure that the skill, emblem, tool, etc., makes perfect sense in the scene in which it first appears. Then, later, when it's needed at an opportune time, readers will think, *Ah. Nice. Yes. I forgot about that!*

If, however, they think, *Well, it's about time. I saw that coming a hundred pages ago*, you're sunk.

They shouldn't see it coming.

But when it does, it should make sense.

Apart from the opening coincidence that initiates your story, coincidences will only serve to undermine believability. We use foreshadowing to remove them.

Coincidences typically happen when an all-too-convenient asset happens to be present, the expert shows up, or the interruption occurs right when the character needs it.

When foreshadowing, you'll want to bring in the object or skill naturally, early in the story, so that when it comes back later it'll make sense.

For example, a plane crashes on the island and a mom screams, "My boy's not breathing!" One of the men rushes over and says, "I'm a paramedic. Let me help him." His skill is needed in that scene, and then later at the climax, when the shark attack happens, readers will recall that this man is a paramedic and they'll easily accept that he knows how to stop the bleeding in the victim's leg. However, if you don't include that moment when he helps the boy and suddenly, after the shark attack, he says, "Step out of the way. I'm a paramedic. I can save him," readers will be thinking, *Oh. Well that's convenient.*

Coincidences often sneak in when you've decided on a plot point and you're trying to get the story to lean in that direction, or when you've written yourself into a corner and you don't want to rework earlier sections of the book to make the next event unexpected and inevitable.

The climax is the most important scene. It should have the least amount of coincidence and will therefore have the most amount of foreshadowing.

We all accept that coincidences start stories, we just don't want them to end them. Here are four ways to use foreshadowing to make *your* climax more believable.

1. Foreshadow the Way the Protagonist Will Triumph

Show the character using what turns out to be an essential skill in a contextually appropriate and meaningful way early on so readers will find it believable when he exhibits this ability at the climax.

For example, your book opens with him hunting elk, so we know he's an expert marksman. Or the girl reads her mom's texts upside down and later uses this skill when she needs to save her mom's life.

2. Foreshadow the Tools that Will Be Significant

You don't want readers to guess how she'll use a specific item, but when she does, they'll realize that the solution was swimming deep within the story the whole time.

For instance, when she dumps her purse out to try to find her cell phone and you mention the purse's contents, readers don't pay particular attention to the lighter and perfume spritz bottle among the list of all the other items, but later in the story when she lights the flammable liquid and sprays the flames at the bad guy to escape, readers will appreciate her cleverness.

3. Foreshadow Who Will Be Present

Don't let saviors pop in to save the day at the climax. If it's absolutely necessary for your character's partner, the intergalactic wizard, S.W.A.T., or a mentor (or whoever) to arrive, foreshadow that they're on their way to the climax's location. Remember, though, it's vital that your protagonist makes the choice that determines the story's outcome.

4. Foreshadow the Location

If your climax is going to occur at an unusual site, have a scene happen there earlier so you can describe the place in detail then, before the final narrative sprint to the story's finish. At that earlier moment, offhandedly mention any assets that might be available so readers will already have a picture of the location in their minds when the climax arrives.

WHY SHOULD I STEER CLEAR OF COINCIDENCES?

Coincidences kill believability. They make readers sigh, scoff, or shake their heads—and that's never the reaction you want. The logic of the story should support the decisions of the characters.

QUICK FIX: Look for places where things seem too easy, too convenient, or too contrived. Solve the issue by foreshadowing or by making promises earlier in the story. Remove chance happenings and coincidences. Foreshadow everything that would strain credulity or that seems too convenient.

- Do the foreshadowed abilities or assets make contextual sense in the scenes when they first appear, or do they stick out like a sore thumb?
- How can I insert scenes to reveal characteristics or emblems that later become essential to the character's success?
- Apart from the coincidence that initiates the story, have I rooted out the other instances of people showing up at exactly the right time or for just the right reason?
- If there's a villain, does the protagonist have an encounter or close call with him at some point in the middle of the book to foreshadow their climactic showdown? If not, where could I add that?
- Do coincidences exist in my character's view of the fictional world? In other words, does she think things in the story are unbelievable? If so, she would naturally seem perplexed or confused. Is that how she responds?

58

VIEWPOINT

One of my office managers was a ballet dancer before she came to work for me. One weekend, our family accompanied her to a ballet performance, the first one I'd ever attended.

Thinking that she would want to get a good view, I said, "Should we sit up close to the stage—maybe the front row?"

"No. We need to move back a little."

"Why?"

"Because up there, with the angle of the stage, we wouldn't be able to see their feet."

• • •

It was natural for someone who'd studied dance to want to see the feet of the dancers, but it hadn't even crossed my mind.

The viewpoint is the set of eyes through which we see a scene occur.

Dancer's eyes.

Writer's eyes.

It makes a difference.

Viewpoint evinces the perspective that grows from the attitude, filters, backstory, desires, agenda, and personality of this character.

It's how that character would perceive, interpret, and process this scene under these circumstances. What will she notice? How will she respond? How is her take on things different from anyone else's?

> The sooner you clarify who the viewpoint character is, the more you help your readers step into the story.

FIXING VIEWPOINT ISSUES

A character can only know for sure what's inside his own head. He can *assume* what others are thinking or feeling, but he cannot *know*. You'll want to avoid making it seem like he knows what he cannot.

For instance, from your viewpoint character's perspective you might write, "From across the room I noticed Jerome idly rubbing his finger against his thumb," but not "From across the room I noticed Jerome subconsciously rubbing his finger against his thumb," since the point-of-view character won't know what Jerome was consciously aware of and what he wasn't.

You wouldn't write, "As I approached the woman, she was wondering who I might be."

But you might write, "As I approached the woman, she looked nervous."

In a similar vein, the viewpoint character might observe, "The woman seemed scared of me," or "The woman was acting like she was scared of me," or "I sensed that I'd hit a nerve," but he couldn't say, "The woman was wondering who I might be," because he can only know what's in his own head.

Is your character psychic?

No?

Well, then don't allow him to read other people's minds.

Typically, in today's marketable fiction, you'll render the scene from the perspective of one of the characters rather than from the viewpoint of a generic, all-knowing voice in the sky (sometimes called the omniscient point of view).

Keep in mind the viewpoint and the verb tense—that is, have these events happened, or are they happening right now?

FIRST-PERSON PRESENT TENSE: I scan the banquet hall looking for the man that the communiqué informed me about. He's here. I know it. And I'm going to find him.

FIRST-PERSON PAST TENSE: I scanned the banquet hall looking for the man that the communiqué had informed me about. He was here. I knew it. And I was going to find him.

SECOND-PERSON PRESENT TENSE: You scan the banquet hall looking for the man that the communiqué informed you about. He's here. You know it. And you're going to find him.

THIRD-PERSON PAST TENSE: She scanned the banquet hall looking for the man that the communiqué had informed her about. He was here. She knew it. And she was going to find him.

Since you mentioned a "communiqué," had this character "scan" the banquet hall, and wrote the sequence with a crisp, brisk pace, readers will likely anticipate that this character is a spy or secret agent.

A five-year-old girl looking for her daddy would use an entirely different vocabulary, sentence structure, and so on.

Again, only include details that are significant to the story and that this character would notice, then allow her to observe them in her own unique way.

For example, a homicide detective assesses a victim at a crime scene:

> He was in his late thirties, Caucasian, slight build, with salt-and-pepper hair and a goatee. A frenzy of blood was spread across his abdomen. And he was now and forever dead.

That's his viewpoint. It's how he thinks. It's how he processes things. The wife of the victim would describe things in a completely different way.

So, when it comes to viewpoint:

1. A character will notice things that are important to her (that is, that matter to her pursuit). What she notices will reveal not only what she's like but what she's seeking.

2. Only flip to another point of view at the end of a chapter or section rather than within the same paragraph.
3. Every viewpoint character will have his own pursuit, setbacks, and resolution.
4. While you're in someone's viewpoint, choose the words, phrases, and figures of speech that character would use.
5. It's hard to sustain second-person point of view through a whole book, so you'll most likely write your story in first person or third person.
6. If you use multiple points of view, consider rendering the main character in first person and the others in third person so it's clear to readers who the protagonist is.

HOW DO I KNOW WHICH POINT OF VIEW TO USE FOR THE NARRATOR?

You might not—at least not until you've finished your first draft. The narrator's point of view will depend on who's present in each scene, whose perspective sheds the most light on that scene, and the narrative voice you choose to tell the story. The more external the struggles, the more impersonal the narrator's viewpoint can be. However, the more your story centers on internal or interpersonal struggles, the more closely it'll be tied to the protagonist's point of view.

QUICK FIX: Ask who could best tell this story. Who's present in this scene? Who do characters want to spend the most time with? Whose perspective matters the most? Limit the number of viewpoint characters, and confirm that each one has a pursuit and, if appropriate, a transformation.

FINE-TUNING MY MANUSCRIPT

- Who is the narrator? Is she reliable? What is she privy to? What restrictions does that put on the story?

- Is there an overriding contextual reason to use more than one narrator in a scene (that is, to render the scene from more than one viewpoint without a section break)? If not, where have I inadvertently done that?
- Is it clear from the beginning of my novel whose viewpoint the story is being told from? Where have I made the viewpoint fuzzy or undermined it by allowing characters to be privy to the thoughts, emotions, or motivation of other characters?
- If I've used multiple points of view, are the transitions between them clear? Do the point-of-view flips contribute to the story or slow it down and make it tedious?
- Will switching to another point of view confuse readers, or will it serve them?
- Do readers care enough about this character to buy into (and want) her point of view?

59

VOICE

"Find a subject you care about and which you in your heart feel others should care about. It is this genuine caring, and not your games with language, which will be the most compelling and seductive element in your style."
—Kurt Vonnegut

When you think of voice, think of distinctiveness. It's your personal style, your passion, and the narrator's singular perspective coming together. Voice is expressed through your unique flavor of word choice, attitude, and viewpoint, and it sets you apart from other writers.

Finding your voice might happen at an early stage as you work on your book, but it's more likely that your voice will develop and mature as you flesh out your story. Because of that, the scenes you wrote most recently will probably be more "in voice" than the ones you wrote months or years ago. For a unified voice, you'll likely need to recast those earlier scenes and descriptions to make sure the voice is consistent throughout the book.

> **Editing isn't just about finding mistakes, it's about contextualizing the voice.**

FIXING VOICE ISSUES

Your voice might be formal or informal.

It might vary from book to book.

It might be short and terse, or wandering and elephantine.

A strong narrative voice is vital, but it is not everything. If your style ever becomes more attention-grabbing than your story, you're no longer serving your readers. Calling attention to yourself isn't what you want, because it's not what *they* want.

It's impossible to completely divorce voice from viewpoint. Each character will have a distinctive voice when we're in his point of view:

A TEENAGE BOY EXPLORING THE FOREST ON HIS BIKE:

You're a junior in high school.

Leaves, dead and brown, swirl on the ground, then skitter around you and across the mountain bike trail in front of you, caught up in little whirlwinds of air. Tiny tornadoes of late fall.

You pedal hard, trying to outrun the coming storm.

A THIRTY-YEAR-OLD WOMAN WHO'S THANKFUL THAT HER RELATIONSHIP WITH HER LOVE INTEREST IS DEVELOPING:

She let her mind walk slowly through all that had happened over the last couple of days. Every moment became another flower, and in her heart she placed them in a vase and began to arrange them in a way that caught all the light she'd ever known.

A SOCIOPATHIC ELEVEN-YEAR-OLD BOY COMMITTING HIS FIRST MURDER:

Giovanni had cut steak; he knew that cutting meat wasn't easy, and that his grandmother's body would have meat on it, that everyone's does, so he expected that it would be difficult to push the knife into her belly, expected that there would be more resistance, but it was much easier than he thought it would be.

TWO ADOLESCENT FRIENDS DOCKING A ROWBOAT ON THE SHORE OF THE LAKE:

Once he was on the bank, Jamaal called to Ariel, "See? No problem." He set the oars beside one of the boulders. "I'll be back in, like, two minutes."

"Be careful."

"My middle name is Mr. Careful."

"That doesn't even make sense."

"I'll see you in a few."

If you introduce a memorable voice, be sure you can carry it believably through the whole story. For example, if you were to start your novel, "I ain't never killt nobody before," you'll need to be able to keep that unique voice alive for the next several hundred pages. The more unusual the voice, the bigger the challenge of staying in it for an entire novel.

Uphold the voice with your metaphors, similes, and other figures of speech. When you compare two things or say that one thing is like another, keep the atmosphere in mind. So, depending on the voice, the roots in the woods might be "thick and bulging like veins on the forest floor," or "look like vipers frozen in mid-slither," or be "gentle living ribbons meandering across the path."

Any of those descriptions could be used to enhance the atmosphere (or ruin it), or reflect the voice (or undermine it).

Let's say we're in a specific character's point of view and you write:

I brushed aside a strand of my light brown hair and sauntered across the room.

Okay, there's a lot wrong with that sentence. First, mentioning the hair color here is intrusive. After all, why would the character suddenly take note of the color of his hair at this moment? Second, he wouldn't describe himself as "sauntering." If he did, he would sound arrogant, losing both status and reader empathy.

When you write without pretense or posturing, and that authenticity meshes seamlessly with the atmosphere of the story and the pursuit of the character, you've found your voice.

The best way for it to emerge?

Don't try to be eloquent.

Don't try to be avant-garde.

Don't emulate others.

Instead, strive to disappear into the story.

The more you can enter your narrator's mind and understand what she would naturally be thinking, doing, observing, and pursuing, the more this book's unique storytelling voice will emerge.

BUT SHOULDN'T I TRY TO BE MORE LITERARY?

Don't try to be anything you're not. Shoot for authenticity. Keep your voice consistent. The more natural it sounds, the less anyone will care about how literary it is.

QUICK FIX: Descriptions are spoiled more often by authors trying to be literary than by those trying to be honest. Read your book from the beginning. Pay particularly close attention to the voice in sections where there are revelations, discoveries, or transformations. Continually ask how the viewpoint character would respond. Often, changing only a few words can lock in and maintain the narrator's voice.

FINE-TUNING MY MANUSCRIPT

- Is my voice consistent from the first page to the last? If not, where do I need to take a closer look at it?
- Have I inadvertently emulated someone else's voice? Am I being derivative?
- How well have I merged voice and viewpoint? When I'm in one specific character's point of view, does his voice come through clearly, or is it lost in the static of authorial intrusion?
- Am I trying too hard to write impressive prose? Where can I let the writing be more honest and less forced?

60

TIMING

We are all prisoners of time.

In a sense, our characters are too.

But our stories are not.

What do I mean? Time in a novel is flexible in the sense that it can be stretched out (a climactic minute or two might take a chapter to play out) or contracted (a century might pass in a single paragraph).

However, it's not flexible in the sense that it passes at the same rate for all the characters. So, if five seconds pass for John, five seconds have passed for his daughter—not two hours. If the phone call between Lacey and Rhonda lasts three minutes, three minutes will have passed for each of them—and for every other character in the book.

Managing the passage of time is often a stumbling block for authors.

....

Time is elastic for the story, but not for the characters. It passes for all of them at the same rate.

....

FIXING TIMING ISSUES

To understand the dynamics of time progression in novels, it's important to consider elasticity, continuity, and the perception readers will have of the passage of time within the story.

Use the Elasticity of Narrative Time to Jump over Dead Spots in the Story

Regarding the flexible nature of time in fiction, if nothing important is happening, don't overwhelm readers with details that'll drag down the story's pace. Don't dwell on things. Move forward.

So, although the previous forty pages might have covered just one hour of the teen protagonist's life, we can zip through the next day to get him on his way to football practice again:

> Thursday. Time whipped by. The history test seemed to go alright. Then Government. Spanish. Study hall. AP Calculus.
>
> Before I knew it, I was on my way to the locker room to get changed for practice when Coach saw me and pulled me aside. "I need to have a word with you. Follow me."

Use the Consistency of Narrative Time to Keep Readers Oriented

During a fight scene, you wouldn't have one character cock his fist back to punch the other guy, and then flip to another point of view for fifteen pages before coming back to the fight and letting Character A punch Character B in the jaw as if no time had passed at all for the two of them.

Don't let any of your characters enter a time warp.

Some authors claim that they use this scene cutting "to create suspense," but it throws readers off, and when they're confused they're not in suspense.

Instead, if you use multiple points of view, cut sideways through time, allowing it to pass for all the characters simultaneously. Don't hopscotch back and forth across it.

Remember That It Takes Time to Read the Scene

Okay, I know, this seems obvious, but don't overlook it.

Reading a scene will take your readers a certain amount of their own time, and the passage of real-life time will affect their perception of the amount of time that should have passed within the narrative world.

So, if it takes them two hours to read a scene that takes place over the course of two minutes, they'll likely get bored and assume that more time *must* have passed just because so much time passed for them in real life.

Ask yourself (1) how long this narrative event takes, (2) how long it will likely take to read about it happening, and (3) how long it will therefore *seem* to have taken. Don't let the gap be too big or readers won't remain engaged.

Use Time Stamps to Your Advantage

As we've examined elsewhere, everything you write carries a promise of significance.

If you include time stamps, some readers will compare them against each other to verify that those events could've actually occurred in that span of time. If readers think it would've taken longer for something to happen, they'll lose faith in the story's believability.

Even if you haven't made a mistake, if they think you have, they'll be distracted. So, only include time stamps if they're vital for keeping readers oriented and if the time passage is accurate and believable.

Concerning countdowns, they'll need to escalate—and there needs to be a payoff. Additionally, monotonous countdowns where every chapter covers one day or one hour grow old fast. The longer the countdown occurs, the more important it is that (1) the timing actually matters, (2) the countdown escalates in intensity, and (3) the final scene is rendered rather than summarized.

HOW MUCH TIME SHOULD MY NOVEL SPAN?

The time span of your story will be contextual. Allow enough of it to pass to keep readers from drowning in tedium, but not so much that they stop caring about the protagonist's pursuit.

QUICK FIX: Use the elasticity of time to your advantage. Milk the parts of the story that are suspenseful (draw them out)

---

and zip through (that is, condense) the parts that are nonessential. Unobtrusively demarcate the passage of time to clarify how much has passed between scenes.

FINE-TUNING MY MANUSCRIPT

- Have I rendered the scenes readers will want to experience? How well have I managed the different aspects of narrative time?
- How can I better express the passage of time to serve the pace by appropriately shrinking or expanding how long events take to occur?
- Have I inadvertently included any time warps in which some characters don't travel through the story at the same rate as others?
- Considering the length of my book and the time span it covers, have I appropriately tackled the transitions of time from one chapter or scene to the next?
- Will readers be annoyed by some sections because they don't think things are moving fast enough? What can I condense to fix that?
- Have I resorted to clichés in the countdowns I've included? Are there other books or movies that have rendered them in the same ways? How could I recast things to be more original?

61

SHOWING VS. TELLING

Writers are often taught, "Show, don't tell!"

But what does that adage mean? Is it universal? How can we discern when to do one rather than the other?

Let's say you have a vampire chasing a man through a moonlit forest. Do you show the chase, or do you summarize it? Under what circumstances would you simply tell readers that it happened?

To *show* is to *render*.

To *tell* is to *summarize*.

Think of how you might reveal that a character is angry. You could simply tell readers:

> Jonathan was furious.

Or you could show that he was furious by his actions and mannerisms:

> Jonathan stomped across the room, threw open the
> door, and hollered for his son to come down the stairs. *Now!*

Readers would infer what's going on and think, *Man, that dude is seriously upset.*

Typically, we're taught that it's better to go the second route (of showing) than the first one (of telling). That's where the "Show, don't tell," advice comes in.

But why is that encouraged?

Well, often, showing makes for more engaging reading, and it demonstrates trust that readers will be able to piece things together from the context and discern the character's mood, feelings, or desire.

Okay, so then are there times when you wouldn't want to show but would want to tell instead?

Yes.

There are.

....

Show struggles. Tell goals.

....

FIXING SHOWING AND TELLING ISSUES

Generally speaking, we *show* characters' emotions by their response to stimuli, but we *tell* (or have them tell) readers their desires.

Showing rather than telling doesn't work well when you're revealing intention. In other words, it's often better to have a character simply and unequivocally state why he's in a scene rather than bending over backward trying to show what he wants without telling readers.

Often, it's stronger and more effective to have a character say, "I came over here today to find out where Alice is, and I'm not leaving until I have some answers," than to try to reveal all of that indirectly.

If you attempt to show desire rather than tell it, you may end up writing unnecessary scenes and needlessly burden the pace of your story.

STORY ELEMENT	SHOW OR TELL?	HOW?
A character's emotional response	Show	Don't tell readers he was ashamed or joyful; show them by how he reacts.
A character's attitude	Show	Rather than explain that he's uptight or judgmental, show him acting that way, or reveal it through his lines of dialogue.
A character's special skills or abilities	Show	Don't tell readers what a great fighter he is; render a scene in which he fights while something meaningful is at stake.

Status (dominance/ submission)	Show	Instead of telling readers which character is in charge or who has the highest status, reveal it through stillness, self-control, confidence, and self-assurance.
Tension and suspense	Show	The more you claim that something is suspenseful or tense, the less it will be. Instead, build tension through engendering reader empathy and concern for characters in peril.
Desire (a character's goal or intention within a scene)	Show or tell	If you show, do so quickly and clearly. Otherwise, just have the character state what he's trying to accomplish.
A progression of events that doesn't change the character's attitude, status, or situation	Tell	If nothing tilts in the scene, don't spend time detailing it. Instead, just summarize what happened and get to the point in the story where things tilt.
A scene that tilts	Show	These are the core scenes of your book. Play them out. Show your characters facing struggles, taking action, meeting setbacks, and recalibrating before moving forward again on their pursuit.
Stakes	Tell	Tell readers what will happen if the characters are unsuccessful. Be as specific as possible, calling attention to deadlines when appropriate.
Decisions	Tell or show	Often, it's best to just tell readers what your characters have decided to do; however, context might provide you unobtrusive ways to show them.

So, back to the vampire.

If it is vital to the story, contextually driven, reveals how a situation is altered, and remains true to the pace, you would show the chase scene and its frightful conclusion in all its bloody glory.

Otherwise, you could simply summarize: "It took Vlad only thirty seconds to find Johnny in the forest and make him one of his own."

HOW CAN I TRUST MY READERS MORE WHEN I'M SHOWING?

Context will make this clear to you. The bigger the promise you've made regarding the importance of a scene, the more vital it is for you to render that scene.

QUICK FIX: Verify that (1) every significant scene is rendered, (2) emotions are honest and evident, and (3) the characters' intentions are clear to readers.

FINE-TUNING MY MANUSCRIPT

- Is there too much telling when it comes to emotion? What about showing when it comes to desire? How can I fix that?
- Have I rendered the most appropriate scenes? Are there any scenes that I'm rendering that I should have just summarized instead?
- Have I been sensitive to the promises that are made by the amount of time I take rendering or summarizing different scenes? Will readers properly anticipate which scenes and turning points are important?
- With the dilemmas I've introduced and the characters I've portrayed as important, what scenes will readers want to see played out? If I'm not giving them that, why not? Will they be captivated and pleased by what I give them instead?
- Concerning intention, is it clear what this character wants and what's stopping him from getting it? If not, how can I better clarify his goals or aspirations?

62

SUBTEXT

The ocean looks so calm out there, hardly a ripple at all. But deep down, all sorts of currents and riptides flow in different directions.

To get to know the ocean, you have to do more than look at the surface.

You have to actually dive in.

Most of the time there's something deeper going on in a story: emotion, pain, passion—flowing, churning, surging right there beneath the surface. A relationship is forming or deteriorating, an attitude is readjusting, a revelation is unfolding.

Subtext is the deeper meaning of a scene, conveyed alongside the surface events that are occurring. When someone refers to "reading between the lines," he's talking about subtext.

Things are not what they appear to be.

What you see is not what you get.

When a scene is built primarily on subtext, you don't trust what's said, you don't trust what's done, you trust what's implied.

Subtext is what's meant but isn't said.

FIXING SUBTEXT ISSUES

Subtext can be present during any type of scene—whether that relies on narration, dialogue, the use of silence, evasion, or the ambiguity of responses.

Subtext in Narration: Use It to Show the Emotion Behind the Action

Think in terms of juxtaposition.

Let's say a woman is digging in the garden, and her husband comes home drunk—again. As they talk, she jams the shovel into the ground, then kicks a clod of dirt out of the way, channeling all of her anger toward him into the way she treats the soil. Consider juxtaposing actions to show something that wouldn't have as much impact if you just let a character say it.

However, be aware of the context. Trying to layer subtext into every scene will actually hurt your story. In some sections, such as fight scenes, chase scenes, or suspenseful climaxes, the presence of subtext will distract readers from what's happening onstage in the story. Let those scenes be about what they appear to be about.

Subtext in Dialogue: Use It to Say What Isn't Being Said

When characters flirt or banter, the conversation isn't typically so much about the surface subject they're discussing or that they're playfully jibing each other about but rather the dynamics of the relationship. The friendship is being solidified or romantic interest is being expressed.

When a scene is rich in subtext, characters will often engage in small talk. They'll joke around, discuss the game or the weather, compliment each other's clothes, and so on. But readers can tell that there are other motives or intentions there beneath the surface that matter more than the trivialities being discussed.

When friends give each other a hard time, often it's not a matter of one-upmanship but rather a way of reaffirming to each other that they are equals. Often, when a woman flirts with a man, she's verbally sparring with him, but she doesn't want to win, she wants to be won over.

Hinting can bring out the romantic subtext:

> "What do you want to do tonight?"
> "I don't know. Use your imagination."
> "We could play a game."
> "I like games."

A double entendre can do so as well:

> "I need to plug in my cord."
> "I'll bet you do."

Often, subtext is used to bring depth to triviality. The more trivial the topic of conversation, the more your readers will expect the subtext to be significant.

Readers know that the scene ought to be about something that matters or else it doesn't belong in the book. Because of this, they naturally look for significance in what is said and done in a story. They're trusting that this scene will carry some importance. If it doesn't, if everything is as shallow as it appears on the surface, they will not be happy.

Subtext Through Silence: Use Pauses to Set up Twists

Pauses can be used to construct two or more storylines that would each be believable. This can be helpful when foreshadowing or setting up a twist:

> "They think I hurt my dad, maybe even killed him. You can't tell them that you're helping me."
> "I'll think of something."
> "I didn't stab him, Kyle."
> "I know."
> "I mean it."
> A slight pause. "I know."

Readers will buy it that Kyle believes his friend, but because of that pause, they would also be willing to accept that he didn't believe him—if that's where the story goes in the following pages.

Subtext Through Evasion: Use Circumvention to Reveal Intention

When a character changes the subject, there's always a reason. Evasion speaks volumes.

If one character asks another a direct question and that person doesn't answer, readers will intuit that there's something more going on.

Subtext Through What's *Almost* Said: Take a Close Look at the Wording

The way things are phrased carries deep meaning and can sometimes contradict what's actually being said. For example, there's a big difference between saying, "I love you, Arianna," and "I do love you, Arianna." The phrases are *almost* the same, but they say two entirely different things.

HOW MUCH SUBTEXT SHOULD I INCLUDE?

It depends on the scene, the characters' attitudes and goals toward each other, and the literary genre in which you're writing. Subtext comes from moments (actions, words, or silences) that can contain more than one meaning or interpretation. It's most prevalent in romance, coming-of-age stories, and novels revolving around interpersonal struggles.

QUICK FIX: Ask yourself what the scene is primarily about—despite what the characters might be saying or doing. What's implied? That's what you want readers to take away from it after reading it. In relationship-centered stories, let a deeper meaning pervade the scenes, but remove subtext from scenes where things actually are what they appear to be.

- If the scene's meaning depends on subtext, is it clear to readers what this scene is principally about? If not, how can I layer more meaning into the silences, dialogue, or actions?
- Have I tried too hard to insert subtext? How is that hurting the story?
- Where have I missed opportunities to weave subtext into the story? How can I take advantage of those moments or story events?
- Did I use juxtaposition for effect? Where can actions convey feelings? Where can they speak louder than words?
- Are there any places where I could have a character answer one way but, based on the context, let readers infer that he really means the opposite of what he said?

63

BALANCE

Recently, I was doing some research on aerodynamics, and I was intrigued to learn that four forces work in concert to allow planes to fly: thrust, drag, lift, and weight.

Thrust is the forward propulsion, drag is the result of friction, lift comes from air traveling over the wings, and weight is, well, weight.

Wings are designed so that while the plane is in motion the air molecules pressing against the bottom of the wing create upward pressure.

Thrust, drag, lift, weight.

If you have too much of any one of them, your plane is likely going to crash or will never even make it off the ground.

• • •

I wouldn't make a very good airplane engineer.

I tend to write by trial and error—I try out a certain wording or scene, then analyze it in context and let that determine if I keep it or not.

If I were designing airplanes, they would keep crashing. "Oops. A little too much drag there, not enough lift. Better try that again."

And so it goes.

Month after month. Until I have a book.

The whole countryside would be littered with crashed first drafts.

Though we're not working in the field of physics, we are working in the realm of narrative forces that press in upon our stories to make them engaging and entertaining. These forces (such as believability, causality, escalation, desire, and the many others we've been exploring) all affect the flight pattern of our stories, and unless they're working in sync with each other, your story is going to be in trouble.

Lots of believability but no escalation? Boooooooring.

Lots of choices but no stakes? Who cares?

Lots of despair but no desire? Way too depressing.

Lots of themes but no truth? Seriously? What's that about?

....

The interplay of narrative forces will affect every scene of your story.

....

FIXING BALANCE ISSUES

Throughout this book, we've covered many different aspects of story craft. Here's an example of just a few narrative forces at play:

> **EXAMPLE 1:** "We have to go," Mr. Zacharias said emphatically.
>
> **EXAMPLE 2:** "We have to go," Mr. Zacharias emphasized.

Typically, when you can use one word to communicate what two are saying, you'll want to revise the sentences and, in the service of brevity, cut the unnecessary word. So, in this case, the second example is more concise.

However … would the narrator really use the verb *emphasized*? It seems a little more formal, maybe authorial. Does it fit with that character's viewpoint and vocabulary?

In this one sentence you have the forces of voice, viewpoint, and brevity all coming to bear on your word choice.

Which example would you use?

It depends.

Writing isn't about formulas—this is where we differ from airplane engineers. Word choice relies on context, instinct, and constant, careful evaluation. For instance:

NARRATIVE FORCES	QUESTION
Causality vs. Twists	How can I keep the twist believable without making it too predictable?
Escalation vs. Believability	How can this character remain believable while doing something that, at the moment, seems "out of character" but is necessary for building the tension?
Vulnerability vs. Status	How can I keep the protagonist's status high while also showing how vulnerable he is?

With practice you can train yourself to more effectively evaluate the way the forces affect each other, but there's no right or wrong here. The issue is what works, what serves the story, and what does not.

Although all of the topics in this book are important, here are a dozen narrative forces that top the list:

1. **UNMET DESIRE:** Your character wants something that he cannot get. This drives his pursuit.
2. **DILEMMA:** His choices are difficult and reveal moral convictions.
3. **BELIEVABILITY:** Everything remains believable throughout the story.
4. **CAUSALITY:** Events are caused by the ones that precede them.
5. **ESCALATION:** The tension continues to tighten until the climax.
6. **TWISTS:** The story turns and pivots forward, believably and unexpectedly.
7. **VOICE:** Your storytelling has a distinctive style that sets it apart.
8. **VIEWPOINT:** Characters express uniqueness through their point of view.
9. **READER CONCERN:** Readers are emotionally engaged and invested in the story's outcome.
10. **SUBTEXT:** A deeper meaning pervades surface events.
11. **PROMISES AND PAYOFF:** You make meaningful promises and then keep them.
12. **TRANSFORMATIONS:** The situation or the character (or both) has changed at the story's end.

HOW DOES BALANCE RELATE TO SUBPLOTS?

If the subplots don't contribute to the main story or end up distracting from it, your book will lack balance. Every conflict that you layer in makes its own promises and contains its own pursuit. While the storylines might be divergent, they should all contribute to the goal that the character is pursuing.

QUICK FIX: Evaluate the importance of each subplot, taking into consideration the narrative weight it bears and its relevance to the main plot. Then look carefully at the list of twelve narrative forces included in this chapter and see how each influences the movement and development of each storyline.

FINE-TUNING MY MANUSCRIPT

- What forces are pressing in on the story on a structural level, and which ones on a line-by-line level? What minute changes do I need to make to move the story toward excellence?
- Looking through my book, which narrative forces have I done a good job of valuing and including? Which ones am I neglecting? How can I balance things out more?
- Considering my genre, what forces will readers be expecting the most: escalation, believability, or internal struggles? How will that affect the climax?
- Where's my story veering off course? Are there places where it's about to crash and burn? How can I recast the scenes by taking more narrative forces into account to keep the story soaring through the air rather than plummeting to the ground?

PART IV
READER ENGAGEMENT

64

EXPECTATIONS

I have a love/hate relationship with movie trailers.

I love it when they intrigue me, but I hate it when they (1) include plot spoilers, (2) give away the entire story, (3) contain lines that don't actually appear in the film, or (4) make a minor storyline seem like a major one, skewing my impression of what the movie is really about.

The first mistake ruins the surprise.

The second steals my curiosity.

The third is a broken promise.

The fourth confuses me and leaves me annoyed.

All four sabotage my enjoyment and undermine the emotional impact of the film.

And all four can also happen with novels when we mislead readers either before, or during, our stories. For instance, consider all the ways readers might learn about your book before they even flip to the first page:

1. **REVIEWS:** Whether positive or negative, ratings and reviews will impact readers' expectations.
2. **BLURBS:** Endorsements (online, on the book cover, on your website, etc.) from other authors will help reassure readers that the book is worth their time and will also set genre expectations.
3. **ONLINE PRESENCE:** What will readers find when they search for your name on the Internet? What sense will they get about your work by reading the Wikipedia article about you, looking at your Facebook page, or scrolling through your website? What impression will they be left with—that you're a pro, or a wannabe? That you strive for excellence or settle for mediocrity? Does your web-

site look like it was thrown together in an afternoon by a college student for a mass communications assignment? All of this will play into readers' expectations regarding the quality of your book.

4. **PACKAGING:** What impression do the title, cover art, and back-cover copy leave? What genre does it pinion your book to?

5. **EXCERPTS:** If readers are able to check out the first chapter online, will they be intrigued enough to want to read more? What genre will they expect? What level of excellence will they expect from the rest of the book? What feeling will they anticipate the book will give them, or what need will they think it's going to fulfill?

....

**Always give readers what they want
or something better.**

....

FIXING EXPECTATION ISSUES

Before the book even gets into your readers' hands, you can:

- Find and disseminate positive reviews.
- Invite other well-respected authors or celebrities to endorse it.
- Ensure that the title and cover design set accurate expectations.
- Include stellar, accurate back-cover copy.
- Monitor your online presence and social media posts to correspond with the image, impression, and brand you're trying to maintain.
- Understand your genre and include key words in the description of the book, your bio, and so on to invite interest and elicit trust from those who enjoy reading novels in that genre.

Okay, all that happens earlier, but now a reader has picked up your book. How do you manage his expectations throughout the story?

Carefully consider the following factors.

The Opening

Readers will expect more of whatever you give them at the start. They also expect that what's important early on will be important later.

Make sure that's the case.

At the opening, give them a true taste of what you're going to be serving during the meal.

Narrative Progression

Readers expect different things at different points in a novel in regard to character, promises, and payoff. For instance, at the story's inception, they expect characters and storylines to be introduced. They recognize that aspects of the different subplots won't always appear to be connected, but they trust that all of the storylines will be somehow related and even dependent on each other.

As the story progresses, they'll anticipate that the protagonist's situation will get worse as he faces and overcomes setbacks, until finally, the various storylines all wrap up in a satisfying way.

Study the promises you're making in your story's opening scene, and evaluate if you've kept them by the book's end. Then make sure that each scene contributes in a meaningful way to the overall progression of the story.

Story Content

Keep readers' expectations in line with what your story delivers.

As they read, their expectations will be in flux as they make predictions and see how (or if) they come true.

You're in the business of trying to get readers to notice certain things and not notice others until the right time. All of this is accomplished by what you call attention to through your use of details, description, and word choice.

Consider when and how you reveal clues, insights, or secrets; the role that they play in moving the story along; and how that affects the transformation of the characters' situation or attitude at the close of the story.

. . .

What are readers coming to your story for? Immersion into another world? A fast-paced read? An escape from the stress of everyday life? A white-knuckle thrill ride? An intriguing puzzle they can attempt to solve before the detective does? Is your story delivering what it promises, or does it promise one thing and deliver another?

In summary:

- Set accurate expectations.
- Manage them throughout the story.
- Write with your readers in mind.
- Fulfill your promises.

WHAT'S THE BEST WAY TO MANAGE READERS' EXPECTATIONS?

Respect your readers, lock in the voice and atmosphere of the book in the first scene, make meaningful promises, and then keep them at the most opportune times.

QUICK FIX: Study other books in this genre to better understand what readers will be anticipating or hoping for. Foreshadow the scenes that veer from genre conventions. Add unexpected twists and turns to avoid clichés. Keep track of the promises inherent in each scene, and make sure that you don't leave questions that readers care about hanging in the air at the story's end.

FINE-TUNING MY MANUSCRIPT

- Based on everything readers know when they open to page 1, what expectations will they have? What genre will they think my book is going to be? Is that what I give them?
- After the first ten pages, who will readers assume the main character is? If that's not who it turns out to be, how will they feel? How can I better prepare them for that reveal?

- Based on the story's opening, what will readers expect in terms of action, suspense, romance, pace, twists, and literary excellence? Have I met those expectations?
- What aspects of the story will readers be dissatisfied with? How can I strengthen the promises regarding those areas?
- How will I overcome any negative attitudes or stereotypes readers might have (it's "genre fiction" or "religious fiction" or "just a beach read") in order to satisfy them more?
- What obligatory scenes are inherent to this genre? How can I render them in a way that isn't clichéd?

65

ANTICIPATION

Imagine that you're a six-year-old looking forward to opening your Christmas presents. For weeks you've seen the gifts from your family members sitting there under the tree, taunting you, tempting you.

You squeeze the packages and shake the boxes, trying to guess what's inside.

Somehow, you want to both guess correctly and get it wrong—because you don't want to ruin the surprise.

Your anticipation heightens … heightens … heightens …

Until finally, the big day arrives.

Anticipation and then payoff—so there better be something good in those presents.

Since stories are more about promises toward something than reflections about something, they rely more on anticipation than on retrospection. So, reading a story is more like looking forward to opening presents on Christmas than it is thinking back to that day six months later.

But sometimes writers don't take into account readers' emerging relationship with the story and how their anticipation relates to their reading experience:

> "Well the writing's not that great, but I started the book, so I might as well finish it."

> "I always give the writer a hundred pages. If he can't keep my attention that long, I set it aside."

> "I think I know where this story is going, but I hope I'm wrong. There better be a twist at the end. If there isn't, I'm gonna be mad."

"Man, this is so good, I just can't put it down. I wonder what's going to happen next!"

Only one of those is the reaction I'm hoping for.

The other three serve as warnings to me.

....

Never tell readers what they already know in a way they already expect.

....

FIXING ANTICIPATION ISSUES

Remember that with every line they read, readers are thinking *something*.

As they move through a story, they're both processing and predicting. Based on the promises and context, they'll be anticipating certain things, evaluating the implications of what happens, and then making predictions once again.

As you craft your scenes and evaluate the balance of how much you want readers to process the scene they're reading or predict the scene that's coming, keep the following points in mind.

Readers Anticipate Cohesion

From the very first scene, readers will be anticipating the last. They won't know exactly what it'll look like, but they do expect that it'll be related to the story's opening *somehow,* so that when they reach the climax and look backward, everything will make sense.

They want the storylines to all tie together, for the novel to feel whole and complete.

Make sure that it does.

Confusion Is Toxic to Your Reader's Engagement

Confusion acts as a drain for all sorts of emotions: fear, worry, joy, etc. If readers don't understand what's going on, they won't be emotionally engaged. Whether you're trying to create tension or empathy or compassion or laughter—or any other reaction—problems with believability, causality, and continuity will never be in your readers' best interest. So, enter their state of mind as you shape scenes, and keep them oriented to the progression of the scenes as they play out.

Incongruous Responses Create Intrigue and Heighten Anticipation

Readers expect that a character's response to a situation will make sense based on the stimulus that prompted it.

If a character has a major reaction to a minor event, readers will assume that there's something else going on. For instance, he stubs his toe and flies into a rage. Why is he wound up so tightly? What's the deal? What's *really* bothering him?

Also, if she has only a slight reaction to something tragic, readers will think there must be a significant reason for that stifled response: She has a miscarriage and simply heads off to work like she would on any other day. What's holding her grief back? When is it going to erupt?

So, whenever characters don't act as readers would anticipate, make sure the reasons that justify those reactions are forthcoming.

We Use Readers' Expectation as Subtext to Create Surprises

Based on their understanding of literature and of this genre, readers will come to a story with certain expectations about what's going to happen, when it'll happen, and how it'll affect the outcome.

When it looks to them like they've come to a clichéd scene, they'll be thinking, *Oh, I know what's going to happen now: a chase/kiss/twist/etc.*

Identify the common or conventional scenes in your genre, and then ask yourself, "Based on readers' expectations at this moment in the story, how can I give them more than they are anticipating?"

• • •

You can also sharpen anticipation by:

• offering a possible solution for a character to resolve a problem. Readers will wonder if (or how) it will work.

- reminding readers about the consequences of failure or the dangers of facing the forces of antagonism.
- escalating the story's narrative promises.
- layering in subplots or additional storylines so there's continually growing tension.

To keep your story from sagging in the middle, don't let the three-act paradigm handcuff your narrative. Insert more acts if it will better serve the story or the readers.

Show your readers the presents under the tree. Tantalize them as the climactic moment comes closer. And then make sure that when they tear off the wrapping paper, they get an even better gift than they were hoping for.

HOW DOES ANTICIPATION RELATE TO CHARACTER DEVELOPMENT?

If your character faces the same challenge over and over, and doesn't change in the way he responds to it, he has no development, no growth, and hasn't learned anything from the last encounter. He's static. He's uninteresting.

QUICK FIX: Readers anticipate that the consequences of failure will affect the story's trajectory. They want to see change, so give it to them. Show the shifting dynamics of relationships: status, desires, needs. Reveal how the character is affected by—and is affecting—his environment. Clarify how his situation needs to change, the steps he takes toward that transformation, and the resultant effect.

FINE-TUNING MY MANUSCRIPT

- Before moments of closure within the story, have I layered in other tension, unresolved issues, or mysteries that will keep readers flipping pages because of anticipation rather than just obligation?
- What are readers thinking at this point? Who do they believe the villain is? What's at the forefront of their minds?

- Is most of my story centered around anticipation of what will come, or reflection on what did? How can I reshape the book so it focuses more on the developing storylines than on reliving ones that have already happened?
- What is my character repressing? How is he overreacting? How will I pay that off later in the story?
- Where have inaccurate promises undermined my readers' anticipation that this book will have an exciting climax?

66

PROMISES

Think about the types of things people say when they're disappointed with a story:

> "The author built up that whole hacking angle, but then it didn't go anywhere. It had nothing to do with the rest of the book!"
>
> "No kidding. And through the whole thing the hero is supposed to be this incredible boxer. I kept waiting for a fight scene, and did it come?"
>
> "Nope. And did you get why that one woman, Julia, kept talking about how she was going to run for Senate and then never did? Oh, and she left her phone in the basement, right?"
>
> "Right."
>
> "So, how did she call 9-1-1 at the climax when she was out in the woods? It didn't make sense. Nothing in that story made any sense."

All of those complaints have to do with the same issue: broken promises.

Promises come in two forms: overt and implied.

Overt promises tell readers straight-out what's coming and create either anticipation or apprehension, depending on the specific promise being made. They often originate from the characters themselves:

> "I'll meet you at ten o'clock for coffee."

> "I'm not going to rest until I catch Ben's killer."

> "His text said to be there at noon, so we still have a few minutes until we need to leave."

Implied promises, on the other hand, come from subtext, backstory, or readers' implicit understanding of story.

For example, if the killer is caught on page 250 of a 500-page novel, readers will think, *Okay, he's either going to escape or get set free on some sort of technicality*. They anticipate this, not because you told them it would happen but because they already instinctively understand narrative progression and principles.

Every time you introduce a character and a struggle (that is, another subplot), you make a promise that there'll be some sort of resolution.

A few common ways writers break promises include (1) elaborating on details that aren't significant, (2) introducing an important character halfway through the book, and (3) having someone else show up to rescue the hero at the climax.

Stories are about more than just what's happening on the page at any given moment. They're about promises, anticipation, fulfillment, and satisfaction.

As you build your story, you'll want to layer in, overlap, and intertwine the overt and implied narrative promises. This way, you'll move readers up to, and then past, moments of resolution or closure that might happen in one of the storylines.

By their very nature, promises create interest and expectation. Readers feel betrayed if you promise something that's never fulfilled. No one will notice if you fail to fulfill your foreshadowing, but everyone will notice if you fail to keep your promises.

....

The bigger the promise, the more important the payoff.

....

FIXING ISSUES WITH PROMISES

When making promises, have characters tell readers their PLANs (and use the following rhyme to remember the four points):

- **PURPOSE:** What are they hoping to do?
- **LONGING:** What do they desire?
- **APPREHENSION:** What are they afraid of?
- **NEEDS:** What do they require?

When readers know a character's PLAN, they know what to look forward to and what to worry about.

Even as you make promises, you'll want to add twists, reveals, setbacks, and subtext to keep your story from becoming too predictable.

For instance, let's say Dad is tucking his eight-year-old son, Joey, in bed:

> "I know I didn't make it to your birthday party today, Joey, but work went late. I'll play catch with you tomorrow night at five. How about that? I'll teach you how to throw a spiral like a pro."
> "Really?"
> "Yes."
> "Promise?"
> "I promise, Son. Nothing could keep me away."

And readers are thinking, *Yeah, right. That guy is never gonna show.*

If the story plays out like they expect—Dad works late (or simply forgets, or gets stuck in traffic, etc.), and Joey is left staring out the window, football in hand, feeling forlorn and forgotten—well, let's just say readers aren't going to consider that to be the most satisfying plot development. Instead, consider the different ways the scene might unfold. (Notice the word *but* in each scenario. That's where the plot pivot lies.):

- Dad makes it home, but while teaching Joey how to throw, he ends up inadvertently insulting him, leading to hurt feelings or misunderstanding.
- They play catch, but subtext makes it clear that this scene has more to do with the strain of their relationship than the football-throwing lesson.
- Dad is there, but Joey never shows—why not? Has something happened to him?

Even if readers aren't aware of it, they are constantly looking for and evaluating the significance of events, details, and characters as they move through the book.

Problems with proportionality occur when something that's promised to be a big deal turns out not to be, or someone who enters the story in the middle ends up becoming more important than he should be.

This doesn't mean he must spend a lot of time on the pages of your story, but if he does, he should matter—and if he doesn't matter, his role should match the degree of importance the rest of the story places on him.

Typically, readers won't notice if you keep your promises too soon, but they'll certainly notice if you keep them too late.

Examine your book's first and last fifty pages. Make a list of four things: (1) the overt and implied promises, (2) when they're introduced, (3) how they're fulfilled, and (4) how they've altered the protagonist's situation, perception of himself, or understanding of the world.

Identify the promises you've made (through specificity or magnitude) that aren't kept, and then recast those descriptions or scenes, add promises that are more relevant to the final payoff, or hone the ending to better fit the promises.

HOW CAN I KEEP READERS FROM GETTING BORED?

Add more promises. Readers will put up with limited action when they trust that the payoff is coming. They don't necessarily want *excitement*, they want *meaningful progression*. Curiosity and concern will keep them flipping pages more than The Constant Clamor of More Things Happening will.

QUICK FIX: To add promises, let readers know (1) what the characters want, (2) what they're planning to do, (3) why it matters, and (4) the painful consequences of failure. Think of action sequences as payoff for the promises made earlier in the story, then pinpoint what needs to happen during the action scenes to pay off those promises. Verify that the promises build toward the climax and aren't fulfilled too early.

FINE-TUNING MY MANUSCRIPT

- Do I have enough clear promises (overt or implied) to keep readers turning pages?
- What promises will readers feel aren't fulfilled at the end of my book? How will I change the ending to fix this or alter the promises made earlier so they don't point in the wrong direction?
- Does each character have the appropriate amount of narrative weight? That is, does each one receive the right amount of words, descriptions, and point-of-view sections for the role she ultimately plays in the story?
- How can I do a better job at keeping both the story's overt and implied promises?
- Am I giving readers what they want, when they want it? If not, why not?
- By the last page, do I satisfactorily answer or resolve the narrative questions my story has brought up?

67

EMOTION

Years ago, I attended an improvisation conference taught by Keith Johnstone, the innovative dramatist and acting coach. He gave us some advice about crafting comedy sketches that I'll never forget: "Don't say, 'Wouldn't it be funny if …?' Say, 'Wouldn't it be true if …?'"

That line came to mind again recently when I read a manual on improv comedy called *Truth in Comedy*. One of the authors, Kim Johnson, writes, "Deliberately trying to be funny or witty is a considerable drawback, and often leads to disaster. Honest responses are simpler and more effective. By the same token, making patterns and connections is much more important than making jokes."

Both Keith and Kim emphasized the importance of truth, and both were giving advice on *comedy*.

Apparently, one of the keys to making people laugh requires us to stop trying to be funny and start telling the truth.

When we talk about truth and honesty in comedy, we're not referring to something being true in the sense that it *happened* but true in the sense that it *happens*. The audience recognizes that this is the way things are in the world: *Yes! That's exactly what it was like to be in high school! He's captured it perfectly.*

And just as humor comes from truth, so does drama.

In a sense, they both involve pointing out truth no one has noticed yet: Comedy points out the irony and absurdity in life, drama draws attention to its tragedy and poignancy.

Wonder.

Glory.

Grief.

Joy.

When it comes right down to it, drama and comedy are both about opening people's eyes.

....

The most direct pathway to emotion is through truth.
....

FIXING EMOTION ISSUES

Of course, laughter and tears aren't the only emotions our writing will evoke, but the principle remains the same: The more that readers identify with the situation because they relate to the struggle, care about the outcome, or see the truth borne out on the page, the more they will *feel*.

The emotion—whether joy or sadness or grief or longing—will grow from the issues that characters whom readers care about are facing.

Melodrama asks readers to feel more than the scene justifies. Readers hate to feel manipulated, so don't try too hard to tug at their heartstrings. Avoid contrived situations, let characters act naturally, and then take things to their logical, painful—or hilarious—conclusion.

Invite emotional investment in your story.

If readers are going to spend a dozen hours of their lives with you and your words, they're going to want to feel something during that time. Because of this, an emotional response is earned through (1) believable storytelling, (2) reader empathy, (3) concern for the character's happiness, and (4) an honest portrayal of human nature.

Creating an emotional response in your readers often comes from restraining the emotional response of your characters. When characters hold back their feelings, it draws feelings out of your readers. Ask:

- What emotion would this event, setting, or conflict evoke in my main character?
- What would his natural reaction be?
- How might he repress that response?

Readers will typically be more apt to cry when the character holds back from crying. A single tear in a character's eye has a lot more power than a whole shower of tears, so use them judiciously. Keep characters from over-emoting. Let the character do whatever he can to avoid weeping so that when he does, it means more.

It's the same with humor: The more you have your characters cracking each other up, the less readers will laugh.

To touch on deeper emotions in your storytelling, take a cue from the two masks of theater—the one smiling, the one crying.

Both responses come from telling the truth.

HOW CAN I LEAD READERS TO AN EMOTIONAL RESPONSE?

Emotions can't be summoned up on command. If someone is depressed, just telling him to grin and bear it, or saying, "Be happy. Now!" probably isn't going to work. No one can order joy. And no one can erase pain with a word.

QUICK FIX: Emotion is earned. An emotional response is the result of identification and concern. Reader emotion is payoff for kept promises. Think of an event in your life (or in another story you've read or a film you've watched) that brought you to tears, that changed your entire outlook, that sent you spiraling into grief or depression, or that made your heart seem to finally awaken to wonder and joy. What caused that powerful response? Is there a way you can lead readers down this same path?

Now, you're not going to insert that exact event. Rather, draw from your experience to evoke that same emotion. Tap into the essence of its impact on you, identify the universal desire or human need that caused it, and weave that into your story.

FINE-TUNING MY MANUSCRIPT

- Where have I resorted to melodrama or clichés? Where am I trying to manipulate emotions rather than tell the truth?

- What emotions will this scene most likely evoke in readers who've never seen these words before? Is that what I want? How can I use this response to the readers' advantage, to entertain them more?
- How have I been too ambiguous in expressing the mood of the scene? Where can I draw it out by tapping more into the truth?
- Does my story delve into profound, universal human desires, or does it just skim along the surface? Where can I take things deeper?
- Where am I undermining reader engagement by having characters over-emote?
- Where have I tried to be funny? How can I find an honest response rather than endeavoring so hard to find a humorous one?

68

LONGING

Think about the times you've longed for things to be different for the people you care about.

A friend's marriage is in crisis, or maybe he loses his job and can't seem to find another one, no matter how hard he tries. You care about him. Your heart aches for him to be at peace, for things to be resolved—but forces beyond his control seem to be making disaster inevitable.

That sense of helplessness, that yearning, is one of the most powerful connections readers can have to the characters in our stories.

Dread and longing are two sides of the same coin.

Dread occurs when readers see where things are going and they don't want them to happen; longing results when readers see where things are going and they yearn for a happy outcome.

For instance, two lovers in your story are facing insurmountable odds toward getting together, but readers care so much for the two that they don't just *want* them to get together, they *long* for them to get together.

Or we care about the character but see that he's pursuing the wrong things, and we long for him to learn his lesson and find what he truly desires—but the whole time he's on a steep downward path that's leading him in the opposite direction.

Or readers see a man spiraling out of control, and they dread what's going to happen to him.

That longing, that dread, is what you're shooting for in fiction when you write dramatic scenes.

And the same forces that create longing and dread in real life create them in readers: concern, compassion, worry, desire for resolution, and the feeling of an impending or inevitable disaster.

....

**The deepest level of reader concern is
the longing for things to be different.**

....

FIXING ISSUES WITH LONGING

Tension, not release, will increase longing. Readers come to fiction with the desire to care about the main character, to worry about her, to feel her pain, to long for her redemption or salvation. If there's no longing, if there's no pain, then there's no tension worth caring about.

Here are six tips for generating longing in your readers:

1. **CREATE "OH, NO" MOMENTS THROUGH FORESHADOWING.**
If we know that the five-year-old girl believes she can walk on the water like Jesus did and her doll falls into the lake off the side of the boat, readers will be anxious as she watches the doll begin to slowly sink. Then, when you show them that the girl's dad is momentarily distracted and has glanced in the other direction and the girl is climbing onto the gunwale of the boat, they're going to feel dread coming on.

   A very big "Oh, no" moment brought on because, going into the scene, readers knew the little girl's beliefs.

2. **USE MULTIPLE POINTS OF VIEW TO CREATE APPREHENSION.** Let's say the detective has planted a camera in his teen daughter's room while another officer poses as a teenager to create a film to catch online predators. However, that officer was supposed to remove the camera but forgets to. Then the detective's daughter finds it. By alternating between the points of view of the father and daughter—showing her feeling of betrayal that her dad put a camera in her room, and his desperate attempts to explain the circumstances—we can create deep tension and the longing in our readers for things to get resolved.

3. **LET READERS SEE THE IMPENDING DISASTER.** Show that the train is going to run off the tracks. If you can make it believable and create a sense of helplessness or hopelessness, you'll dial up readers' dread.

4. **CAPITALIZE ON MISUNDERSTANDINGS.** He's leaving her alone after the argument because he thinks she wants space and that it'll help her relax or blow off steam, but she takes it to mean that he doesn't care about her or love her any more.

5. **SHOW THE TRAJECTORY OF HOW THE STORY IS GOING IN THE WRONG DIRECTION.** Readers watch the character making the wrong decisions or coming face to face with setbacks that drive her deeper into despair. When these two things come together—concern for a character and seeing that the direction of the story is pointing toward the demise of her dreams—deeper longing will emerge.

6. **WRITE YOURSELF TO TEARS.** It happens to me about once a year, and when it does, I know the scene has an emotional depth and resonance that will touch a lot of readers.

Create longing in your readers by helping them care more about the well-being of the character and remain on her side even when she doesn't make wise decisions—that is, her decisions continue to make sense based on the circumstances, even if they aren't healthy or beneficial for her. In other words, keep the story believable so readers feel the character is justified in making her choices and isn't stupid for doing so.

When readers see negative choices continuing to spiral the character deeper into a negative situation, they'll become more tense.

- Keep readers guessing through twists, plot turns, mysteries, secrets, and revelations.
- Keep them caring by creating characters worthy of their attention, emotion, and time.
- Keep them worrying by having danger crouch in the background or start rolling in across the horizon.

Sometimes we produce longing by letting readers know something that the character doesn't know (which is a type of irony). For example, they realize that the e-mail that could end the lovers' relationship was sent because of a misunderstanding, and now it's about to be read. Or that the apology he mailed remains unnoticed and unopened in the pile of junk mail she just threw in the trash.

Strive to do more than induce readers to care about your character. Take it deeper. Skewer them on the longing they have for those characters to achieve their unmet desires. Let that longing lead them through the story.

If readers know what the desire is, they can be worried or concerned about whether or not the character they care so much about fulfills it. If readers don't know what the desire is, they won't be worried but will search for a reason to explain his behavior. So, with each scene and with each action your character takes, ask yourself if you want readers to be wondering (out of curiosity), "Why is this happening?" or (out of concern), "Will he be alright?"

DOES LONGING REALLY MATTER?

Yes. It creates moments that readers will remember for a lifetime. Longing is almost a visceral reaction, a deep, gut-level yearning. The more readers care about the character and the more hopeless her situation appears, the more they'll long for a happy ending. Typically, more longing is produced when the main struggle centers on internal or interpersonal struggles rather than on external ones.

QUICK FIX: Show the character making natural choices and suffering devastating setbacks. If you give him a wound that readers share, they'll immediately be drawn to him. To develop concern, sharpen the desire, make the results of failure more catastrophic, or enhance the reader's compassion for, or empathy with, the character.

FINE-TUNING MY MANUSCRIPT

- Since my protagonist needs to struggle with something that readers care about, how can I invite them to invest more deeply in her pursuit? What profound human desires or dreams do my readers and my character share?
- How do the story elements work together to create longing in readers? Where have I dropped the ball and failed to do so?
- Are these characters ones that my readers will cheer for or weep over? If not, how can I add more struggles readers identify with?
- How can I reshape the scenes to deepen my readers' yearning for things to be in balance again, for there to be a happy ending?
- Have I brought dread and longing into my story? Where can I facilitate them by drawing readers more intimately into the narrative?

69

TRUST

Once, when I was reading a novel and the character started making bone-headed decisions, it occurred to me that there's a simple way to test whether I trust an author.

If the protagonist acts in an unbelievable manner and I get mad at her: "No! Don't go into that building! Don't leave your son in the car!" then I trust the writer.

However, if I get mad at the author: "No, that would never happen. She would never leave her son in there. I don't buy it," then I don't trust him.

Same scene. Same choice for the character.

Completely opposite reader response.

All because of trust.

• • •

Trust can overcome a multitude of sins. When readers feel like they're in the hands of a confident, competent storyteller, they'll bear with all sorts of seeming plot incongruities because they know you'll wrap up the storylines in the end.

However, as soon as they stop trusting you as their guide through the story, those plot flaws will become more and more evident and irritating—like a sliver, getting driven deeper and deeper into their skin.

**It takes only one word to lose readers' trust,
and often even five hundred pages won't be
enough to earn it back.**

FIXING TRUST ISSUES

Trust is interwoven with many of the other principles in this book. As you read through the following chart, relate the solutions with the information included in previous chapters.

PROBLEM	SOLUTION
Broken promises	Track your promises regarding each character, and then make sure they're all fulfilled.
A character acts in an unbelievable way	Verify that every response, every choice, makes contextual sense and reveals what that character is truly like. Making an obvious mistake early in your book is the fastest way to lose your readers' trust.
Things happen for no reason	Work on causality. Move the story along, cause to effect, both sentence by sentence and scene by scene. Focus on the logic of the scene progression and on building a world of inevitability.
Too predictable	Think of ways to pivot the plot, reveal insights, and propel the story forward. Keep your promises in ways readers don't expect.
Including scenes that have nothing to do with the story	Some scenes contribute through their entertainment value (they're so hilarious or so gripping that readers will forgive you for not making them necessary); most contribute through their vital integration with the plot. Cut every scene that doesn't enrich the story.
Introducing storylines that go nowhere	Confirm that every storyline (that is, subplot) has its own resolution.
Emphasizing a struggle that you don't resolve	Even if a storyline is going to carry over to your next book, it needs to be satisfactorily dealt with in this one or readers will get annoyed.

Mood is off	Verify that every word upholds the atmosphere (the mood, tone, and voice) of the scene. Cut or recast those that don't.
De-escalation	Tighten the tension. Remove unnecessary action. Promise more peril, and then deliver.
Sloppy fact-checking	Be attentive to details, especially the expectations readers have for fiction in this genre. They'll be unforgiving if you make mistakes in their field of expertise.
Poor editing	Sharpen your grammar and punctuation skills, cut unnecessary words, have another person edit the manuscript to locate mistakes you may have missed.

Sometimes, scenes that appear to be dead-ends are false leads or red herrings. They foreshadow important events that come up later, or they set the stage for future conflicts—but remember, readers won't know any of that when they're reading those scenes. They need to trust that you're not wasting their time.

If readers become too distracted, confused by too many characters, or bored by a languid storyline, they'll put your book aside.

Readers today are narratively astute and are used to storylines in television shows that span dozens, if not hundreds, of hours. If your readers trust you, they'll stick with you. Then, when the big narrative reveals come, they'll go back and mentally fill in the things they didn't understand earlier. Emmy award–winning screenwriter John Tinker refers to this as "backfilling."

When readers trust an author, they'll keep telling themselves, "Well, he's a good writer, so I know this is going somewhere. I just don't know where yet." The more readers trust you, the more willing they'll be to backfill.

Earn their trust. Keep their trust. Tell stories in ways that invite engagement, and then make it all worthwhile.

HOW IMPORTANT IS TRUST?

As soon as readers stop trusting you, the jig is up. If they continue reading, it'll be in the hope that things turn around, but most likely they won't stick with the book all the way to the end. Even if readers *think* you've broken a promise, they'll lose trust. "But," you might say, "I resolve that plot thread on page 300 when you find out the pro football player is really a woman." Well, that won't matter if readers never make it that far because they've stopped trusting you.

QUICK FIX: Trust is engendered when we, as storytellers, keep our promises. When you portray something as significant, make sure that it is. Promise struggles, desire, and transformation. Then deliver.

FINE-TUNING MY MANUSCRIPT

- Have I developed readers' trust enough so that when things don't go as they expect, they'll continue reading, knowing that a satisfying resolution is coming?
- Where am I undermining trust in what I include—or in what I don't?
- How can I show more confidence in the story by writing with measured assurance and authenticity?
- Where have I strayed into any of the eleven classic trust-destroying areas listed in the chart?
- How much does the story depend on backfilling? How is it entertaining as it stands already? Are there any changes that I need to make?
- How can I do a better job of earning trust early by keeping promises in the first fifty pages?

70

EMPATHY

Years ago I heard a story about a little girl who was late getting home. When her mother asked why she was late, she replied, "There was a boy on the beach who fell down, and he was crying."

"So, did you stop to help him up?"

"No," the girl said. "I stopped to help him cry."

• • •

Empathy occurs when readers feel the pain, grasp the questions, or relate to the wounds of the character, vicariously, through the story.

You'll often hear writing instructors claim that readers need to have empathy for the protagonist. While that's somewhat debatable (after all, I don't have a lot of empathy for a super spy, yet I enjoy spy stories), in most genres, reader empathy does strengthen your story—especially when the character is facing meaningful internal or inter-personal struggles.

To evaluate whether you have empathy with someone, ask the following questions:

- Can I see this event from the perspective of the person/character experiencing it?
- Do I feel the same things that this person/character is feeling?
- Can I identify with her emotions?

....

Empathy is caring enough about someone to hurt, or rejoice, with him.

....

FIXING EMPATHY ISSUES

For readers to care about a story, they must care about the main character.

Decide which of these responses you want from readers:

- **SYMPATHY:** "I feel sorry for you."
- **EMPATHY:** "I feel sorry with you."
- **ANTIPATHY:** "I feel angry at you."

Readers will only identify with the person who has the problem, not the person with all the answers. So, don't build your story around the necessity of readers identifying with the answer-giver. Instead, draw them into the world of the problem-haver:

- He's trying to make his marriage work, but it's slipping away.
- She's trying to be a better mom, but her son resents the time she spends at work.
- He's dealing with shame over his porn addiction.
- She's sacrificing her time to tutor inner-city teens but isn't seeing any tangible results.

Typically, when readers are clued in to a character's struggles, they'll empathize when they see him wrestling with doing the right thing. You can use this technique to create more empathy for your protagonist, and even for your antagonist.

To develop empathy, consider tapping into the inherent emotion contained in acts of kindness:

- **TO THE PLANET:** He plants one tree every weekend, talks to his houseplants, grows a vegetable garden.
- **TO AN ANIMAL:** He brings in a stray cat or dog and cares for it.
- **TO A PERSON WHO'LL NEVER KNOW ABOUT IT:** He anonymously donates to the shelter for battered women—and makes sure the contributions remain anonymous.

- **TO A PERSON WHO CAN'T PAY HIM BACK:** He volunteers at the soup kitchen to help those who can't return the favor.

Identify an emotional state: that unsettling sense that you might have hurt a friend's feelings in a way that can't be fixed, being left out of the "in" group, wondering if there's "more to life than this," feeling alone in a world filled with billions of souls, finding yourself holding a grudge even though you know it's not helping either of you heal, or secretly celebrating someone else's misfortune even though you don't want to.

Now, consider what led to that emotional state. Where does your character or your reader's life parallel those experiences?

Prod at yourself. Where are you sore? Where are you tender? What wounds are still raw and fresh? Grief over the death of a friend, a marriage, a dream? Shame from the secrets you continue to keep hidden? Loss of confidence in that one thing you held so dear?

Look there, under the surface—not necessarily for something you can define, but rather for something you can dip into.

Storytellers make a living trafficking pain. If you don't want to feel the deep yearning of a character facing an impossible situation, you might be better off becoming a furniture salesperson or an accountant instead of a novelist.

HOW CAN I CREATE MORE READER EMPATHY?

The better you're able to pinpoint specific emotional responses that you have, the more you'll be able to tap into them to write scenes that create empathy with your readers.

QUICK FIX: When a character feels self-conscious (too old, too skinny, too ugly because of that scar or zit or rash, etc.) readers quickly empathize with her. Give your character (1) a struggle readers have, (2) a cause they believe in, (3) a wound they share, or (4) a mission or objective they value.

FINE-TUNING MY MANUSCRIPT

- Is my main character empathetic in the sense that readers will be concerned about what happens to her and whether she gets what she wants?
- Will they truly invest in this story? If not, how can I give her an emotional or psychological wound my readers will share?
- Who am I asking readers to identify with? How can I write this scene more honestly and empathetically?
- Have I developed the appropriate amount of reader sympathy and/or empathy for the protagonist? Will readers be able to see through his eyes, feel his emotions, and relate to his struggle?
- Where can I draw from my own heartaches, grief, or regret as I show the desires of this character? How can I avoid emotional manipulation but instead draw readers into her struggle through personal identification?

71

TRUTH

The way that you portray virtue and vice in your story will end up making a statement about life and morality:

1. Redemption is not necessary.
2. Redemption is necessary but not available.
3. Redemption is necessary and available.

Let's say your story deals with incest.

Does the book take the viewpoint that redemption isn't necessary for those who rape their children? That cultures differ about this issue, and that incest has been accepted at certain places and at certain times in the past, so there's really nothing wrong with it? In that case, your story would be saying that redemption is not necessary.

Or do you show the consequences of incest and write from the perspective that it's so disastrous that whoever engages in it has committed a crime that he cannot be forgiven for? Then your story would be acknowledging that we hurt others by our actions but also would be claiming that there's nothing that can be done about that guilt. At least in the case of incest, the book would be asserting that redemption is necessary but not available.

Or does your story come from the perspective that incest is devastating and deserves to be punished but that forgiveness is possible? If so, you're stating that redemption is necessary and also available. The story can end with hope through forgiveness, justice, penance, etc.

....

**Truth, beauty, tragedy, redemption—these are
four hallmarks of powerful storytelling.**

....

FIXING TRUTH ISSUES

Don't be afraid to celebrate virtue.

You don't have to be an ethicist to know what's virtuous and what isn't. You just have to be a human being.

So, where do you start?

Here are three universal virtues you can explore: courage, respect, and responsibility. Or take a cue from three prominent philosophers:

- In *Nicomachean Ethics*, Aristotle listed virtues such as temperance, patience, truthfulness, wittiness, modesty, and righteous indignation.
- In *Six Great Ideas*, Mortimer J. Adler lists truth, goodness, beauty, liberty, equality, and justice.
- In *Back to Virtue*, Peter Kreeft lists the Four Cardinal Virtues as justice, courage, wisdom, moderation, and the Three Theological Virtues as faith, hope, and love.

More than half of the world's population believes that the Hebrew Old Testament was inspired by God. And, when it comes to living a virtuous life, three things top the Old Testament's list: justice, mercy, and humility: "What is good; and what doth the Lord require of thee, but to do justly, and to love mercy, and to walk humbly with thy God?" (Micah 6:8).

For thousands of years, Christians have acknowledged the "Fruit of the Spirit" as evidence of God's work in someone's life: love, joy, peace, patience, kindness, goodness, faithfulness, gentleness, and self-control. (These are from Paul's letter to the Galatians 5:22-23.)

On the other end of the spectrum, the Seven Deadly Sins are vices you'll likely want to avoid celebrating in your story: avarice (greed), envy, anger, sloth, lust, gluttony, and pride.

Some people might say that the most profound ideas must be able to be stated simply, but simplicity isn't the measure of a great idea—or even a true one. Truth can be complex and isn't always as pithy as we would like it to be.

Novels can express complex, even paradoxical, truths in a complicated world. All too often people who work from a theme statement end up writing simplistic stories that portray only caricatures of the truth, such as, "Be nice."

Go deeper: When shouldn't you be nice? What trumps being nice? When have you been thankful that someone wasn't nice to you?

Stories that ultimately matter help readers see the world as it truly is, neither through the lens of wishful thinking nor through the lens of nihilism. They address the deep and meaningful issues of life: dreams, mystery, tragedy, death, significance, hope.

Redemption always comes with a price. How much it costs will make a statement to readers about how much it's worth: If it's cheap, it means little. If it's costly, it means much.

How deeply will you burrow into the truth about human nature? Only far enough to make readers experience the shallow glow of veneer happiness? Or deep enough to make them drop to their knees in awe?

Stop telling timid, tepid stories.

Let your novel ring with truth.

Franz Kafka said, "A book must be an ice-axe to break the seas frozen in our souls."

Alright then. Go ahead.

Pick up your axe.

WHY DO MORAL ISSUES MATTER?

Because life either does matter or it doesn't—and if it doesn't, then there's not much of a reason for you to spend a thousand hours on your story. Deep inside the soul of humanity, at the core of our pain, our stories of hope and loss all intersect. We all understand and yearn for stories of love and restoration and redemption. That's how we know we're human.

QUICK FIX: Sometimes it's helpful to think about the things that might be keeping you from probing into the places of raw, real honesty. In what ways are you holding your story or your prose back? Why? What are you afraid of? Write a paragraph

about a time when you felt hopeless. Allow yourself to feel dis-
comfort. Explore it. Become aware of it.

Now, write about a time when you felt triumphant and confident. Use both paragraphs as fodder for the emotional core of
your story.

FINE-TUNING MY MANUSCRIPT

- Do I show the consequences of choices, the effect of tragedy and loss, or do I gloss over those things in the service of being avant-garde?
- Effective stories show us our own, and our culture's, blind spots rather than make them larger. What does my novel do? Overall, does the story reinforce societal clichés, or does it explore and expose truth instead?
- Does my story offer readers a chance to ask meaningful questions? Does it honestly explore the human condition or attempt to proselytize people to my point of view? What's my intent behind this story?
- What moral impressions are left at the end of this story? How will that affect readers? What virtues were held up as ideal and worth pursuing?
- Does the story ultimately come from the perspective that redemption isn't necessary, that it isn't available, or that it is both necessary and available? Is that what I want? If not, how do I need to reorient my story (or myself)?

PART V
STYLE AND FINESSE

72

RECEPTIVITY

On February 2, 2014, *The Sunday Times* related an interview with J.K. Rowling in which she admitted that she wrote the Hermione and Ron relationship as a form of wish fulfillment.

"That's how it was conceived, really," she said. "For reasons that have very little to do with literature and far more to do with me clinging to the plot as I first imagined it, Hermione ended up with Ron. … It was a choice I made for very personal reasons, not for reasons of credibility."

When she clung to her preconceived plot idea, it led her away from, not toward, credibility.

Often, when authors work from an outline, the choices that characters make end up being dictated not by the context of the scene— what makes sense in that moment—but from an authorial preconception of where things ought to go.

It's just so tempting to default to our ideas of what "should" happen and to cling to those initial concepts—even when the story is straining at its reins to go in another direction altogether.

....

Don't ask, "What should this character do?" but "What would this character do if I got out of the way?"

....

FIXING RECEPTIVITY ISSUES

While teaching at a writing conference in Anchorage, Alaska, I met a woman who was a painter. After hearing me share how important it is to be responsive to a story as it emerges and not to follow an outline, she told me that in her life she'd painted one thousand paintings.

"And before I started each of them," she said, "I knew what it was going to look like."

"Okay." I thought she was going to contradict what I'd just taught, but then she went on: "But when I was done, not a single one of them looked like I'd pictured."

And so it is with writing. This is the creative process. It involves discovery and adaptation, exploration and response. Your story will look different at the end than what you had in mind when you started it—or you're quite possibly not telling the right story.

Lots of people will offer you templates, outlines, plot formulas: "At 22 percent of the way into the book, introduce subplot B. And be sure to write a thousand words a day! So, if the book is 85,000 words long, then you'll finish it in eighty-five days. Voilà. You're done."

Don't listen to any of that nonsense. The logic of the story will determine the flow, when the subplots should be initiated, the number of words you can write each day, the number of drafts you'll have to go through, and so on.

Throughout the process of writing, be receptive to new ideas, new directions, twists, and turns.

Focus on Story, Not Plot

As we've reviewed elsewhere, the character's pursuit, driven by desire, escalates as he faces mounting setbacks on the way to a satisfying climax.

So, look carefully at the actions your character takes in pursuit of his unmet desire. Let every choice in every scene be shaped by that pursuit, not by your preconception of what should happen "to get to the next plot point."

You won't know what impact a scene will have on a character, or how much time it'll take him to process the setbacks he just encountered, until you read that scene in context. Trust the context over your outline every time.

Sketch out Obligatory Scenes

Sometimes when you're writing, you won't know exactly what needs to happen, but you can still work on the scene and be responsive to the direction it's heading.

When I was writing my novel *Fury*, I wasn't sure exactly what the antagonist wanted or how he was going to pursue it. I did know he was a chronobiologist researching ways organisms process the passage of time. A scene in the first draft occurred while he was in his laboratory:

> That's where he used the electrodes to stimulate different parts of the brain that processed memory in his subjects. The Defense Department had been secretly experimenting for years to find ways to alter, implant, or erase people's memories.
>
> Things had come a long way in the last decade.
>
> He crossed through the room to the something to get something to take an action that leads to him accomplishing his goal.

Yeah, that's actually what I typed in. I had no idea what the details or intentions would be, but I trusted the process and moved on, knowing that the story would reveal itself as I worked on it.

Later, as I discovered his agenda and how he was trying to accomplish it, I went back to fill in what needed to happen in that scene—but I didn't learn those details until I'd fleshed out more of the story.

This is the organic process of crafting stories rather than plotting them out.

It's thrilling, intriguing, freeing, and, for most writers I talk to, a lot more enjoyable than working under the burden of an outline.

Organic writing involves (1) trusting your instincts over your road map, (2) going where the story is leading you, (3) and being willing to follow characters wherever believability takes them.

Don't concern yourself with how many drafts your book takes or how many words a day you need to write.

Think about excellence.

Put your effort there.

Don't end up in a place where you have to apologize to your fans that you led a story to a certain conclusion because, for personal reasons, you clung to your plot rather than writing in the service of credibility.

IF I DON'T OUTLINE, HOW WILL I KNOW WHAT TO WRITE?

If you understand the narrative forces that direct and influence your story (i.e., the ones we've been examining in this book), you won't have to follow formulas and outlines.

QUICK FIX: Ask: "What would this character naturally do?" "How could I include a twist?" and "How can I make things worse?" With these questions, you'll tap into some of the most essential narrative forces: believability, causality, twists, and escalation. Almost every plot problem can be fixed and every scene improved by letting those three questions impact how the story plays out.

FINE-TUNING MY MANUSCRIPT

- Have I responded to the forces that press in on a story to form it, or have I tried to place a preordained agenda or plot outline on the story?
- How receptive have I been to the way that the painting is progressing? Am I imposing or responding?
- Where do I need to step out of the way and let the characters have more space, more freedom, more of a say in where the story goes?
- Has credibility or believability suffered because of my commitment to a plot idea I just won't let go of? What will I do about that?
- Where can I allow the narrative forces of believability, causality, twists, and escalation to make more of an impact on my scene progression?

73

CONTEXT

You're a movie star.

Over the course of the past twelve months you've been filming the next big blockbuster. But the director doesn't always film scenes in order, and one day she tells you that she needs to reshoot one you did last fall.

You return to the set. Makeup and wardrobe do an incredible job, and you look exactly as you did during the first shoot.

What's going through your mind as you rehearse your lines and prepare to do the scene?

You're probably not thinking about the end of the movie or where everything is heading, but rather you'll be focusing on getting this scene right. I'm guessing you'll be asking questions that relate to three areas:

- **CONTEXT:** What was my character just doing? How will that affect his choices, attitude, and demeanor in this scene?
- **INTENTION:** Why is he here, in this scene, right now? What is he hoping to accomplish?
- **EMOTION:** How does he feel about the other characters with him right now? What's going through his mind?

To play the scene well, you'll have to step back in time, imagine yourself in that situation with that scene-specific set of goals, emotions, and desires.

Well, as an author, this is what you'll be doing as you write and edit your book.

But you won't just need to do it with one character or one scene. You'll do it with every character, in every situation, in every scene, throughout the entire novel.

....

**The secret to what comes next lies in
the promises that come before.**

....

FIXING CONTEXT ISSUES

Without taking context into consideration, you won't have the right state of mind for your character, and without that, the believability and continuity will be off.

Often, if something doesn't feel quite right on a page, it's because something other than context is dictating what you wrote. The more of the story's context you're able to consider as you edit a scene, the better it's going to be.

There've been times with some of my longer books when I've spent the first twelve hours of my writing day reviewing the story to get the context in mind for the new scene that I'm working on.

Think about that character in that scene and ask, "Given what just happened, what would she be thinking? What would her first response be? Feeling as she does, how would she act? What's she planning? What is she concerned with? If she could tell me anything right now, in this moment, what would it be?"

When in doubt, listen to the context to tell you the next word.

Listen carefully.

It's there, and the story wants to tell it to you.

But you'll have to be attentive to hear it.

Edit with the Big Picture in Mind

If you gave any scene from any of my published novels to a writer's critique group and told them to have at it, I'm sure they would be able to find plenty "wrong" with it:

"Steven, I don't understand who this character is."

"Oh, he was introduced a couple hundred pages ago. He's the main bad guy."

"I can't really picture him."

"I never describe him—at least not what he looks like. It's still a secret who he is. It'll only be revealed in the twist at the end."

"Oh. I think you need more details for this setting. I mean, is it night? Day? When?"

"It's night. The whole—"

"Well, you need to describe it better."

"I did when they first got there in the previous chapter, but as I was saying, the whole book takes place over the course of one night, so—"

"The pace is too slow."

"They're regrouping after one of the major chase scenes."

"None of this is working for me. I'm afraid this book will never see its day in print."

To properly analyze or understand any scene, you'll need to read it in context. Print out your book. Read it from the beginning. Analyze every scene. The context is vital to making each one of them work.

Study the End to Find the Beginning

You won't be able to tell what's vital to the story until you've finished telling it.

Why?

Because only then will you be able to see where you've added too much detail, or where you haven't included enough; where you've made promises the story doesn't keep; and where you've failed to promise pivotal events that the story relies on.

Make the Hard Decisions

Every word is a decision. Every punctuation mark is a decision—and this is the case with every draft you go through. Two. Five. Fifty. A novel is a million decisions waiting to be made, and every one of them is interrelated to and interdependent on the others.

Every word influences the next.

Every choice is determined by the rest.

If you don't want to make decisions, don't become a novelist.

Be Wary of Good Ideas

Ideas love to flirt with writers. They try to convince us that they're the best ideas we've had in years (maybe that anyone has ever had!). They'll want us to commit to them, and then they'll want to move in with us. Those are usually the ideas you'll want to avoid.

Watch out for those clever scenes, those phrases that sparkle, those words that shine. Don't get enamored of them. They'll try to insert themselves into your book, even if the context doesn't quite work.

Continually Ask Where You're Going and How It Relates to Where You've Been

Enter your character's state of mind—what he would naturally be anticipating, worrying about, reflecting on, hoping for, or questioning at this moment in the story, based on every moment that has preceded it.

Then ask the same questions in regard to your readers. For every scene you write, consider how their expectations about the story affect their current participation in the story.

So, to summarize:

- Question your assumptions. Pay attention to the context. Sometimes what you thought was the core of your story needs to get jettisoned because it was actually only the seed of the real story.
- Everything in your story is nestled in context. Every choice. Every emotion. Every action.
- You can't write a scene in isolation, stick it in your story, and expect that it'll have the right pace, texture, and tone.
- Context will lead you closer to the heart of the scene and reveal the story's truest path.

HOW DOES CONTEXT AFFECT CONTENT?

Context affects everything. Every word of your story that isn't contextually appropriate will become a snag for your readers.

QUICK FIX: When you're editing your book, review at least the preceding fifty pages before working on a new scene. Evaluate every character's state of mind as he enters that scene. What is he thinking, feeling, dwelling on—*based on what he just experienced*? How will that affect his choices and responses? Avoid having a critique group analyze isolated scenes. Without considering the broader context, their advice will almost always lead you in the wrong direction.

FINE-TUNING MY MANUSCRIPT

- Where have I failed to let context influence the direction of a scene, a line of dialogue, or a character's thoughts?
- Looking back at what I've written over the past few months, how has the pace or voice of the book changed? What will I do about that?
- What's holding me back from making the necessary changes to my manuscript, based on the context of each scene?
- Considering what's on my character's mind right now, in this scene, how would she respond? Is that what I show her doing?
- What scenes have I edited out of context? In what ways will that be evident to readers? What changes do I need to make?

74

CONTINUITY

A few years ago I watched a movie that involved a cross-country road trip from Texas to New York City.

As the characters drive along, the filmmakers showed exit signs off the highway to indicate their progress. The road trippers passed the exit to Johnson City, Tennessee, where I live, and then they passed the exit to Knoxville.

Except Knoxville is actually *west* of Johnson City. The actors were heading in the wrong direction—toward Texas rather than away from it.

Whoever edited the film must have just pieced together the footage without bothering to look at a map to verify that the characters were driving past the exits in the correct order.

I don't remember the name of the movie.

I don't remember any of the characters or anything else from the plot.

All I remember is that mistake.

> **Your book is only as good as the mistakes it doesn't make.**

FIXING CONTINUITY ISSUES

Readers will remember your mistakes longer than they'll remember your plot.

When your story has continuity, everything that happens does so for a reason, and all of those meaningful moments flow seamlessly together to portray the characters' pursuits. But when you make a glaring error, it'll stick out like a sore thumb.

I've made my own fair share of them.

In one of my book series, a character ended up changing names from one book to the next. (Don't even ask me how that happened.) Another character actually got younger by about a decade when I forgot to fact-check his age. Once, during a chase scene, I had a character punch the gas pedal to the floor, and then a few lines later, he hit the gas. I'm not sure if his foot went through the car's floor at that point or not.

Even though those mistakes happened over the course of thirteen novels and about 1.5 million words, I still remember them.

In some books I've read, characters suddenly have a different hair color from earlier in the story or magically grow enough arms to be able to carry groceries, talk on the phone, take their son's hand, and open the door to the house all at the same time.

To avoid these gaffes in your own story, pay particular attention to objects, people, and emotional states.

Objects

Readers get distracted when characters pick up objects and never put them down again, answer the phone but never hang it up, pull out their gun but never holster it again, and so on.

Have your characters put stuff away. If a character is holding something, readers will assume he's still holding it until he sets it down.

People

Keep track of your character's physical characteristics, quirks, name, and so on, in whatever way works for you: charts, graphs, lists … it really doesn't matter. Just keep the characters differentiated and consistent, and avoid similarly spelled or similar-sounding names.

Also, manage who's onstage. If you bring a character into a scene, let her contribute to it. If she just appears, doesn't say anything, and then disappears, readers will wonder what happened to her and why she was there in the first place.

If she's irrelevant, she doesn't belong.

Keep those characters who are integral to the scene involved, and get those who aren't off the stage.

Emotion

Typically, since characters are in scenes with other characters with whom they have dynamic, volatile, and sometimes adversarial relationships (and are in settings they all have a specific attitude toward), there'll be more than one emotion present in the scene.

Rather than trying to define how your protagonist feels, identify how he would naturally respond, even if you can't precisely quantify things: *I'd say his primary emotion is fear, at 60 percent, but he's also feeling 20 percent disgusted and 20 percent intrigued.* Focus instead on encapsulating a response that honestly portrays those varied emotions, a response that emerges naturally and contiguously from the context.

• • •

During your editing read-throughs, fact-check everything, make sure the chapter numbers are correct, and verify:

- the spelling of all names and locations
- physical attributes of each character
- what the character is holding at different times and what he does with those objects when he's done with them
- the progression of events
- inconsistencies, including references to the wrong person (especially in dialogue)

Don't pass the wrong exit ramp at the wrong time.

And don't let continuity errors become what readers remember most about your book.

ARE THERE ANY CONTINUITY ERRORS THAT AREN'T A BIG DEAL?

Whenever something distracts readers, it's a big deal. Even if you're writing a mind-bending story that twists back and forth through time, you'll need to be aware of continuity issues (perhaps even more so, since readers will be paying closer attention to the progression, timing, and how the storylines are related). Remove or fix anything that would come between your readers and the story.

QUICK FIX: Follow the characters as they move through the book, tracking what they hold, where they stand, and where they walk. Pay particular attention to continuity during chase scenes and action sequences to avoid repetitive events.

FINE-TUNING MY MANUSCRIPT

- Does my story have continuity problems or glitches in timing that will throw readers off? If so, how can I alter what has happened in the previous pages or what happens in the following ones to fix them?
- Have I forgotten to have characters complete actions, put things down or away, etc.?
- Where does the progression from scene to scene not make sense?
- Are the names, dates, times, and descriptions of people and places consistent throughout the story?
- If I've used nicknames for any of the characters, have I made it clear who they are and locked in that nickname early enough so readers aren't confused?

75

UNOBTRUSIVENESS

Readers come to fiction to be impressed by the author's vocabulary.

They want to be converted to his political perspective.

They hope he'll beat them over the head with his social agenda.

They love to see him get on his soapbox.

Or maybe they don't.

Maybe they come to our books to be entertained, but they get all that other stuff instead.

• • •

People read novels so they can feel tension, danger, longing, heartache, grief—and, paradoxically, feel safe at the same time.

Readers want believable stories that touch them on a deep emotional level, that are honest explorations of the human condition. Sometimes they want to laugh. Sometimes cry. Sometimes bite their fingernails with apprehension. Sometimes cringe.

Most of the time, though, more than anything else they want to be swept away: perhaps through a narrative puzzle, or an adrenaline rush, or an escape to a magical, fantastical world.

Your job: to become invisible and let that happen.

....

**Don't intrude on your readers' experience.
Their agenda, not yours, is what matters—
and their agenda centers on being entertained.**

....

FIXING OBTRUSIVENESS ISSUES

You'll tell yourself all sorts of things to try to justify including material that you know doesn't fit:

- You plotted out the book, and you're defaulting to your outline rather than responding to the characters' desires and choices.
- You wrote up a history of this character (just like the seminar teacher at that last writers conference told you to do), and you want to include every last detail.
- You have a personal agenda that's more important to you than entertaining your readers.
- You found out all that stuff about eighteenth-century buttons in France, and you're not about to let it "go to waste."
- You're passionate about something, and you want to share your passion.
- You are a cop/surgeon/scientist/carpenter/interior decorator, and you're going to make sure every reader realizes how much you know about that topic.
- You're trying to convince readers of something, and rather than write a nonfiction book, you decided to dress your argument up as a story and pass it off as a novel.

Authenticity doesn't require you to be eloquent or to have an extensive vocabulary or even to come up with the world's greatest plot twists. It simply calls for you to write genuine prose that readers want to be a part of.

Eloquence is invisible.

Remember, you're here to entertain readers, not to make a point, show how clever you are, or break the rules for the sake of being "literary" or "innovative."

You'll be tempted to find a way to use that witty phrase, that stirring description, that interesting but insignificant detail that you dug up over your long hours of research, even though you know it doesn't quite fit. Yet you keep trying to make it fit. Twisting and turning the prose around to get it in there.

Let it go. Stop.

Let your goal be telling a story in a way that moves people to the place where they can encounter truth. If you want to get something off your chest, write a blog.

If you want to spread a message, send a tweet.

If you want people to know how great you are, post a selfie.

If you want to open the gates of emotion and set the truth free, write a novel.

HOW CAN I AVOID INTRUDING ON THE STORY?

Identify and recast sections of your manuscript where you go into more detail than necessary or where your desire to take a stand regarding a social or political agenda overshadows what will benefit your readers. Usually, these are issues you're the most passionate about or have spent the most time developing or researching. However, the more compelling your urge to include something, the more leery you should be about doing so.

QUICK FIX: Stop trying to impress readers, educate them, or convince them of something. Don't try to prove your thesis or promote a certain social agenda. Stop drawing attention to yourself. Get out of the way.

FINE-TUNING MY MANUSCRIPT

- Do I have an agenda with this story, beyond exploring truth in an emotionally resonant, entertaining way? How can I reshape the story so that it's dilemma driven rather than didactic?
- Will readers be able to tell what religious, moral, or political views I hold? Is that what I want?
- Am I writing this story to get people to agree with me about something? If so, how will that affect readers who *don't* agree?

- Why have I chosen this topic, this scene, this word? Where have I overloaded readers with research, unnecessary detail, or irrelevant information about a character's history?
- At what moment will readers be tempted to put my book down? What scenes might drive them out of the story? Are those necessary, or not? What will I do about that?

76

TEXTURE

You're a composer, and you decide to change a note in the middle of your symphony.

What will happen to the notes surrounding it?

Well, they'll quite obviously be impacted as well.

If you leave them as is, that part of the symphony will likely sound off-key.

In a novel, just as in a musical composition, one change affects everything around it.

Every word is inextricably tied to the rest of the story. Remove one of them, change a *said* to a *told*, and the effect will ripple across the page, the chapter, the story as a whole.

If you make a change and it doesn't cause any other changes, you may not be looking closely enough at your novel.

Every word affects the texture of the story.

FIXING TEXTURE ISSUES

Review the chapters on atmosphere, details, and description—all of those principles apply as you edit your story and finalize its texture, scene by scene, word by word.

Be Cognizant of the Lighting

Readers need to be able to see what's happening.

If a scene happens in the dark, perhaps mention the moonlight seeping through the window, the night-light in the hallway, or the illuminated glow of the digital clock on the microwave. Any time the lighting isn't implied by the setting, give readers something specific so they know how to visualize the scene.

Select the Right Word

Carefully consider word choice and connotation.

Is he "lean" or "gaunt-faced"? Does she "weep" or "cry"? Does he "judge" the situation or "evaluate" it?

It matters.

Keep in mind the subtlety of every word's meaning.

For example, even the prepositions *to* and *toward* have different meanings and significantly affect the flow of a story.

- "I walked to the store," indicates an action that was initiated and then completed. The next sentence or scene would occur inside the store.
- "I walked toward the store," indicates an action that was initiated and is still in progress. The next sentence or scene would occur while the character is en route.

Keep the Voice Consistent

You've worked hard to unearth an authentic voice for this story, so don't shatter it with one poorly rendered scene or ill-chosen word. Keep the voice sharp. Keep it alive. And stay in the viewpoint you've established for this section of the story.

Choose Strong Verbs

Avoid starting a sentence (rather than a question) with *what, where, when, why,* or *how.*

For example, "What we're going to do is provide free meals." "Where we're going to go is the beach." "When we're going to have our meeting is after lunch." If you find instances of these, recast them: "We'll provide free meals," "We're going to go to the beach," or "Let's meet after lunch."

Also, search for *is to*, *was to*, *is that*, *was that*, *is because*, and *was because*. If you find these phrases, you can probably improve the sentence. For instance, "The problem that we have here is that there aren't enough jobs." Change to "There aren't enough jobs," or "We don't have enough jobs. That's a problem."

Avoid sentences that start with *all* or *one*. When you use them, you force yourself to use a weak verb. For instance, "All you have to do is eat your supper." Change to "Eat your supper." Or "One thing you have to do is count your blessings." Change to "Count your blessings." Weed out all those instances of *to do is*.

Remove Echoes

A callback is an idea or insight restated for effect. An echo is an inadvertent repetition of a word or phrase. Remove echoes, and judiciously use callbacks for humor and during moments of revelation.

Often, I find echoes in sections of dialogue where the author is trying to find something for the characters to do while they're talking. They might sit down or stand, lean forward or backward in a chair, walk across the room toward the window, and so on. In many cases, the author inadvertently has the character repeat the action a few lines down.

Most writers have common words or phrases that they subconsciously default to when crafting scenes. Train your eye to find yours. Keep a list, then search your manuscript for them and recast the sentence to eliminate them.

Avoid the following echoes:

- **DIALOGUE:** Starting too many sentences with the words *so*, *then*, *well*, *okay*, *alright*, *listen*, *of course*, or *I mean*. In real life, we use these words, so you might want to include them sparingly, but they often get overused. In the service of brevity, drop most of them.
- **CELL PHONES:** Always having people "pull out" or "scroll across" or "hang up" their phones.
- **ACTIONS:** Having characters "turn," "spin," "whip around," "approach," or "arrive."

- **QUESTIONS:** Don't overuse "What are you doing?" or "What do you want?"
- **ADVERBS:** Check for overuse of *actually, quickly, suddenly, finally,* and *very.*
- **VIEWPOINT:** Depending on the point of view you're writing from, you'll likely start too many paragraphs with *I, He,* or *She,* in your first draft. Look for ways to vary your sentence structure.

Cut the Over-Emoting

Often, aspiring writers focus too much on the minutia of body language.

Eyes widen and narrow and snap open. Hands twitch and quiver. People smile and giggle and gasp and chortle, as tears run down their cheeks.

And for some reason, unpublished authors seem to be in love with eyebrows. They endlessly arch and dive and furrow. They peak and shoot upward. Limit yourself to one eyebrow reference every 100,000 words. That's all I'm going to give you.

For the most part you can trust the dialogue and context to reveal facial expressions.

Generally, the more your characters emote, the less your readers feel. In most novels, people smile too much, which makes them seem more like caricatures and lowers their status. Instead, to maintain the tension, let the characters hold back from emoting and let their words and actions convey their emotions.

Eliminate Sensory Words

Most of the time you can drop descriptions of how a character uses his five senses.

So, rather than writing, "He smelled the sad ripe odor of death filling the air," write, "The sad ripe odor of death filled the air." Instead of "She saw an eagle in the sky," write, "An eagle soared high overhead." Instead of "I notice the vampire step out of the shadows and smile," write, "The vampire steps out of the shadows and smiles."

IS IT POSSIBLE TO OVER-EDIT?

Yes, but it rarely happens. You probably don't need to be wary of over-editing, but you should be on the constant lookout for its opposite. To over-edit would involve continuing to work on something after it's the best you have to offer—and why would anyone ever do that?

QUICK FIX: Scrutinize every word, every punctuation mark. Do they uphold the atmosphere? Do they help the flow? Remember that every choice a character makes has a consequence, every act an implication. Let them play out honestly in your story, even if it means abandoning your outline. The more discerning you are in your revisions, the more regard you're showing for your readers.

FINE-TUNING MY MANUSCRIPT

- Have I rewritten each scene until I can see it, sense it, hear it? Have I climbed into the story, looked around, and written what I experience?
- Where do I focus too much on the minutia of body language? How can I show more respect for readers by tweaking these sections?
- Would this character really think that? Say that? Do that? Would he describe things in that way at this moment in the story?
- How can I show tension without overdoing a hammering heart, racing pulse, narrowing gaze, tightening jaw, or a hand forming into a fist? Where can I take things deeper?
- Did I make everything significant? Where do I need to cut words that aren't essential or add details that are?
- Where have I overused certain words or phrases? Is there a contextually imperative reason to do so? If not, how will I alter the wording to trim out the echoes?

77

BREVITY

Letter XVI
TO THE REVEREND FATHERS, THE JESUITS
December 4, 1656

> Reverend fathers, my letters were not wont either to be so prolix, or to follow so closely on one another. Want of time must plead my excuse for both of these faults. The present letter is a very long one, simply because I had no leisure to make it shorter.

—Blaise Pascal

I love how the author and mathematician Blaise Pascal apologized for not having enough time to write a shorter letter.

Sorry, no time to be concise today. Please forgive me.

Some people might assume that it would be the other way around—that the more time we have to write, the longer the letter. But Pascal understood: Brevity—cutting whatever's unnecessary, crafting every word—takes time.

Brevity is a way of showing respect for your readers.

FIXING BREVITY ISSUES

Every unnecessary scene you include, every unnecessary *word*, wastes your readers' time.

No matter what genre you write in, it's easy to lose readers with long sections of meandering prose. Opt for sharp, distinct writing instead.

Often, you can drop words that readers already know, especially in action sequences.

> "He ran to the door. He threw it open. He leapt into the night."

> "He ran to the door, threw it open, and leapt into the night."

> "He ran to the door. Threw it open. Leapt into the night."

Everything else being equal, the first example is cluttered and too repetitive, the second is smooth and even-flowing but doesn't carry a lot of urgency. The third, however, leaves out every unnecessary word and conveys the frantic action of the scene.

Lean toward economy of language, especially in the final push to the finish as you build to the climax:

> Brown.
> Stucco. Two story.
> Around us, twilight in the city.

• • •

Shaving unnecessary words is part of the process. It's not a waste of time. The wood shavings in a carpenter's shop aren't evidence that he wasted wood, they're simply the result of him doing his job. Same with *word* shavings. You'll have some left over at the end. Get used to it. It's just evidence that you're doing your job.

Authors tend to fall into five traps, each of which can be an enemy of brevity.

Time

Just like Pascal when he was rushed in his letter writing, authors today often don't take the time to trim their work. They haven't found a concise way of stating something, and they don't want to print out the whole book from the beginning (again!) and edit it. Go on. Take the time. Do it. Edit it. While keeping the story's essence in mind, trim it down—not to the bone, but to the truth.

Uncertainty

They don't know what to write, and they're working out the scene on the page, shaping it as they craft it. There's nothing wrong with this approach—in fact it's the one I suggest—but after you've unearthed the scene, condense the language to bring what truly matters to the forefront.

Certainty

They know precisely where they want things to go but don't take the time to readjust based on the context and readers' evolving expectations.

Instead, be flexible, intuitive, receptive. Some of the content you thought was brilliant, essential, and nonnegotiable six months ago won't be necessary—or might not even fit now as the true shape of the novel begins to emerge.

Respond to the developing narrative. The more you try to call the shots, the more likely you'll intrude on your story.

Descriptions

Authors tend to get carried away describing clothes, weather (especially sunsets), characters' physical characteristics, locales, and meals. Instead, trust your readers to use their imaginations. As we explored in chapter fifty-two, when you do include descriptions, use them to evoke, not just depict.

Filler

Let's just be honest here, some authors use more words than necessary just so they can meet the manuscript length stated in their contract. Tell the story as it should be told, not in a way that precisely fits into a predetermined mold. Don't include fluff. In fact, de-fluff scenes whenever possible. In the end, your editor—and your readers—will thank you.

• • •

Three closing thoughts:

1. Logic trumps length. If everything makes sense, readers will stick with a longer story. Some stories bore me within ten pages. With others, I find myself at page 600 and wonder what happened to the last two days of my life.
2. Story is tension and pursuit, not reflection and indecision. Don't get caught up in reverie. Instead, direct scenes toward choices, actions, and consequences that move the story forward.
3. There are probably places where you're overdescribing or overshowing. (Flip to chapter sixty-one to learn how to fix this.)

Time is precious.

Don't waste your readers' time with words that don't matter or stories that aren't worth reading.

WHY DO SO MANY WRITING INSTRUCTORS EMPHASIZE BREVITY?

Most novels are far too long. There isn't enough story to support that much narrative weight, so the author resorts to unnecessary filler, which never serves readers.

QUICK FIX: Cut out sections where you needlessly included (1) a character's life history; (2) rumination about insignificant events; (3) debate over easy decisions; (4) detailed descriptions of negligible people, places, or objects; and (5) irrelevant subplots. Don't try to stretch things out. Snip off extraneous threads. Make every word count.

FINE-TUNING MY MANUSCRIPT

- Does my book contain any unnecessary words? Why?
- Does this scene really contribute to readers' entertainment, or am I letting my own laziness keep me from taking the time to slice it from the story?

- Have I included any actions that aren't vital? How will ambiguous events be interpreted by readers? For example, if my character folds his arms, is he doing so because he's confident, or as a way of hiding? How will my readers know?
- Are there places where I could describe something more succinctly, clearly, or evocatively?
- Where have I overdescribed something—particularly in moments of tension or during the push to the climax?
- Where does my story wander and need to be trimmed? Where is it unfocused? Where can it be sharpened?

78

GRAMMAR AND FORMAT

When my daughter was in eighth grade, her teacher told her that a sentence needed a noun and a verb. "Really," she said skeptically.

"Yes," the teacher responded.

"Huh," my daughter replied.

"That's an exception."

"Oh. Okay."

● ● ●

All of my daughter's replies were sentences.

A sentence doesn't always have a noun and a verb. Instead, a sentence is a word or unit of words that conveys a complete thought *within that specific context*:

> "Pass the salt."
> "Huh?"
> "The salt. Please."
> "Oh. Here."
> "Thanks."
> "Sure. Pepper?"
> "Naw."

To use traditional "complete sentences" wouldn't just be unnecessary for this exchange, it would make the dialogue sound stilted and unnatural:

"Pass the salt."

"What did you say?"

"I would like the salt. Please pass it to me."

"I will gladly pass you the salt."

"I'm thankful."

"Being helpful is what I'm here for. Would you like some pepper as well?"

"No, I won't be needing the pepper."

Concentrate more on communicating clear ideas than on writing complete sentences. Sometimes you might purposely opt for fragments in the service of the energy or urgency of the scene:

As Daniel tried to thread through the gap, his tires spun on the ice and the car whipped around.

Everything outside the window was whirling.

Turning.

A smear of white.

And then.

The jolt of impact as the car collided sideways into Dr. Fromke's car, pinning the doctor between the two vehicles.

....

Grammar isn't about rules—it's about allowing the story to do its job.

....

FIXING GRAMMAR ISSUES

While a basic grasp of grammar is essential for getting your work traditionally published, when revising your novel, devote more attention to how various parts of speech (nouns, verbs, adjectives, etc.) serve your story, and less attention to following every grammar-related "rule."

PARTS OF SPEECH	WHAT TO REMEMBER
Nouns	Many nouns are mood-neutral, so the context will determine the connotation. Take a careful look at the adjectives and verbs that refer to your nouns to get a better feel for the scene's atmosphere.
Verbs	Use the right verb and you'll sustain the atmosphere; use the wrong one and you'll undermine it.
Adjectives	Look for adjectives that point out aspects of something that readers might not have noticed. When describing a noun, don't try to tell readers what that thing is like. Try to induce an emotion.
Adverbs	If you have an adverb beside a verb, you can often improve the writing by choosing a verb that carries the meaning of both words. So, rather than writing, "He looked carefully," you might write, "He scrutinized." Instead of "He drank thirstily," you could write, "He guzzled." Often, the presence of an adverb simply means that you haven't yet chosen the most appropriate verb.
Prepositions	Typically, you won't use two or more prepositions in a row. So, "She ran back around the cabin," becomes, "She ran past the cabin." In the service of brevity, cut extra prepositions. Also, don't pile on too many prepositional phrases, as in "He went behind the barn, into the field, over the hill, through the woods, to Grandmother's house." It disrupts the flow. Slice the action into several sentences.

Typically, you'll want to go with what sounds natural rather than what might be considered "proper." For example, it might be proper English to write, "It is I," rather than "It's me." But if you hear a knock on the door and you call out, "Who's there?" and someone replies, "It is I," he would sound presumptuous. Instead, he would probably say, "It's me."

Also, stop worrying about ending sentences with a preposition. It's just not something readers really care about. (See—if that last sentence was written formally, it would have read, "It's just not something about which readers care," and that sounds incredibly awkward.)

Don't fret about starting a sentence with the word *there*. It's perfectly fine to write, "There's an old saying about that," rather than "An old saying about that exists."

As soon as proper grammar gets in the way of the story, abandon it.

By the way, when choosing verbs, go with active over passive voice:

PASSIVE: A great time was had by all.
ACTIVE: Everyone had a great time.

PASSIVE: My foot was the place on which the anvil fell.
ACTIVE: The anvil fell on my foot.

PASSIVE: The ray guns were carried by the aliens.
ACTIVE: The aliens carried the ray guns.

The active voice is stronger, more present, more concise. Because of this, it's usually a better option.

FIXING FORMAT ISSUES

As you tell your story, let every sentence break, section break, and chapter break work in your favor.

The number of chapters, whether you title them or not, their length, the number of point-of-view characters you use—all of this will grow out of your encounter with the story, not the other way around.

As you understand your story's shape, be responsive to the flow of the book and how things are moving, and then determine your chapter breaks and lengths.

Keep in mind that readers rarely complain that a chapter is too short. Ask:

• Would a chapter break here serve my readers?
• Will readers be thankful or annoyed that I inserted this break?
• Does it orient or disorient them?

Also, regarding formulas, the more you follow a template (three acts, archetypes, mythic structure, etc.) the less likely you'll tell original stories.

If you're self-publishing, you can format your book any way you like. If you're writing for a publisher, you'll want to remove any extraneous formatting. Take out tabs, and use the hanging indent function instead. Choose one font size and style, and remove bold lettering and random capitalization. Include page numbers. Double-space your manuscript. Remove extra spaces and left justify rather than full justify the text.

Every formatting choice you make should be done in the service of your readers—to engage them in the story, to draw them deeper in, and to provide a more satisfying emotional experience.

HOW SHOULD I LAY OUT MY CHAPTERS?

Lay out your book in whatever way best serves and orients your readers. In some novels, every chapter is labeled. In some, they're numbered. Some contain no chapter breaks at all.

QUICK FIX: Choose your breaks carefully. Use them to propel the story forward rather than to provide a resting spot for readers. Don't give them any excuse to set the book down. End your chapters with a revelation, a discovery, or a decision. Let the breaks become integral to the story's flow rather than a distraction from it.

FINE-TUNING MY MANUSCRIPT

- Is the grammar serving the scene? Does it convey the right voice and sense of urgency?
- Have I weeded out extra prepositions, needless adverbs, weak adjectives?
- Does the writing sound too formal? Where can I write in a more natural and less pretentious way?

- Are my chapters relatively consistent in length? If not, is there a good reason for the exceptions?
- Are the chapters the length that readers of this genre would expect? If not, how can I overcome that potential drawback by shaping the story so it won't create a distraction?
- Am I placing this scene here because it's convenient for me or because it contributes to the story?

79

PUNCTUATION

Punctuation marks are like traffic signs: They differ from state to state, there's no "right" speed limit, and no matter what the sign says, it's better to break the rules than to run over a pedestrian.

If the punctuation gets in the way, change it. If it's not in the way, leave it.

Everything that has the potential to mislead readers or drive them out of the story matters. Punctuation exists to serve them. Incorrect or missing punctuation may confuse them. Obvious errors will also make them lose trust in your writing ability.

With so many online writing resources at your fingertips, there's no excuse for sloppy punctuation. Some punctuation is subjective (commas, colons, and em dashes, for example). Use only what contributes to the flow and pace of your story.

....

Strive for readability and consistency, but opt for context over convention every time.

....

FIXING PUNCTUATION ISSUES

Noticeable mistakes—whether in consistency, continuity, or punctuation—will distract readers. Six things to keep in mind:

1. Rules are in flux. What's common usage today might not be tomorrow.
2. There's no such thing as "proper" punctuation. It's a little like dialect—there are styles of speaking, but no dialect is "right."
3. If a punctuation mark might throw readers off, don't use it.

4. If you invent a convention (such as not using quotations marks or not including any commas in your book, etc.), do it in the service of the story, not out of novelty.
5. Every publishing company will have its own preferences.
6. Every choice regarding punctuation should be made in the service of your readers.

Here's what will make you look stupid: apostrophes in the wrong place, misspelled words, and timing that's off (especially when you use multiple point-of-view characters).

Run-on sentences will often annoy readers. Judiciously used sentence fragments usually won't bother them.

Check your quotes to make sure they're all "smart" (curly) or all neutral (straight). Often, for whatever reason, authors end up with a combination of the two in their manuscripts.

Regarding question marks: When a character should be coming to a conclusion, don't have him ask a question. It makes him look stupid and lowers his status. Context will determine this. So, you might write:

> "That's a one-way mirror, so he can't see us?"
> "Correct. All he sees is a mirror."
> "It's cracked on his side of the glass."
> "That's from the chair."
> "So, he's been trying to break out."
> "Yes."

But not:

> "That's a one-way mirror, so he can't see us?"
> "Correct. All he sees is a mirror."
> "It's cracked on his side of the glass."
> "That's from the chair."
> "So, he's been trying to break out?"
> "Yes."

See how, in that second to last line, the question mark makes the person seem dim-witted? Clearly the prisoner tried to break out. A question mark wouldn't be the best choice in this instance.

PUNCTUATION MARK	WHAT THE STYLEBOOKS AREN'T TELLING YOU
Commas	Commas are subjective. One editor says this, another says that, you go back and forth; it can be exhausting. In the end, it's up to you. Use them to manage the flow of your sentences. Trust your instinct—but take the time to hone that instinct first. (And be aware that it might need a lot of honing.)
Semicolons	Remove them from sections of dialogue. People don't usually talk in semicolons unless they're trying to hide something. Most of the time, a full stop (period) rather than a semicolon will do the trick.
Question Marks	These are used to show the upward inflection at the end of a sentence. When someone is coming to a conclusion, rather than asking a question, use a period instead of a question mark.
Exclamation Points	Usually, they lower the status of a character who uses them all the time, since they show loss of control. In a series of commands, because of escalation, the last one might have an exclamation point, but not the first. So, you might write, "Swim faster. Hurry!" but not "Swim faster! Hurry."
Italics	Use italics to denote thoughts and quotation marks to distinguish between speakers during dialogue. Using quotation marks for thoughts confuses readers because they won't know right away if someone is talking or thinking.

Em Dashes	In dialogue, use an em dash to show someone getting cut off:
	    "Come here."
	    "No, I—"
	    "I said come here!"

Ellipses	Use ellipses to show that someone's thoughts are trailing off: "Come here." "No, I ..." A pause. "You what?" "Oh, sorry, I lost my train of thought."

WHAT STYLE MANUAL SHOULD I USE?

If you're working with an established publisher, they'll have an in-house style manual. If you're self-publishing, you'll want to find a contemporary one and stick to it so your punctuation is consistent.

QUICK FIX: While there are plenty of stylebooks available, trends are constantly changing and many style manuals that were published more than five years ago contain conventions that are no longer common in today's marketable fiction. Keep an eye on current trends, and check online grammar guru sites for the most current information. The book *Painless Grammar* by Rebecca Elliott PhD is one of the most practical and contemporary resources I've found. Check the publication date of any style manual you use, and go for the most recent edition.

FINE-TUNING MY MANUSCRIPT

- If I haven't followed current punctuation conventions, why haven't I? Is it to remove distractions and serve readers, or is it to be "experimental"? What am I going to do about that?
- Is my punctuation usage consistent?
- What stupid mistakes do I keep making? What steps will I take to address that?
- Where does my punctuation (especially exclamation points that show lack of self-control and question marks for conclusions) undermine the status of my characters?
- Are my punctuation choices well informed and appropriate? Where am I following the rules of the road so much that I'm running over my readers in my quest to follow proper punctuation?

80

REVISIONS

A well-crafted book will appear to move along effortlessly, just like a skilled rock climber scaling a cliff. But is it effortless? No, of course not. His grace was earned through hundreds of hours of training and hard work.

So, brace yourself.

To make your story appear effortless, it's probably going to require hundreds of hours of hard work—maybe thousands.

You'll have to tunnel through a mountain of words to find the path to the ones that'll best fit in this story, in this context. Words that'll ring true. That'll be vibrant. Alive. Authentic.

While there's a point of diminishing returns, for the most part, the more time you spend crafting your story, the less time it'll take someone to read it because you'll have removed the plot snags, mistakes, and continuity errors.

....

Most of editing is deciding what not to put on the page.

....

FIXING REVISION ISSUES

Perspective is huge.

Set the story aside for a week or two, and then come back with fresh eyes. Step into the scenes and try to experience them as if you were reading them for the first time.

Fact-check, spell-check, and proofread everything.

Beyond that, keep these principles in mind:

Weed out Minutia

Details direct attention. Minutia distracts from the scene, weighs the story down, and kills the pace. Not everything is important enough to earn the right to have vivid information about it included.

Stop Trying So Hard

Does her voice become a blade? Do her words bludgeon you, scorch the air, writhe from her mouth, drip like water from a leaky faucet? Or does she just say them?

You might write:

> She stared at him and waited for him to reply.
> A dark silence invaded the room.
> "Well?" she said at last. "Are you going to tell me her name?"

Okay, so, why a "dark" silence? Why did it "invade" the room? The scene might be more effective if you just rendered it like this:

> She stared at him and waited for him to reply.
> Silence.
> "Well?" she said at last. "Are you going to tell me her name?"

Very often, authors overwrite in early drafts and the editing process isn't so much changing the story as it is trimming what's unnecessary so the words that are left have a greater impact.

Curtail Speaker Tags

Often, in final edits you'll find yourself removing speaker attributions. That's natural. Cut them whenever you can, as long as it's still clear who's talking.

Save the Best for Last

The best twist, the greatest moral dilemma, the funniest punch line comes at, or near, the climax. Otherwise, your story will be de-escalating in intensity, humor, or suspense.

Make Every Action Purposeful

As we covered in previous chapters, action without intention is a distraction. Stories aren't simply about personality or activity. They're not just descriptions or accounts of movement. They always involve intention with direction.

If you've had to reverse cause/effect order in certain places in your story, you can help the flow by inserting, "After all." For example, "He brought her roses. After all, it was their anniversary, and he'd forgotten it the last two years. This year he wanted to get things right."

Keep Everything Believable

Here's a quick believability test: If you read a tense scene and find yourself thinking, *Yeah, right*, it's not believable. If, on the other hand, you're thinking, *Oh, no*, it is.

If something strains credibility, have the point-of-view character acknowledge that he doesn't know why it happened:

> **EXAMPLE 1:** Alisha put on her sunglasses even though the room was dark. I had no idea what she was thinking.
>
> **EXAMPLE 2:** For the life of me I couldn't figure out why he was so angry, but things were happening way too fast right now to dwell on that.

When Necessary, Leave out the Good Stuff

You came up with that killer phrase. You chipped it out of the universe of ideas, but deep down, you know it isn't quite right for this story. Yet, you've been hanging onto it. You've kept it in your book. Guess what? It needs to go.

Editing is distillation. It's sifting through what could be and finding what should be. Often, it involves leaving out some sparkling gems that just don't fit in this piece of jewelry.

Make Sure the Book Has a Broad Internal Consistency

Keep the amount of thoughts (or internal dialogue) relatively consistent throughout the book. If you use a lot of them at one point, don't stop using them in others. This is a common problem when authors edit scenes in isolation rather than in context.

Check Proportionality and Congruence

Memorability makes a promise to readers. The more interesting you make a character, the more readers will want to be with him. When you set expectations, you need to fulfill them.

For example, every scar has a story. So does every tattoo. If you mention a scar or tattoo, what will readers want to hear about?

Exactly.

The story behind it.

So, if you bring up something unique like this about a character, be prepared to fulfill the implied promise you've made and include the backstory of how he got that scar or why the tattoo is significant.

• • •

There's an old writing dictum: "Leave out what the reader can fill in."

Do that, and you'll be well on your way.

HOW DO I KNOW WHEN I'M DONE?

When you can read the whole book through the eyes of a first-time reader, as well as through the eyes of a seasoned editor, and not find anything to improve, your manuscript is done. If you can improve it, do it. Then read it again and evaluate if it's ready.

QUICK FIX: There isn't a fixed number of drafts that you'll need to go through to tell a great story. Some writers need one. Others need sixty. Remember, every time you make even a slight change, you send ripples across the surface of your story. Reprint that section and make sure the context supports the change. Don't let the fact that you've been through a dozen drafts keep you from making the courageous decisions that will improve your story.

FINE-TUNING MY MANUSCRIPT

- Where are characters acting in ways that are incongruent with their personality, situation, priorities, or mindset?
- Are characters suddenly prioritizing things that wouldn't be important in that situation? (For example, would she really stop for a meal at this time? Would he really take that phone call right now?) What will I do about this?
- Would a different opening serve the story better? Does this one set the wrong tone, give the wrong impression, or introduce things that aren't essential within the story's broader context?
- Where have I cut corners in my manuscript or my storytelling?
- Does the story's ending tie in inextricably with the beginning? Does it fulfill all the promises I've made? Is the protagonist's life transformed in a way that satisfies readers?

CONCLUSION

Years ago, when I was dreaming of becoming a writer, I went to a seminar by best-selling novelist Davis Bunn. He told the story of how, at his first book signing, a much more famous author was seated beside him and had a long line of people waiting to get their books signed.

No one was lining up at Davis's end of the table.

Finally, a devout Mennonite woman came walking up to him, reverently carrying a copy of his book with both hands. She asked him, "Sir, is this a worthy book?"

"Yes," he told her. "It is."

"Then would you kindly sign it for me?"

When Davis told that story, I vowed that if I ever wrote a novel, I would pour everything I had into it, and I wouldn't offer anything less than my best. I wanted to be able to look anyone who might ask me in the eye and tell her, "Yes, this is a worthy book."

What if the novel you're working on right now was the last thing you ever wrote? What if it was the way the world remembered you—would they remember a hack, a rushed attempt at zipping something off into the self-published fray, a mediocre swing at the ball, or would they agree that it is a worthy book?

Will you leave behind a legacy of mediocrity or of excellence?

Let your book matter.

With today's technology, you could have your novel published in the next hour by dumping the text into one of the many online templates floating around out there. By suppertime you could be selling your book on Amazon.

What's holding you back?

I'm guessing that since you've read this far, you have a deep and profound desire to make this novel of yours the best it can possibly be.

That'll take time. Revisions. Months. Maybe years.

The writing process isn't about how few drafts you can get by with or whether you hit your daily word count, it's about if you are producing a worthy book.

If you read at an average speed, from the time you began this book until now, more than two thousand books have been self-published in the United States.

And that number is rising every month.

What will set yours apart?

What will make it stand out?

You can certainly do everything within reason to market your book: the branding and the interviews and the social media posts and the guest blog entries. However, in the end, you have no control over who buys or doesn't buy your book, or what Hollywood does or doesn't do with your book.

The only thing you have control over is the quality of the work you do today.

Why not go ahead and make it count?

Weep, scream, *feel*. Snatch those words out of the air. Love them onto the page. Don't cage the story. Set it free. This might be the last book you ever write. Let it be the best, most worthy story you have to offer the world.

INDEX

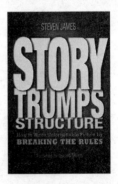